In *Bed* *with the* ATLANTIC

Kitiara Pascoe

FERNHURST
BOOKS

Published in 2018 by Fernhurst Books Limited

The Windmill, Mill Lane, Harbury, Leamington Spa, Warwickshire, CV33 9HP,

UK Tel: +44 (0) 1926 337488 | www.fernhurstbooks.com

A catalogue record for this book is available from the British Library

ISBN 978-1-912177-16-5

Front cover photograph: © Alex Francis

Other photography © Alex Francis and Kitiara Pascoe as indicated

Designed & typeset by Daniel Stephen

Maps by Maggie Nelson

Printed in Bulgaria by Alliance Print Ltd

In Bed
with the
ATLANTIC

Making Waves

The real lives of sporting heroes on, in & under the water

Also in this series...

more to follow

For *Berwick Maid* and her
wonderful captain Alex

Contents

List of stop-overs

EUROPE

England	Southampton
	Dartmouth
	Salcombe
	Mullion Cove
	Helford River
	Falmouth
Spain	A Coruña
	Ares
	Laxe
	Camarinas
	Muros
	Bornalle
	Ribeira
	Pobra do
	Caraminal
	Baiona
Portugal	Povoa de Varzim
Porto Santo	Vila Baleira
Madeira	Canical

Canary Islands

Lanzarote	Arrecife
	Playa Blanca
Graciosa	Playa La Francesa
Fuerteventura	Gran Tarajal
Tenerife	Santa Cruz
La Gomera	San Sebastian
Gran Canaria	Las Palmas

CARIBBEAN

Grenada	Prickly Bay
	St George's
	Dragon Bay
Carriacou	Tyrell Bay
	Hilsborough

St Vincent and the Grenadines

Union Island	Clifton
	Frigate Island
Mayreau	Saline Bay
Tobago Cays	Petit Rameau
Canuoan	Tamarind Beach
Bequia	Port Elizabeth
St Vincent	Wallilabou Bay
St Lucia	Rodney Bay
Martinique	Fort-de-France
	L'Anse Martin
	Sainte-Anne
	Le Marin
	Le Robert
	St Pierre
Guadeloupe	Deshaies
Antigua	Falmouth
	Harbour
St Martin	Marigot

CENTRAL AMERICA

Panama	Bocas del Toro
	Red Frog Marina
Colombia	Isla Providencia

NORTH AMERICA
Bahamas

Great Inagua	Matthew Town
Mayaguana	Abrahams Bay
Long Island	Clarence Town
Great Exuma	George Town
	Elizabeth Island
Exumas	Rat Cay
	Lee Stocking Island
	Norman's Pond Cay
	Rudder Cut Cay
	Great Guana Cay
	Staniel Cay
	Pig Beach
Cat Island	The Bight Settlement
Eleuthera	Rock Sound
Great Abaco	Marsh Harbour
	Man-O-War Cay
	Elbow Cay
Great Exuma	George Town
Rum Cay	Nesbitt Point

EUROPE
Azores

Flores	Lajes das Flores
Sao Jorge	Velas
Terceira	Praia da Vitoria
Spain	Punta de Sardineiro, Finisterre
	Muxia
	A Coruña
	Sada
France	Kerdivizian (Brest Estuary)
England	Dartmouth
	Studland
	Newtown
	Southampton

Chapter 1

I Bought A Boat

I'll never know, and neither will you, of the life you don't choose.
Cheryl Strayed

"I would hope that we won't capsize but, if we do, you need to grab Freddy and swim out from underneath," said my dad as we sat huddled in the Wayfarer.

I looked at my stepbrother, he was eight, I was sixteen. He didn't look as concerned about this as I was. I hoped that sisterly instinct would kick in should we be plunged into the Solent's chilly May water and that I'd focus more on saving his life than panicking about my own. I eyed up the Lymington to Yarmouth ferry as it trundled past in a mess of wash and prayed we'd never have to find out.

I don't remember much of that sail except for the tension that filled my body as we spent a freezing hour avoiding gigantic ferries and seeing my discomfort mirrored in the face of my stepmother. We didn't capsize and instead retired quickly to the yacht club where I could focus on more important things like catching the eye of the barman who'd been a few years ahead of me in school.

I'd never really been on a boat before that day, with the exception of the town-sized cross-Channel ferries to mainland Europe, and I had absolutely no intention of repeating the experience. I made sure I was always working when it looked like my dad might remember he had a dinghy and generally steered clear of any activity that would involve getting into the steel grey Atlantic.

Despite my reticence about the sea, I never lived far from it and was brought up a mere mile or two from the Solent's busy shores. When it came to choosing a university I knew I couldn't bear to be inland, I needed to be able to walk to the sea, I needed it near me.

I eventually studied in Plymouth, a seafaring city only second to the twins of Southampton and Portsmouth. The sea wasn't just in my vicinity though – it was in my blood.

My grandfather was a naval architect in Southampton for decades and retired when the company moved to Portsmouth; he still sails in the Solent. His brother, my great uncle is Dick Holness, the author of the East Coast Pilot who spends his free time happily sailing Kent waters. But the connection goes further: just a couple of generations back on my family tree was Ernest Holness, the stoker onboard Shackleton's extraordinary and ill-fated 1914 expedition to the South Pole.

Even my mother spent her childhood messing about in the family dinghy and did I mention my father was in the Navy? Considering Britain has cold and temperamental waters, it surprised me that anyone learns to sail there, let alone numerous members of my own family.

I was quite happy having missed the family sailing gene, happy to spend my time outdoors rock climbing, ambling up mountains and cycling in the flat and friendly New Forest. I didn't know that the world was plotting something behind my back; blood is thicker than water they say, well I didn't stand a chance when my blood was water. Seawater.

It wasn't until 2013 that my fate was sealed and I found myself with a boat. I'd picked up Alex at a party in Plymouth quite accidentally in 2011. He was dressed as a pirate and I was dressed as a cabin boy complete with eyeliner moustache; tied around his waist was the same British ensign that we would fly three years later all the way to Central America.

Together we returned to the Solent, where he'd grown up too, except that he hadn't avoided sailing as deftly as I had. In fact, he'd grown up sailing on board his parents' Moody 34, *Isabella*.

He had come to the same conclusion though that I had on that cold day in the Wayfarer; sailing in England was simply too grey, too wet and too cold. Still, after crewing on a tall ship from New Zealand to

Fiji, he knew what sailing could be like.

"I bought a boat," he said as I shut the car door against the February wind. I looked at him.

"Actually?"

"Actually," he said with a grin.

We had discussed the buying of the boat but, at the time, I was living in Exeter for work and he had been viewing yachts alone. It seemed far away and disconnected and, to be honest, I really hadn't taken it very seriously.

We'd spent many conversations in the last two years talking about sailing around the world, or, after looking at the size of the Pacific, sailing to the Caribbean. The idea of sailing around tropical islands appealed to me and it wasn't like you could backpack through the Caribbean very easily.

I'd read as many sailing accounts as I could find, amazed at how many of them had been sitting in my dad's bookshelves for all those years, waiting for me. While the conditions at sea in all those books sounded terrifying for someone who still believed yachts naturally wanted to be upside down, the theme of exploration and freedom pierced through those pages with such force that I soon became convinced.

Life got in the way though: masters degrees, office jobs and the millions of other tiny things that hook you into the ground and make you think you can't leave. But two years after we'd met we were in the same position, bored and ill contented. We didn't want to buy a house, we didn't want to work for other people and we didn't want to stay in one place. But we didn't want to backpack either, finding hostels, waiting for buses and stuffing our lives into bags every few days.

We were waved past by security in a disused power station and the huge neglected chimney, that Solent sailors had used for decades as navigation, stood cold and empty above us. The weather-beaten warehouses and sprawling outbuildings sat upon vast pipes that lead to the nearby oil refinery and in hidden tunnels across the water.

An abandoned icon in Southampton's history, Fawley was now in stasis, a shadow of the once thriving industry that brought thousands of workers and their families here in the 70s. With a workforce of just a handful of security guards, the power station's unique yacht club had been put on notice. The boats of the long retired workers needed to be gone.

The car crunched over icy gravel and I saw the boat on crumbling concrete, propped upright by planks of wood, her full keel patchy with red paint. She looked sad, cold and alone. I still knew very little about yachts and she struck me as tiny and old, nothing like the white, luxurious creatures that the term 'yacht' had always brought to my mind.

I got out of the car with great reticence. It was, unbelievably, snowing very lightly, a phenomenon almost unknown in Southampton. It was one of the coldest Februaries I had ever known and it didn't exactly shine a light on my first impressions of our new yacht.

With white, numb hands I climbed the ladder and found myself in the cockpit of this 1974 Nicholson 32 Mark X. I didn't know what to do. I sat on a moulding, peeling cockpit locker lid and grimaced unintentionally at my surroundings.

There was algae and mildew everywhere, the once-off-white vinyl inside had long since slipped onto another Dulux colour chart and a gimballed microwave sat forlornly on its studs. The whole boat smelt of damp, homesick teak.

I suppose I was mainly surprised about the size of the interior. With a beam of only 2.8 m at the widest part, the inside consisted of a narrow saloon, a tiny bathroom and long forepeak, open all the way to the very bow. Three 'rooms'. That was it. My confidence had been dulled and I simply couldn't imagine living aboard. There was nothing inside but dust, nothing to make it look like a home.

And yet, as I stood in ski socks and four layers of clothing in the middle of the saloon floor, a tremor of excitement tapped out a melody on my bones. Like a newlywed couple with the blueprints of the house they'd build, I felt as though something was starting here, something with a force all of its own.

Within weeks it was clear that living three hours apart was simply not working and so I handed my resignation in at my office and began working my month's notice.

I wasn't exactly shouting our pelagic plans from the rooftops but I was close to the colleagues in my team and they were aware that I planned to sail to the tropics.

One of the more irritating aspects of my job was to collect paperwork and cheques from the accounts department and deliver them to the desks of the lawyers they belonged to. It was in these instances, three times a day, that I could really see the thousands I'd spent on university tuition paying off. I still thought then that a piece of paper somehow made me more deserving of respect.

I leafed through a small mountain of papers slumped over my arm and extracted a handful to pass to a lawyer not on my team but situated a few desks over. At that moment a secretary I worked closely with bustled over with something for him to sign.

I don't use the term 'bustled' as a cliché, she literally did bustle, she was a bustler. She was also the kind of person you'd describe as having a 'heart of gold' and was the most shocked by my ocean-going ambitions.

"Did you hear Kit's going to sail to Australia?" she said to the lawyer as he scrawled on a dotted line. He sniggered.

"Seriously?" he asked me.

"Well not Australia necessarily but hopefully to the Caribbean," I said, my stomach tightening.

He looked at me and laughed a short, ugly laugh, "I bet you haven't even sailed across the Channel," he said.

I felt liked I'd been slapped across the face; the derision that sat heavy in his words was not only unexpected but downright rude from someone I considered only one degree short of being a stranger.

But mainly I felt humiliated because he was right. I raised an eyebrow and returned to my desk as though I considered it so obvious I'd sailed across the Channel that I didn't feel it necessary to defend myself. I stared at my screen and the text swam in front of my eyes. Is that what everyone thought of me? That I was just some naïve 20-something with big, stupid dreams?

I hadn't 'even' sailed across the Channel; I hadn't sailed at all. I hadn't exactly made this known because I didn't want to be met with any more scepticism than I already was but this guy just came right out with it, laughing and shaking his head like I was a fool. The worst part was that he was merely saying exactly what I felt. I couldn't do it, I hadn't done anything like it, what on earth was I doing continuing with this outlandish and crazy ruse? I wasn't a sailor and only sailors sailed across the Atlantic.

I rattled my nails on my desk and tried to remember that he was always the grumpiest solicitor on the floor and clearly hated his job in construction law. It fired me up as I looked over my shoulder at him, sat in his window desk doing endless paperwork and helping development companies sue each other.

If I stayed and got the promotion I'd been going for, I would end up living a life of what-if. Maybe I'd even end up like him, laughing at the aims of strangers. Well, I wasn't going to be swayed by his negativity, no way.

Suddenly I was more dedicated to sailing to the tropics than I ever had been before. For everyone who rolled their eyes, laughed at me or said in a chandlery that I'd 'never leave the Solent', I was going to get on that boat and go south until the butter melted. I looked around at the desk debris I'd collected over the last year and wondered if this was all I thought I was capable of, a job that didn't even require you to finish school. Sod solicitors, I thought, I'm going to go sailing for me.

By April I had left my job in Exeter and moved into Alex's house, which he was housesitting for his retired parents who were themselves away cruising for a few years.

I installed myself at the kitchen table and worked as a freelance copywriter while Alex spent all of his time at the new boatyard in Portsmouth, refitting the boat.

I went down there often to wiggle into small spaces, swing about at the top of the mast to change the rigging two stays at a time or manhandle a paint brush but, as anyone who has renovated anything will know, you have to make it much worse before you make it better.

I had no idea what I was doing, taking instruction from Alex and trusting him when he said, 'you can remove two stays easily and the mast won't fall down'. He'd never refitted a boat before but his attitude that one can learn anything meant that no task was too difficult, too complex. With a keel-stepped mast, it indeed didn't fall down as I changed the rigging, two by two.

The boat had been originally fitted out for day sailing only and, aside from a very occasional cross-Channel trip, had spent its life dawdling about the Solent. Thus its fittings weren't suitable for us and Alex stripped out everything... everything... and started from scratch.

He built lockers into cavernous spaces, added another bookshelf to stop me weeping over the lack of book space, turned the forepeak into a double bed with storage underneath, removed the microwave and installed a gas system and stove and rebuilt the entire interior piece by piece.

Every afternoon he'd park on the drive, our estate car packed full of teak in need of restoration and disappear into the workshop in the garden well into the evening.

When it became obvious that the rudder was dangerously weak and saturated with water, he removed it, cut it open and rebuilt it. He replaced every inch of wiring and created a whole new switch panel. He sat drawing diagrams for me after dinner, teaching me things that I struggled to understand.

"Wait, so the buses go to the bus station from the city and then they all split up and go to different suburbs?" I asked, searching for a metaphor that would transform my understanding of the electrical system.

"Sure," he said, "like the lighting suburb or the AIS suburb or the

17

navigation light suburb."

"And the bus station is the switch panel?" I found it amazing that I'd ever got a B in physics.

The refit wasn't just rebuilding and adding new shelves and lockers though, there was so much else. Lacking an autopilot, we researched for months before concluding that every sailor in the books we'd read had troubles with their autopilots, so we needed something that was not only as reliable as possible, but also fixable mid-ocean.

We settled on an Aries wind vane, accepting that whenever we motored we'd have to hand-steer. The fuel tank, built into the depths of the bilge, only had a 60-litre capacity anyway and we weren't intending to use the engine much. It was only when we started talking about autopilots that I even learnt we wouldn't be hand-steering 24/7 anyway. I had never realised that you allowed something else to steer offshore – it was immensely relieving but also highlighted again how little I knew. In fact, the entire refit showed me how little I knew.

As I typed madly for ten hours a day, writing all sorts of copy for various companies, I would be answering the doorbell every hour or two and signing for parcels.

At first I felt a little sheepish, seeing the same UPS man for three days in a row, but then it became ridiculous. With almost all of our boat bits, everything from nuts and bolts to a liferaft and aluminium poles coming from eBay, Amazon and online chandleries, I began seeing the delivery men more and more often.

I was only 24 at this point but regularly got asked if I was 17 and could only imagine what the line of UPS, DHL, FedEx and other couriers thought I was buying. 'Poor girl, she'll be bankrupting her parents with that shopping addiction, shouldn't she be in college or something?'

This was compounded by the fact that the house was at the end of a cul-de-sac almost exclusively inhabited by retirees. Huge delivery vans and even small lorries would find themselves having to do ten-point turns just to get out again and the amount of noise they made alerted everyone on the road that I had a delivery. Chandleries, it turned out, do not send small vehicles.

It became a game of time and curtain-twitching; the UPS man always showed up around 11am and was usually the first of the day. That meant I could safely shower in the morning but when a spate of work came in with extraordinarily tight deadlines, I would shower after 2pm instead. This lead to a series of embarrassing towel related incidents I'd rather not go into. Suffice to say, taking parcels and having to sign for them while wearing a towel requires more hands than I possessed.

The liferaft was actually delivered to a neighbour as I had chanced a mere thirty minutes out to go to the supermarket. But delivery men have a knack of turning up at inopportune moments and I returned home to find a 'we missed you...' note on the doormat.

I took a deep breath and headed over to number 14, ready to profusely apologise for dragging them into my Cirque de Delivery, especially since I was aware that the raft would weigh upwards of 20 kilos.

The neighbour was pruning her hedges around the back and it took a few doorbell rings for her to hear me. She was tiny and smiley, batting away my apologies with her secateurs. The liferaft had been left just round the side and it was soon apparent that I would seriously struggle carrying it back across the road and up the slope to the house.

I considered asking her if I could leave it there until Alex returned home but I already felt bad about troubling her with it. She had other ideas though and said she'd help me carry it across. Now I was in trouble, I thought. Not only had some FedEx guy got her to sign for a 23 kg liferaft, but she would have to somehow help me carry it up a hill.

She wouldn't have me refuse though and we took a strap each and lifted. Now I consider myself reasonably strong, I'm a rock climber and have little trouble hefting around boxes. But the liferaft was an awkward and dense object to carry and it would've taken me stop-starting it across the road. My small, retired neighbour, however, picked up the strap with one hand and lifted.

"Ready?" she said. I nodded, wide eyed.

Out of the two of us, I'd freely admit that she carried it with greater ease than I and she merely dusted herself off when we reach my patio and said no trouble, she'd sign for anything if I was out again.

She went off down the drive, back to her hedges and I wondered if she had a secret weights room out the back. Never underestimate the strength of your elders. We still send her postcards.

It took a year for us to complete the refit as far as completion was possible anyway. Boatyards and marinas are full of yachts that just need a 'few more jobs' doing before they are 'ready'. But then you've worked on through the season and maybe you'll be ready next year instead.

We did not want that to be us for several reasons. Firstly, we wanted to be sailing south, not working away through another British winter and secondly, boats are expensive things and we could only afford to have one if we lived on it. No more car, no more bills, no more excess that life in a house encourages. We had to move onto the boat ASAP and be on our way to places where we could anchor for free.

This was the party line, we were sticking to it. But in my head the constant worries repeated themselves and the bizarre double-crosses of my thoughts created an on-going internal battle. Maybe there'd be a huge storm, the boat would fall over and this whole thing would be abandoned. Maybe Alex would get sick of the relentless fiddly jobs to do and we'd just sell her. Maybe I wouldn't have to go to sea, something I still couldn't even comprehend. No one was holding a gun to my head except me though. At any time I could've stepped in and said, 'I don't think I want to do this', but I didn't.

I didn't say it not only because I was deeply afraid of what it would mean for us as a couple, but also because it wasn't even true. It was a sentence that in some way described how I was feeling but it wasn't complete. I did want to sail around exotic islands and swim in warm waters. I did want to experience the pure adventure of being out on the ocean thousands of miles from land. What the real sentence should've read was, 'I don't think I can do this'.

But saying you don't want to do something implies integrity, decision-making and strength; no one can argue with that. However, saying you don't think you're capable of doing something is much more easily countered because it's a weak statement easily batted away with, 'why not?'

While I tend to live my life with as much organisation as group of drunken students, Alex is the sort of person who knows what a Gant chart is. Every month he'd tick off his boat projects and tasks and be more on less bang-on schedule. I would watch over his shoulder with my jaw on the floor; I knew you could plan things, but I didn't realise that it actually worked.

If I write a to-do list I'll populate it with things I know are within easy reach; buy bread, reply to editor, text Sophie. Alex creates a time estimate and difficulty rating for each task and performs it with rationality and enthusiasm. He'll even break down tasks into smaller ones.

It was this attitude and drive that allowed us to put the yacht into the water just two weeks later than had been planned a year before. She'd been in the water for three months the previous summer and we'd ventured on brief day sails around the Solent, but this was it, this was the launch.

When people go off on gap years or leave to move to another country, there are parties and farewells. After all, it's an easily categorisable event. You are getting on a plane in a week and won't return for a year or two, let's throw a goodbye party on the Friday before!

But sailing isn't like that, not our kind of sailing. For all of Alex's enthusiasm, he knew perfectly well that something might go wrong and we'd be back in a month. Or perhaps we wouldn't end up leaving Britain's shores at all. Maybe we'd only get to Falmouth. And from my point of view, I just didn't believe we'd get any further than France. I couldn't imagine it, besides, I'd always lived in the UK, how did it even work, to be nomadic?

Neither of us knew how long we would be gone for or where we would end up. We reassured each other that simply spending a summer sailing to Portugal and back would be fun. If we made it to the Canaries then the Atlantic might beckon but I wasn't so sure. Either way, we made no official date for 'leaving' and were purposefully vague about our departure. If for no other reason than a cruising departure isn't really a departure anyway, we might launch from Portsmouth only to spend several days in an anchorage a few miles away and then we'd spend a month or so pottering along the English coastline before even attempting a channel crossing. We didn't know when we would leave leave. So we didn't really tell anybody.

We stayed on the mooring for just three days until we left in a force six that Alex optimistically said would only be a nice force five once we got out of the harbour. We were heading for Newtown Creek, it was Wednesday the 7th May 2014 and it was our three-year anniversary.

"Something's wrong," I said a few miles into tacking to windward. "The wheel feels loose."

We swapped places and Alex told me to get 'the number thirteen spanner' and fast. The boat was speeding towards Gilkicker Point at 6 knots but at least the boat was balanced, an important quality in a boat without steering.

Alex knew exactly what the problem was instantly, mainly because it was something that he'd sort of caused. The wheel and the rudder had disconnected, the rudder stock having slipped after being altered slightly in the course of the rudder being re-built.

Alex fixed it quickly as my heart was hammering in my ears, audible against the howl of the wind and we tacked at the last second, a dog walker on the beach looking at us, probably with the kind of expression people get when they're about to see something they should film and put on YouTube. A yacht hurtling towards the beach, improbably close.

The wind was a steady force seven and we were the only yacht out in the Solent, which was refreshing. The busiest shipping channel in the world, the Solent is normally chock-a-block with people on every waterborne object imaginable with a few container ships and cruise liners thrown in for good measure. It's not even unknown for clusters of people to swim across it (I should know, my mother's done it) with a kayaker or two as escorts.

While this was only day one of our adventure, I'd already had many sailors nod appreciatively at our little boat on the pontoon and say, 'real round-the-world boat you got there.' This day of ploughing head first into a 27 knot south-westerly certainly did incline me to agree. Sure there was no ocean swell but the yacht didn't seem to mind about the nasty chop or the raging wind, if nothing else, she seemed to relish it.

I huddled in the corner under the spray hood as Alex helmed in his genuine Guy Coton yellow jacket, fresh from France, making him look like a traditional fisherman. I unfolded my cold body only to tack and each time Alex talked me through it — I still had almost no idea how to sail.

Portsmouth Harbour to Newtown Creek is 11 nautical miles on a good day but, when we finally dropped our anchor in the soft, black mud, we'd done 45. The harbour master appeared in his RIB, gobsmacked to find a yacht in his midst when it was gusting force 7.

He repeatedly reassured us that we could pick up a buoy for free any time we felt the wind was too strong and were we quite sure that we were alright? I felt bad that he'd come all the way out in such weather but I was so happy to finally be stopped that I was almost swinging from the rigging.

In those early sails, arriving at anchor made me giddy with achievement and filled with the happiness that you only get from coming in from the cold to warm your hands on the fire or, in my case, the engine bay.

We stayed in Newtown Creek for a wild and windy week, trapped by a gale that made us thankful for thick Isle of Wight mud. We escaped once by dinghy and walked to the local pub. We were only a few miles from where I grew up across the water, but the sense of adventure I felt merely from having sailed there myself was overwhelming.

There was very little that had previously excited me about the Isle of Wight, it being an ever-present sight throughout my childhood. I'd been there plenty of times before but now that'd I'd battled wind and waves to get there, it became a Blyton-esque treasure island where every footpath lead past Kirrin cottage and every shore could hide adventure. In short, sailing reverted me to an excitable form of childhood.

While this was supposed to be the start of our 'shakedown' cruise, we realised that an adjustment needed to be made to the rudder stock to prevent it slipping ever again and plunging us suddenly into danger. That would require finding a welder and so, when the wind chilled out, we sailed across the water to Hythe, a town in Southampton Water.

After the previous year of refitting, Alex had got a feel for the industrial parks around southern Hampshire and within a week we were off for shakedown cruise part deux with the rudder stock altered.

This time we were to attempt a journey that had been weighing on my mind for months. A Channel crossing.

By this point I'd still never left the Solent. We'd practised picking up buoys in Portsmouth Harbour, I'd raised the mainsail a few times and I could reef the genoa. But that was about it. I believed even the slightest wash would threaten us with capsize (even after Alex explained that it was incomprehensibly difficult to capsize a boat like ours and basically impossible to do so in sheltered water. Not to mention that our righting angle was 160° so 'if we did capsize, which we never will, we'd pop right back up anyway').

We anchored in Totland Bay on the western end of the Isle of Wight and set sail at 6:30am with a friendly westerly wind. I'd been diligently making passage plans for every tiny sail we'd done so far, mainly because Solent and Channel tides are a force to be reckoned with, and was pleased with the apparent simplicity of the crossing.

It would take around twelve hours and the Channel tides are semi-diurnal, meaning that for half the journey you'd be swept to the side in one direction and the next half you'd be swept to the side in the other direction. Thus the tides politely cancelled each other out. A unique attribute to the Channel, it seemed as though the tides had created themselves purely for the pleasure of English and French sailors. The crossing was north to south, the tides east to west.

We hopped on the ebb tide that rushed between Hurst Narrows

where the Isle of Wight and the mainland sit closest to each other. A few miles offshore Alex taught me how to hove-to, something which I promptly forgot mainly because I really needed to pee and we'd been on an uncomfortable tack for the toilet.

Beam reaching the whole way, I was surprisingly not nauseous at all even though I often had been when rolling about in the chop off Portsmouth Harbour on previous trips out. I slept on the leeward cockpit seat for a couple of hours, lulled by the soporific motion of the sea and Freya, our wind vane, steered us with ease.

As we closed in on the island of Alderney, heavy clouds crept up from the south and lightning began to appear. Of all the things that freaked me out about sailing, the idea of being struck by lightning was one of the main ones. Wind and waves were manageable to an extent but lightning was nature set to random and it made me nervous.

The current around Alderney is a determined thing and while Alex was concentrating on directing me so that we wouldn't be set down too far east, I was busy praying to a God that I didn't believe in that we wouldn't be struck by lightning. After all, out there you can't help feeling that you're a ten-metre lightning rod in an empty sea.

We arrived in Alderney Harbour at 8pm and anchored, avoiding the mooring buoys and their charges. The water taxi came out to us, following a downpour and the woman cheerfully welcomed us to the island and gave us a couple of leaflets, one detailing the protocols for ordering duty-free alcohol. It was obvious why most British sailors hopped over to Alderney for the weekend.

I was salty and windblown but drumming my hands on the walls in excitement; this was more than sailing to the Isle of Wight, this was a new country! Well, not a new country exactly as Alderney exists in the strange, semi-autonomous archipelago of the Channel Islands and uses the pound but still, it wasn't England per se. It wasn't even EU.

The magic of Enid Blyton had followed me well and truly to the Channel Islands, especially as Alderney was riddled with wartime fortifications that were either abandoned or seriously eerie. With hidden tunnels and wild, overgrown fields, it was a windswept place with a beauty all of its own.

We sailed to Sark a week later and the feeling was compounded. Sark was still based on a feudal system and seemed to exist wholly outside of the world as we knew it. Relying on supply ships from the larger islands, Sark had a tiny population and no motorised vehicles. We stayed for a lumpy two nights before catching a weather forecast while paying exorbitant 3G roaming fees and prepared to flee for Guernsey.

Because of an increase in swell the night before, Alex had rowed out a kedge anchor to keep us bows-to the incoming swell. The bottom was thick, heavy kelp and we had a significantly more comfortable night than we would otherwise have had.

I stowed things for sea while Alex rowed back out to retrieve it. He returned quickly with a whole load of chain but no anchor.

"I forgot to cable-tie the shackle," he said dumping the chain into the cockpit, "I'm going to have to dive for it."

I did not envy him the task of getting into Sark water and he donned his ancient winter wetsuit, complete with its holes, and jumped overboard with a dive torch. He swam until he was numb but the kelp had long since absorbed the anchor into its dense, oceanic meadow.

We figured the swell must have steadily rocked the shackle pin loose as we slept but kept repeating 'what are the chances'. It wasn't a mistake we ever made again.

We set off into the increasing swell for the shelter of Guernsey and were only mildly comforted by the fact that the anchor had been free from a friend. Still, it would be expensive to replace.

Within a couple of hours we were nestled in Fermain Bay, a shallow cove with a small and pretty beach just to the south of St Peter Port. We were the only yacht there and we'd arrived early evening when Sark became untenable.

I was in bed by 10pm and the night was still and moonlit in the shelter of the bay. We'd tucked close into the shore and checked the tidal range but a while later Alex poked his head into the forepeak and told me he thought we might ground – he'd miscalculated.

He said he'd re-anchor himself, the water was smooth and there wasn't even the smallest hint of wind. I closed my eyes again and kept an ear out for the activity on deck.

By the sounds the engine was making, it was clear that all was not going to plan. I hopped out of bed as Alex called to me and went to investigate.

The anchor was stuck on something on the seabed and the tide had dropped, fast. We were minutes from grounding and after one last attempt to free it from the surface, we were forced to tie a fender onto the end of the chain and throw it overboard. Anchorless, we retreated to an unused fishing boat mooring buoy and tied the boat on.

The moon was almost full and lit up the still water. The white fender looked grey in the half-light, a ghost sitting firmly on the surface. We decided that we couldn't stay on the buoy all night; we had no idea what sized boat it was designed for but probably not an 8-ton yacht.

"I'll have to dive for it," said Alex, heading for the wetsuit cupboard for the second time that day. I pulled a face, I wanted to help but there wasn't a chance I was going to get into that temperature water. Just thinking about it, I could feel the freezing water leaking into my wetsuit around the neck. I shivered.

We pumped up the dinghy and left *Berwick Maid* silently sat on the buoy, her halogen deck light creating an almost biblical beam of light onto the foredeck.

We hauled the fender into the dinghy and Alex went over the side. I pulled the chain into the dinghy, just a few metres to keep the dinghy in one place, and watched as Alex tracked the chain back to the anchor with his dive torch.

I hauled in a couple more metres, the chain lying across the width of the dinghy. A link pushed against the air bung and knocked it out as I squealed with surprise. A precarious thing at best, the bung could be knocked out with a fierce look and the inner mechanism had long been broken, allowing air to whoosh out. I scrambled for the bung, now somewhere in the bottom of the dinghy and felt the tubes begin to soften. I grabbed it, dropped it and grabbed it again, ramming it back into the hole. What else could possibly go wrong?

"It's caught through some kind of iron loop," he said as he swam back to the dinghy. "I'll detach the anchor and pull the chain through one side and the anchor out the other." I passed him a pair of pliers to cut the cable tie around the anchor shackle and he disappeared again.

For some reason, we loaded most of the chain into the dinghy before he went to retrieve the anchor and the dinghy started drifting, ever so slightly back towards the boat.

His huge free diving fins were kicking up billowing clouds of sand as he tried to stay above the water helping me with the chain and by the time he turned to get the anchor, it was obscured in a pale and opaque mist.

There was a few metres of chain out, anchoring the dinghy, but our movement had still allowed it to drift. He swam frantically with his torch trying to locate the anchor but each kick sent more sediment into the water.

I sat in the dinghy with wide eyes, running through the consequences of losing our anchor again. This time we didn't have a spare. We'd have to motor up to St Peter Port and tie up to a pontoon. How much did new anchors cost?

The was a splash and a shout and I realised that I was still drifting slowly, the weight of the chain in the dinghy too heavy for the remaining chain to hold still.

"I found it!" he called. He swam the 15 kg anchor back to the dinghy and loaded it in, I was overwhelmed with relief. We rowed a slightly soggy dinghy back to the boat and re-anchored in deeper water.

When we arrived in the Solent after two weeks exploring the Channel Islands, I finally felt like this was something I could see myself doing. By this point I had yet to experience any ocean swell but at least I had made peace with the idea of living on a boat. Besides, if I'd known what how hard it was going to be, then I probably would've needed a lot more convincing.

We spent a further two weeks in Hythe Marina, seeing friends and tying up the last loose ends. By this point we had no idea how long we'd be away – I think I thought it was going to be more like a few months than a few years. But we had no real reference points because we didn't really know where we'd end up going. This made saying goodbye or explaining the situation to banks all the more difficult.

We made no fuss of actually leaving. Leaving, leaving. In the back of my mind was the very real possibility that we'd get to Cornwall and think, 'screw this' and just go for a nice summer trip to the Scillies before coming home. I liked the idea of living on the boat now, but I still wasn't all that sure it was a long-term situation.

The boat was full of food, tinned and fresh. The water tank was full, as was the fuel. We'd closed up the house and said goodbye to friends and family. We slipped our mooring, negotiated the lock out of Hythe Marina and headed out down Southampton Water.

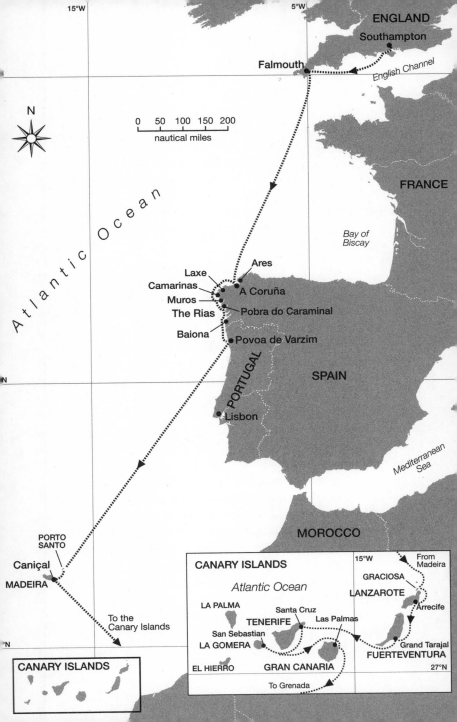

Chapter 2

Spanish Horizons

You didn't come into this world. You came out of it, like a wave from the ocean. You are not a stranger here.

Alan Watts

We are innately drawn to water. Even I, with my uncertainty and reticence, am drawn to water. To me there has never been anything more beautiful than rivers, lakes and oceans, whether I wanted to be in them or not.

In my early teens it was to the clifftops that my mother would take us to watch lightning storms roll in up the Channel. And the clifftops were only a mile from our house. And, looking back, that's always been the case.

Despite being an island, it's still easy to live an inconvenient distance from the sea although almost impossible to do so from some water source. I always grew up within walking distance from the sea in three different houses and it was only when I first went to university that I made the unwise decision to leave it.

I didn't go far from my childhood hunting grounds even though I'd always imagined I would. University was the escape on the horizon, my way out of a confusing youth. But I not only left the sea, but I left myself too, choosing to follow a boyfriend to Winchester and hemming myself in in more than one sense.

To the inlander it may sound preposterous, Winchester, after all, is not very far from the sea. But to someone who's grown up walking to the churning ocean, it was an impossible distance.

I felt it more than I thought about it. I never thought, 'the sea is far'. Instead I'd find myself on the willow-strewn banks of the Itchen as it chortled its way through the ancient city after another argument. But there was something lacking about the intrepid river as it disappeared round the bend into forests and fields. It didn't have the expanse, the pull or the depth that the ocean gave me.

I felt claustrophobic in Winchester even though I loved its soul and beauty. History didn't so much seep out of walls and buildings as flood. I lived on the high street opposite the 15th Century Buttercross statue and spent evenings running my hands along the stone walls of Winchester College, founded in 1382.

I love history. I love the endless, mesmerising depths of it and moreover, I love how easy it is to touch in England. In Winchester you could walk anywhere within the city walls and, if you stopped and reached out, you could touch something improbably old. You'd be walking near Roman walls, over medieval graves and above lost escape tunnels leading once upon a time from the castle.

But Winchester was small and coddled and presumptuous about itself and its inhabitants. There was no escape. There was no ocean. Living inland was like living in a room without a window while living on the coast was having one of those walls knocked clean away.

I didn't know I needed the ocean literally next to me until I went to explore Plymouth University in the summer of my first year. I stood on the Hoe, a ten-minute walk from student halls, and looked out to sea.

I went through the process of transferring from Winchester to Plymouth in time to enter my second year at my new university. Winchester's student welfare officer leaned forward in her chair, 'are you sure you're not running away?' she asked me.

No. I had already run away, I thought, this is me going back.

The deep pull the ocean had on me from the cliffs was not the same effect it had on me as we sailed from Falmouth to the Galician port of A Coruña. I hadn't done an overnight passage beforehand and this was my first, at five days long.

Biscay to me was the absolute test to overcome, the pinnacle of difficulty that, if conquered, would open up the entirety of Europe.

After all, once you've crossed Biscay, you can technically day sail almost all the way into the Mediterranean. We may've been heading for the Caribbean but I only had the capacity to worry about one offshore passage at a time.

Cold and afraid, I spent the first two nights offshore wearing as many clothes as humanly possible and scrunched up in the corner of the cockpit on my night watches.

It was a crash course in ship avoidance as not only did we straightaway have to deal with crossing the shipping channels of the English Channel, but we then had to either go inside or outside the channels off Ushant.

While over a year later we'd be freely sailing in empty Caribbean shipping channels, those in northern Europe were more akin in motorways. Weaving our way across them in the daylight was hard enough, at night it was exhausting.

With an AIS receiver, we could see the name, speed and heading of commercial shipping within a half to 16-mile radius depending on the waves and strength of signal.

Broadly speaking, yachts under sail have right of way against ships under power, but in the face of a Panamax doing 18 knots on a tight schedule, we ballet danced across lanes to stay out of their way.

On the third night we were into Biscay proper and, with hundreds of miles of space and multiple routes, the shipping lanes had eroded and lights on the horizon were fewer and further between.

I was nauseous and chilled at 8pm. The incessant grey waves were chipping away at my enthusiasm not with rock hammers but with mighty pickaxes. It was almost time for me to go off watch for two hours and I'd just put down my bowl of rice after two spoonfuls.

We're making progress, I thought, that's all that matters. This will end.

The last 24 hours had been rough. A short, sharp chop had sprouted up from the beam and, despite Alex's assertions that the waves were small, to me they felt and looked monstrous.

Alex put away the dishes and I stared out across the greyness. There was nothing out there, I thought, how would we ever reach Spain? We had hove-to to eat, not something we ever made a habit of but that evening it made cooking and eating much more comfortable. It involved the two sails to be set against each other, cancelling out any forward motion.

I closed my eyes and tried not to think about feeling sick. Was I even sick? Was it just worry? Was it the cold? I opened my eyes again and caught something in the ruffled sea. I saw things all the time, things that weren't there. This was something that would continue for the entire voyage and something every offshore sailor can relate to. You hallucinate at sea, your brain constantly creating things out of spray and waves and haze.

I saw it again. A shot of black. I sat up a little, it really did seem real. Again. Not just one, but tens. Tens of dark triangles zooming towards us at impossible speeds, like distance and waves were nothing at all.

I gasped and pushed myself out of my corner and over to the port side of the cockpit. Alex leapt out, thinking something was wrong.

"What?" he said, prepared for anything.

"Dolphins!"

They were around us in moments, shooting out of the water and crashing down with the flair of circus performers. They were innumerable, leaping and spinning in twos and threes. Racing around us and rolling under the waves. I stared over the side, the sea less than a metre from my face as a dolphin swam along on its side, it's right eye looking right back at me.

I clipped on and crawled to the bow, there's even a photograph of me, sumo-shaped in countless layers and clinging to the pulpit – this was a time before I'd learnt to walk on deck at sea. I'm cold and exhausted but I'm grinning with unadulterated joy because beneath me are dolphins playing under the bow as we slop around in the chop.

It was only months later, when I'd had so many dolphin encounters that I began to understand their behaviour, that I realised this first, seminal incident was strange.

After that dolphins never came to the boat if she was doing less than

4 knots. If she was racing along at 6 they'd race alongside with us but if the wind dropped and we went to 3 knots, they'd get quickly bored and leave.

Dolphins never came to us when we were slow, they loved the speed and playfulness of the bow wave and the Aries fin on the stern. So out of character were the first Biscay dolphins, staying with us hove-to and continuing with us for a further hour of slow sailing, that I eventually concluded that they were either very bored, very hyper or had been sent to me by the ocean, the lifting of the first of many curtains.

As I tucked myself up in bed the following evening around the same time, we had another visitor.

"Come look who's here!" said Alex from the cockpit. I had just got into bed and we were still only doing two-hour watches at this stage as I simply wasn't confident enough to do more.

I didn't want to get out of bed. There was a timer ticking in my head, counting down the minutes until I had to get up again.

"What is it?" I called, sceptical.

"Come look," said Alex, never one to give the game away. I sighed, and pushed back the blanket and sleeping bag that I'd entrenched myself in. I was still fully dressed for two reasons. Firstly, I was cold and secondly, I felt it important to be prepared to leap outside at any moment.

Alex was sat on starboard looking at the boom. We were almost broad-reaching and the boom was out over the sea. There, between the topping lift end and the mainsail clew, was a pigeon.

A very, very sad pigeon. Ruffled feathers and unsure of his footing, the pigeon looked at us mournfully as he swayed back and forth with the motion of the boat. As the waves were fairly beam on, the boom bounced occasionally causing the bird to extend his feathers for balance and stumble on the polished surface.

I was beside myself with love. There is nothing so heart-breaking as a dishevelled animal in human territory. Despite being only a metre or two away from us, the pigeon showed no signs of flying away. Clearly being on something floating, anything at all, was better than falling into the drink.

But the waves kept slamming the side of the boat and the boom swung slightly and banged, despite the preventer we'd tied on. It didn't take long for the pigeon to lose his footing entirely and land in the cockpit.

"He's a racing pigeon," I said, seeing the little plastic ring around his ankle. This was not the first racing pigeon to have landed in my charge, although he was certainly the most unhappy.

The house I grew up in, a tiny cottage in Hampshire, was near a racing pigeon breeder although whether it was his pigeons I never found out. We had several racing pigeons land on the patio, each helping themselves freely to our bird table. One showed so little inclination to leave that my father put it in a box and took it to the local RSPB. I had a fondness for them and all hungry birds actually.

After falling repeatedly about the cockpit combing and hitting the guard wires as he attempted to fly back to the boom, the pigeon eventually landed at our feet in the bottom of the cockpit and decided to stay there.

With the cockpit floor only being 1 x 1.5 metres with a teak grating, there was less space for him to slide around and he soon tucked up into the corner. The waves still rolled him and he was clearly going to get zero rest having to keep his balance. As much as I wanted to spend my time cooing at him, I also wanted to get back into bed.

"He can't have flown from England, they don't fly that far do they?" asked Alex.

"I don't know, probably not," I said. "I guess he's probably French." I took one last look at the pigeon we'd by now named Bill and went to bed.

As I tucked myself back in and tightened the lee-cloth, I could hear Alex speaking to Bill.

"Ou est ton bateau eh? D'ou viens tu?" I could hear him saying. I didn't hear the response.

As I lay in bed thinking about the pigeon, the thought of him rolling exhaustedly around the cockpit was too much. I remembered a shoebox that I'd kept recently on the basis that it was a really-useful-looking-box and pushed back the covers.

"Here," I said, presenting the shoe box to Alex, "put him in that."

"You think?" he said, taking the box.

"He's a racing pigeon, he's used to being in a box, it'll probably make him feel at home." The pigeon had no issue with being put in the box and immediately settled down in an unkempt ball of feathers, his head as far down into his body as he could get it. There was no protestation when the lid went on either.

Talking, thinking and checking on Bill got me through my two night watches in a far more enjoyable manner than the preceding ones. Although I tried to limit my peeking, I couldn't bear the thought of lifting the lid in the morning only to find two curled feet sticking up in the air. Each time I lifted the lid, my head torch beam to the side so as to not blind him, I found him just the same, peering up with a querying expression.

As the sun rose on my first morning watch, there was the occasional scuffle from inside the box. I opened the lid and found Bill finely groomed and bright eyed. Where before he'd been rumpled feathers and decidedly bushy, he was now neat and sleek with a spark of attitude in his eyes. He half jumped, half flew out of the box.

I had tried to feed him during the night with Cheerios (wholegrain, I'm not a heathen) but we decided that he must be a highly disciplined racer as he didn't touch the sugary cereal. I'd also tried to give him capfuls of water but whether he managed to drink any I don't know, the motion was increasingly violent.

Now he strutted around the cockpit, evacuating his bowels, clearly having not wanted to dirty his sleeping arrangement. This pigeon had pedigree. As he explored the terrain and took a wind reading, I followed around after him, clearing up in case bird shit stained the gelcoat.

A larger yacht had appeared on the horizon at dawn and was steadily gaining on us. It would only be another hour or so until we were in visual distance of Spain and this prompted Alex to raise a point.

"Look, what are we going to do with him, we can't turn up in a foreign country with an animal," he said.

I hadn't thought about that. Not only was our arrival in Spain still not registering as even possible in my head, but I also hadn't really considered Bill as a domestic animal. He was a bird. Birds did what they liked. But Alex had a point.

Neither of us knew what the customs situation was in A Coruña or how closely incoming yachts were monitored. Besides, surely as soon as we docked he would fly away?

We didn't need to worry about it for long though was Bill had clearly been brought up on golden Niger seeds and spied the larger, newer, shinier looking yacht as it started to overtake us a few miles away.

Without so much as a goodbye, he emptied his bowels once more over the cockpit seat and took off eastwards. Where he'd come from we couldn't imagine as he'd landed when we were around 100 miles from Spain and almost 300 from France. I was sad to see him go, but he wouldn't be the last bird to leave his mark in our cockpit.

I spotted land on the horizon in the early afternoon and the feeling was momentous. This wasn't the Spain of my childhood; the Spain of 14-hour drives south from Calais. This was the Spain of the wilderness explorer, a wild, new land that could contain anything.

Firstly, I hadn't been expecting what looked like mountainous green cliffs. I don't know what I'd expected but I think much lower land, possible even beaches. Having only travelled to Catalonia and the Pyrenees before, my general impression of the rest of Spain had always been fairly arid.

But what I saw now was verdant and towering, only adding to the strange sense of exoticness that I felt. This couldn't be exotic, I thought, it's only Spain. But it wasn't only Spain, it was a Spain I'd sailed to.

The swell grew throughout the day, transatlantic waves building as they reached land and the wind shot up as we neared the coastline. I spent the afternoon in a heightened state of anticipation, always dancing on the edge between excitement, relief and fear.

I was forced to takeover from the Aries as we turned downwind to head down to A Coruña. The following waves threatened to slew the boat over as she rushed down the faces. These were the biggest waves I had come across so far and I rejected Alex's offer to steer, I had to do it myself, I was simply too afraid to relinquish control.

As the wind hit force 6, we had just a scrap of genoa out and I was determined not to look behind me. The waves were likes walls rushing up on us and I plugged myself into my iPod, letting the music keep me believing that this was all okay, we were okay.

Every time I felt the stern being picked up I'd turn the boat down the face and wait for the whoosh and the wallow as she slumped back off the top of the wave and watched it roar onwards. Then I'd resume my course, slightly across the waves, towards the harbour entrance.

As the seabed shallowed towards in the entrance to the port, I genuinely feared for our lives. My inexperience was still at the stage where capsizing was often near the forefront of my mind, but I still remember those waves as being huge now, even with my subsequent experiences.

As I steered us past the first breakwater, heart in my throat, lips jammed together with tension and barely remembering to breathe, a trawler trundled out past us, smashing repeatedly into the oncoming waves. With its bow rising to the peaks and crashing off the backs, I was overwhelmed with relief that we were going in. A large part of me believed we would face those same waves whenever we chose to leave though.

The water was immediately and impossibly calm the moment we passed the breakwater. The difference was astounding and I laughed out loud at how frightened I'd been just moments before.

As we slid inelegantly into our berth that evening, I jumped onto the pontoon to tie on the bow line and skidded to my knees on the damp wood. But I was on land – as good as anyway – and that was all that mattered.

No matter how far offshore you are when you spot land, it always takes hours more than you would've thought to reach the anchorage or berth. In good visibility, you might see the harbour 8 hours before you reach it and by the time we'd tied up in A Coruña, it was almost 9pm.

After a quick shower before the block closed for the night and ten minutes of customs paperwork in the marina office, we were sat outside a tiny shop clinking icy bottles of Estrella Galicia, the first of an Atlantic's worth of local lagers.

A Coruña is a historic city set on a peninsula at the opening of an estuary or, in this case, a Spanish ria. With its winding streets and labyrinthine pedestrianised alleys, it was an immensely perfect place to make our first landfall.

I spent the next week wandering around the cobbled city with its flaking paint and its endless street cafes. If A Coruña sounds like a stereotype of a European city then that's because it kind of is. Except for the tourists. A Coruña seemed to have only Spanish tourists and so to us, it felt like it had no tourists at all.

Small and shoved in the far corner of Galicia, Spain's most north-westerly autonomous region, A Coruña doesn't have the heat of Mediterranean Spain nor the loud look-at-me of Madrid, Barcelona or Seville.

But it did have streets of tapas bars where we ordered back-to-back plates of calamari and spent three days working out how exactly one orders draught beer (caña, as it transpired).

After having spent what felt like weeks at sea – but only 5 days – we bought baguette after baguette and gorged on chorizo, jamón, cheese and wine. Finally, affordable wine! Finding a supermarket in a new place was, as we'd discover, one of a sailor's favourite activities.

As someone who's not only categorically under appreciated food for most of her life but also seen eating as an activity bordering on time-wasting, sailing was already beginning to change the way I lived my life. I would go on to develop a productive and healthy relationship with food but those early days in Spain, after 5 days of nausea and seriously sub-standard nutrition, set the ball rolling.

With many climates and landscapes, Spain has an amazing

abundance of temperate and sub-tropical fruits and vegetables and it was the first place I ever saw kiwi vines and avocado trees growing casually in gardens.

Suffice to say, I ate everything I could find in that first week and I felt cleansed and triumphant having, in my mind, already accomplished the hardest voyage in the world; the Biscay crossing. No, the beginner's Biscay crossing.

I wasn't always this afraid and when I think about myself before the age of twenty one, I don't see an anxious person, always assuming the worst. I remember flamboyancy, extroversion and daring through the majority of my teenage years at least. I know this isn't the full picture because I found diaries I'd kept diligently throughout my childhood and within minutes was tearing them up, ripping them into tiny shreds because I was so horrified with what I saw there. Pages of depression, of misery, of casual desperation.

Did that mean I wasn't a happy child? I spent most of my teens forging a path into the theatre, always happy to be on stage, always happy to spend hours memorising lines and always wanting to be in the middle of everything. When I was thirteen I went and made a list of my favourite actors and researched their lives, seeing how they did it, how they made it. There wasn't much method or even consistency. Kate Moss was 'discovered' at 14 walking down the street. I had a year to be found in the same way before I'd have to write her off as better than me. Orlando Bloom was in the National Youth Theatre, I went for an audition. Kirsten Dunst started as a child actor, I had to cross her off straight away, I was too late for that.

At sixteen I'd put myself on trains to London and trail around the city looking for the alley entrances to audition rooms. I was confident, I felt confident, I didn't doubt myself. I remember that feeling of the world being laid out before me and even though I hadn't really got anywhere, I was certain I would.

In my first year of college I caught a train to London and found myself glued to a map trying to find Ealing Studios. I was studying performing arts and, as far as I could see, being sixteen and auditioning on top of studying was as professional as it got.

I buzzed the studio when I got to the gate and met the director, herself a student at the Metropolitan Film School. But to me she was an adult, a way in. I read for the part, a bitchy schoolgirl with a boyfriend and a bullying streak. It was just me and the director and I loved every second of it, nerves never really playing a part.

I walked back across the small green to the station and a man stopped me. He was tall, smart coat, dark skin.

"Hello, have you ever thought about being a model?" he asked. I stopped too, not wanting to be rude. I laughed my polite, I'm-an-adult laugh.

"I'm not tall enough," I said (I'd done my research, I was a realist at 5'3". Funnily enough, I'd never thought about my face which, looking back, wouldn't have stood a chance even if I had been a giraffe).

"Not all models are catwalk tall you know," he said and got out his wallet. "Here, take my card and give me a call."

I took it and looked at it.

"Just ignore what it says there, that's just my side business, I'm also a model scout."

Life isn't *Sliding Doors*, thankfully because that film only serves to suggest there are no happy endings. But if my life was *Sliding Doors*, this is where it would have split initially. One path would've led me to being tied up and murdered and one path would've been where I am today.

Okay I'm almost certainly exaggerating but I look back to that day and I see who I was at that age. And I miss her. I looked at his card on the tube. It was a business card for a luxury chauffeur. I briefly considered all plausible reasons why a genuine model scout might also be a luxury chauffeur who happened to be walking through Ealing in the middle of a weekday. There were no plausible reasons. I did not call him.

I didn't feel disappointed or even have the remotest temptation to call and see what he said. I had long before decided I was not model material by any shake of the magic stick and so being told something

43

different by a strange man on the street was only the same as being told I could be an Olympic gymnast. The only thing I did wonder with any real concern was what he was actually up to and just how easy was it to get lured in by a stranger. My mother had taught me that men in general were to be treated with caution, let alone stranger older men on the street. Nevertheless, I kept the card in the back of my wallet for many years, a cautionary reminder.

I saw myself as a savvy teenager although I certainly did not exercise the same judgement consistently. But I made decisions with conviction, even if they were the wrong ones. In the year after I graduated from university, that girl was all but gone.

I'd succeeded at partying through my years at Plymouth University but I almost failed my degree doing so. For a girl who'd believed herself intelligent, the scathing dismissal of my dissertation and my 2:2 degree left me embarrassed. But I'd known it was coming. I'd received two minimum pass marks for two entire modules because I didn't turn up to a single lecture or seminar. A single one. I didn't even know what my tutors looked like. Why?

On the first day of the term I stood outside the seminar room but I couldn't turn the handle. I couldn't face walking in. I had joined the university in my second year and was terrified of being the odd one out. It didn't even make sense, because students choose different modules, making the class at least a third strangers to each other anyway. But something inside me stopped me at the last minute and I stepped back from the edge. And that's the thing about giving up on something, it becomes easier and easier to give up on everything else.

I hid my many academic failures from everyone, even my housemates, my closest friends didn't know the extent of it. I became perpetually afraid of being found out, of someone turning around and saying, 'you're not intelligent enough to be here, you can't write'.

I passed by completing the bare minimum of work and down to the fact that I did well in a small selection of classes I did attend due to bizarre and short-lived spurts of hard work and dedication. I liked discussions where I cared about the text, where I could voice my opinion because I was confident in it. But the moment I let doubt creep in I bolted for the nearest exit, the nearest bar. My housemate partied as much as I did but got up every day at 7am to complete her medical degree. She qualified as a doctor while I lay in bed and hid from an English degree. I couldn't blame my failures on my love of a good night out.

I could've stopped the downward spiral at any time by just taking responsibility for my actions. By, as someone said years later, 'just doing the right thing'. But I didn't. I hid for years. I formed an impenetrable barrier of self-doubt and shielded myself from the reality of my emptiness by drinking and being the chaotic girl that everybody patted on the head. I was following a path built from paper, each step hastily pasted onto the next with an ever-decreasing amount of glue. At some point I would inevitably fall through.

Chapter 3

A Secret Island

We travel, initially, to lose ourselves; and we travel, next to find ourselves.

Pico Iyer

It was 1st September when we arrived in Porto Santo. We'd spent eight days at sea, sailing from the northern Portuguese city of Povoa de Varzim. It had taken longer than I'd expected as we'd been becalmed four days out and drifted for 36 hours on a perfectly calm ocean. Something I hadn't even known existed at sea.

As the wind had picked up and boat with it, I'd lain in my bunk during off-watches and listened to the sound of water racing along the hull. It was inches from my ear, my face, my bed. The thinnest of membranes separated me from the great swirling ocean, from a whole other world.

When dolphins came, they too swam inches from my face. I could hear them squeaking in their indecipherable language to one another as though they were deliberately speaking right to me. They were closer than partners lie in bed.

At the very most, the boat was what my sister would call an 'inside-outside' space. If the hatch boards were ever closed it was for the duration of a squall as we sailed downwind, it was too hot otherwise. As we trundled deeper into the subtropics, the boat was more like a solid tent than a house.

I washed up in seawater, hurling a bucket on a rope overboard and heaving it back up against 5 knots of water. Only a few times did I throw out the dirty water with a fork or spoon still in it.

But on passage we only used freshwater for drinking and cooking, saltwater washed us, bore us and was always just a second away. The sea was as much on me and in me as I was on and in it.

There are yachts that are far more separate from the water, perhaps most, when you look at the average Caribbean cruising yacht. But we had low sides and I could touch the water just by reaching over the cockpit sides. I sometimes leant over and washed my mug out that way.

I would never have dreamed that I'd become so comfortable living so close to the water or that I'd come to rely on its motions, sounds and abilities. It wasn't until I stayed on land during a brief trip to Peru halfway through our voyage around the Atlantic that I realised how reassuring the constant noise of water was. In a hostel bed, the silence could be absolute in a way that it could never be on board the boat. There was always the sound of water against the hull, even in a calm anchorage. The Atlantic was always there, in bed with me.

When we arrived in Porto Santo, the island clearly lived for, by and with the ocean as well. Its supplies came by sea, its tourists came by sea, it's very geology was carved by the ocean that ravaged its shores. It was impossible to be anywhere on the island and not see, hear and at least smell the ocean. Volcanic, the island had even come from the sea, thrusting up from the seabed.

'I decided that travel was flight and pursuit in equal parts,' wrote Theroux in his astounding *Great Railway Bazaar* and I felt it more than ever as we dallied in Porto Santo.

I had begun writing a novel a few days into our stay in the island's marina, a fevered, obsessive form of writing that forced me to the saloon table for most of every day. While Alex spearfished and continued on his endless task of boat maintenance, I wrote.

I finished it in three weeks. It wasn't a good novel, its 85,000 words were lazy and rushed but I wrote it because I needed, very urgently, to do something. Simply sailing was not enough, but in whose eyes?

I'd begun writing a novel but a few weeks before I'd come up with the ingenious idea of retraining in dietetics upon our return. Our return? We'd only just left!

So desperate was I to reassure myself that I wasn't running away, that I was making ridiculous plans for when we got back. Knowing by now that we wouldn't be back for a long time.

It was as though I needed something in the future that was... respectable. As though I was telling myself over and over that this voyage of impromptu and absurd nature was just a temporary thing, that I had an honest, sensible plan, that this was just the thing before that.

These weren't even half-hearted ideas, I would grab them with full force for the day or two after they'd occurred to me. During my time in Porto Santo I had a dream that I was at medical school and so strong was the feeling of challenge and happiness I awoke with, that I spent two days researching just how someone with a BTEC in performing arts and a degree in creative writing could possibly re-train as a doctor.

A doctor. It took me a long time to come to terms with our departure not just from England, but from the assumption I'd always had of getting a 'proper job'. I had never wanted one, but I had always assumed that I would have one.

Alex lived each day as it was supposed to be lived, with curiosity and enthusiasm and deep consideration over the flavours he added to his increasingly elaborate dinners. While he looked and touched and smelt everything around him in our new surroundings, I worried about what I was going to do with my life.

"But you're doing this," he would say, baffled. I wasn't, I was doing a thousand things but I wasn't doing the one thing that mattered. I wasn't there, present.

Doubt nagged at me. I should be making an amazing blog, I thought. I should be videoing this stuff. I should be a happy, bouncy traveller photographed in all the cool places I was visiting. Why wasn't I doing any of that? I constantly looked at other people's lives and wondered if I could do that, be that. I could never pin down who I was. I loathed the idea of travelling to 'find yourself'. I fought it on every front. But I was travelling and I wasn't finding myself, I was finding a gaping hole where I should've been.

The only thing that could drag me out of my self-involved loop was newness. I needed the shock and surprise of new landscapes, the touch of new plants and the sight of new shores. Each time I felt embedded in the own mess of my head, I was pulled out and dumped in a new environment like staring at a screen and, after hours, realising you can look out of the window and see something real.

We had hired a moped on the second day of being in Porto Santo and drove around the island. While Madeira is wet, lush and high, Porto Santo is fundamentally low-lying although it has a good handful of peaks up to 517 m.

The only plants are palms and scrub and, as we drove along the north-eastern coast, I was amazed at the harshness of the landscape with the road cut savagely into the sides of the volcanic hills.

Porto Santo has a strange geography which became more and more apparent as we circled the island. One tourism website said, 'Porto Santo is one long beach with a bit of an island attached', which, in my opinion, couldn't be further from the truth.

Compared to Madeira's exclusively rocky coastline, Porto Santo's 9km beach does draw its fair share of tourists, especially Madeirans, but it's the rest of the island that holds all of its secrets. It's the rest that drew me in and made me realise that the island is a place all by itself.

The basalt columns of Pico do Ana Ferreira rise unexpectedly out from a hill overlooking an abandoned housing estate. These vast columns stand tall, shunted up from the earth by tremendous geological force and are one of Porto Santo's major tourist sights but looking down, I could see the perfect roads, crisp markings and even garden paths to non-existent houses.

It made a good place to learn to drive a moped but gave an eerie atmosphere to what should be an impressive geological landmark. The island managed to sustain its organ pipe rocks for millions of years and yet humans couldn't even finish a housing development.

There were natural swimming baths on the north west coast although the sea still wasn't particularly warm down there and the stone seawater baths were exposed to the ocean. They weren't man-made and instead were rough pools, worn in by the centuries of Atlantic swells.

Accessed down a steep path and shadowed from the sun by huge cliffs, I didn't fancy dipping a toe in there. Much later in the trip I discovered similar creations in the Azores, where the sea-hewn rock baths were complimented by food huts and handrails.

There was something magical about the island, young compared to the landmasses of nearby continental Europe and Africa at just 8 million years old, or so. It seemed... secret and unique and, once again, I felt as though I was in the middle of a Blyton plot.

It was Alex's birthday and, Porto Santo being a miniature island, there was only a couple of particularly celebrated restaurants, all supremely authentic.

With a terrace out on the roadside, Bar Joao da Cabeco had a similar menu to everywhere else we'd seen in Portugal and was just as cheap. The birthday boy ordered Chouriço Assado.

Portuguese food is almost always a variation of the same thing and counts carbohydrate as at least 60% of each meal. It wasn't unusual to be presented with a plate including potatoes, chips and rice along with whatever the centrepiece was (so to speak) such as fish or meat. More often than not there'd also be a fried egg on top and a small salad fitted miraculously on the side. In these instances it would be impossible to actually eat any part of the meal without a reasonable quantity of rice or a section of chips falling onto the table. All for €5.

Just when I'd gotten used to this sort of lunch and could order appropriately, something came along which is quite literally just what the menu says. In this case, roast sausage.

My fish burger arrived with the expected quantity of extras piled high and another waitress brought out Alex's dish. It was laid down in front of him, an entire 15 inch chorizo looped on a terracotta pig-shaped dish. The waitress searched in the front pocket of her apron and, pulling out a lighter, proceeded to set the thing on fire and abandon us to the flaming sausage.

The blue flame barely garnered looks from the Portuguese around us, although it was beginning to melt the Coca-Cola sponsored napkin holder beside it. We looked at each other.

"Blow it out," I said.

"But I don't know what's making it burn, if I blow it out now it might leave unburnt chemicals on the sausage," Alex pointed out. The fire continued.

"Do you think it'll burn itself out?" I asked, gazing at the terracotta pig and gently crisping sausage. It was also, I couldn't help noticing, an entire sausage by itself. No bread to ease you into it, no carbohydrates to help you mop up the grease. Just one giant, flaming sausage. We started sniggering.

I began on my own food and Alex looked around him and leant forwards, blowing the flame out. It didn't put up much of a fight and he began his half an hour long battle to cut the tough sausage and eat it, sharing my ginormous plate of carbs.

I lay on the sand while Alex swam off the meat. Porto Santo had seemingly endless beaches on its south coast, or rather, one seemingly endless beach. It seemed to be the main reason why so many Madeirans spend their summers there, catching the ferry from their own island just 20 miles away. A native Porto Santo islander told me the Madeirans come to get away from the business of Madeira as well as for the beach and the parties they bring with them. Madeira has over double the population density of Porto Santo but, ironically, Porto Santo's population increases by so much in the summer months. The tourists bring the crowds they're trying to escape.

I wasn't much of a sunbather. Perhaps it was due to the paleness of my skin and proclivity to burn but I think it was mainly boredom. I didn't see how anyone could just lie on the sand for hours at a time, or even more than ten minutes. I spent enough of my time thinking, mulling, daydreaming and worrying as it was. When I did force myself into a quiet place to meditate, I certainly didn't want it to be under the direct gaze of a subtropical sun.

I couldn't read on the beach because I could never get comfortable and I was always too hot or too cold. To me, beaches were for walking on, for barbecues and for easing your body onto land from the water. I loved beaches but I loved them for movement, for beach ball, for the graduations between ocean, sand and the tree line.

To me they're not for lying, spreadeagled trying to balance the risk of skin cancer with the status of a suntan. If you ever find me lying prone on a beach it's because I'm watching a crab clear out its burrow.

But people flock to beaches. The sun collects there, the sand and sea doing a good job of reflecting it and of course the ever-present desire to look good in a bikini or at least have the money to have the opportunity. But is that really why everybody goes to the beach? After all, people still flocked to the beach before 'bikini bodies' even really existed – at least not in the manner they do now.

The coast has always been a useful place, a place to fish, to import and export and nowhere in the UK is more than 70 miles from the coastline, so it's natural that we all know it to some extent. But no matter how hard I try to go inland, I always get dragged back to the shore. And I think it's the same for others as well. The throngs of people lying in the sun aren't just here for a tan, they're here for the sound of the sea doing its tireless job of rearranging the coastline. After all, the beach is the only real place on earth where you can see geological change on a minute by minute scale.

We, as islanders, maybe as humans, need the coastline as fundamentally as we need the trees. It connects us cleanly to nature.

The wind picked up after our first week in Porto Santo, just around the time we wanted to head south. It was a fearsome south-westerly, who knows where from. The tourists had all gone from the island and the tiny marina was full of long-distance sailors waiting to leave. I could climb up the towering breakwater that separated the beach from the marina and watch as the waves piled onto the shore and ripped the sand away.

Every morning the beach was a different place. Some days it looked like it'd been robbed of half its sand, a deep high tide mark cut and scraped. Then other days the sand was back, asking for footprints as though it had never left. These islands were forced violently out of the earth's mantle but they were in a constant state of change and the beach was the only place to see it.

Porto Santo was full of hidden places though. Once I followed a dirt track down the side of the airstrip and discovered Porto Santo's desert. One moment I was surrounded by low hilly scrubland and the next I'd wandered into a scene straight out of the Star Wars film where Anakin raced pod cars. So immediate was the change that when I came across the wildly unexpected landscape, I thought it was man-made.

With towering, jagged walls of brittle sand and several dunes, I found myself running up and down the desert's curves in wonder. It was a secret place or at least had that feel. Of course, there couldn't be any secret places on an island that small but the fact that an island of just 16 square miles could retain that impression was incredible.

In fact, I found a paper written by the botanist T. D. A. Cockerell while I was looking into the history of Porto Santo and his words so tallied with my experiences that I couldn't tell how long ago he was even writing until I got to the end. He wrote about the endemic snails, dating back to the Pleistocene period as well as the flora of the island and surrounding islets. The desert retains fossils from these ancient periods, the desert itself untouched by much human interference. He goes on to describe the isolation:

My wife and I were two weeks in Porto Santo, during which time we were entirely cut off from the rest of the world. There is no means of communication by telegraph or wireless, and the town, Villa Baleira, seems to be little altered from the time when Columbus walked the streets and married the daughter of the Governor... We found the people most friendly, and left them with regret. Owing to the magnificent bathing beach (something that Madeira lacks) there is now much talk of building a fashionable hotel for summer tourists. Very likely a few years will see a complete change in the character of the place, and though prosperity may come thereby, something will be lost, which we – and Columbus – loved in our time.

Flora of Porto Santo, T. D. A. Cockerell, Torreya Journal (1922)

Cockerell and his wife would perhaps then be pleased to know that Porto Santo simply hadn't changed very much since he wrote his paper in 1922. There were small hotels although certainly no large luxury ones and the action was very much centred in the one and only town, Villa Baleira, which had barely expanded at all. The rest of the island, with its smattering of traditional houses and a single golf course, was almost deserted outside of the summer season. Bumbling around the island on our moped, I saw just one other driver and a couple of horses.

Porto Santo, with all its craggy edges and serenity, couldn't hold my attention for more than ten days. I was developing itchy feet, something that increased the further I sailed and the more islands I visited. It seemed to strike all sailors and travellers at some point, the ceaseless desire to move somewhere new.

After two weeks another English sailor washed up on Porto Santo's shores, a retired GP called Murray.

"So I hear you've been writing?" Murray asked me as I sipped a gin and tonic in his cockpit one evening. I explained a little about my work and he told me that he was also funding his sailing by having written something. "Just a little medical textbook," he said.

The little textbook turned out to be one of the most popular books for British medical students. It was, as my doctor friend Jess told me later, 'the bible'.

"It was actually banned for a while by the examining boards because apparently it made the exams too easy to pass," Murray told us, "but you know what? Nothing boosts sales like a book being banned!"

Murray was heading to New Zealand, having read an article about a particularly beautiful archipelago of islands and deciding that sailing there was as good as any other method. He was the only other sailor I met that admitted to altering course for a celestial body, in his case the moon, in mine, Jupiter.

The trouble with sailing at night is that you become very attuned to the slightest light on the horizon. Despite Jupiter rising at the same time each night in the same place for a period, I still saw it and thought it was a ship coming ever closer the higher the light got. Sometimes it would send me into something bordering on panic as I contemplated whether to wake Alex up. Then it would always rise too high for a yacht and continue on its merry way in the star-filled sky.

Murray also had an interesting theory on whales, as every long distance sailor seemed to. Dolphins and whales are intelligent in a way that is undeniable. They turn on their sides as they come alongside the boat to look at you right in the eye. A long, thoughtful look and if you go below they'll disappear, not performing without an audience.

Murray had been sat in his hammock, tied up between the forestay and the mast, reading his book on his voyage from the Azores south. He'd put the kettle on and could hear it begin to whistle.

"The thing was though, I was nearing the end of a very gripping chapter and I thought, 'well I put plenty of water in so I'll let it whistle a bit until I get to the end.' And the next thing I knew there was a great whoosh of spray alongside and there he was, a huge whale!" Murray figured the whistling kettle had attracted the curious cetacean, something that could easily be true. Sound travels well through the hulls of boats and I've stood on deck in bored moments and shouted, 'where are my dolphins!' at the waves, only to find a pod surrounding us within moments. Although, granted, the two times that worked could have been coincidences.

Still, the ocean is a big place and houses many troupes of inquisitive creatures. A travelling yacht picks up more than its fair share of followers on a daily basis, almost like the pied piper. Tiny fish use it as shelter, larger fish use it for hunting, birds use it to flush out flying fish, dolphins use it as a large, floating toy and whales turn up just to see what the fuss is about. No matter how isolated and lonely you may feel mid-ocean, you can bet that you are far from alone.

We were in Porto Santo for almost a month before heading south to Madeira for just two days and then the Canaries. Madeira, with its heavily volcanic cliffs and lack of beaches was no place to anchor and we were forced into an expensive, soulless marina at the most eastern end. A bus journey to busy Funchal was all we needed to ready ourselves for the short, three day voyage to Spain's Canary Islands.

I left Porto Santo with mixed emotion. On one hand, we'd been there a long time and it was only a small island, I wanted a new place. But on the other hand, the island had something magical to it, a sense of far-awayness that I had never experienced before. It was almost other-worldly.

As we sailed south past Madeira's Islas Desertas, towering, uninhabited rocky islands, the sun was fading and I was preparing for the first night at sea for a month. I was due off-watch at 8pm and could feel my bunk calling to me when I noticed an odd cloud to port. Alex was napping before his watch started and Freya, the wind vane, was steering.

I watched the cloud, a normal small cumulus, as something strange happened beneath it. I could see a straight line. Of cloud. It was a beautiful evening, 30% cloud cover and a good force 3. The sea was flat and there was nothing ominous in sight, so I could not understand what I was seeing. It was as though the cloud had a single, dead straight strand coming out of. But clouds couldn't have straight lines, could they?

With the clouds travelling east to west and us going south, this bizarre shape-shifting cloud was coming towards us and the closer it got the more confused I became. Suddenly the strand got much longer, reaching a third of the way from the cloud base to the sea. My stomach twisted. I slotted the throttle from reverse to its starting position and continued to watch.

It was quarter to eight when my suspicions were confirmed. I could see, less than half a mile off the port bow, a swirling mass in the water.

"Alex," I said, not wanting to alarm him, but he could hear it in my voice and was in the cockpit in a flash. I pointed.

"We have a waterspout," I said. As I was speaking, the spout visibly reached from the cloud to the water and we rolled up the sails, mostly to slow us down but also to prevent them from ripping if it hit us. The base wasn't huge but it was not much smaller than the boat's footprint and I didn't fancy it. As the boat slowed and slopped along, the waterspout trundled across in front of us, its unstable spout appearing and disappearing. Once I saw that it would miss us, I could begin to appreciate it for what it was, a true natural phenomenon, connecting the sky to ocean in a swirling, dancing tube. It was alone, performing for no one on its way west across the serene Atlantic. It was perfect and perfectly alien to me.

Part of the reason, maybe the whole reason, that I found the ocean so frightening was the otherness of it. There was nothing familiar out at sea except for the boat I was in – but I still didn't know her that well either. I felt a much deeper sense of safety and reassurance when we were less than a day sail away from habitable land and it took me a long time to work out why.

A man and his son had been killed the year before, trying to enter the harbour at Povoa de Varzim where we'd stayed in Portugal before sailing to Porto Santo. Their boat had been smashed against the breakwater in the storm they were fleeing from. Harbours are dangerous in storms and Povoa de Varzim is particularly dangerous with swell and surge.

"They'd have been safer at sea," Alex had told me at the time, "If we're out in a storm, we'll hove-to or take the sails down and wait it out, there's nothing to hit out there." While I nodded my understanding, I couldn't imagine how frightening it would be to stay out in a storm at sea, every fibre of my body would want to head for land, for a safe harbour. I don't know why they attempted such a hideously dangerous entrance, but I wonder if, like me, they just associated land with safety, harbours with safety. If they could just get in past the second breakwater they would be safe. If if just just.

But Alex often pointed out instances in which being at sea was preferable. In an anchorage with strong winds coming from the sea and not the land – we would be safer at sea. Because if we found ourselves at anchor and winds pushing us inland, we could be wrecked on the rocks with ease and our engine would struggle to push us through wind and waves. Far better to prepare and go 20+ miles offshore to wait it out. The reasoning made sense but I hated the thought of it, leaving the safety of land for the strange, raging ocean.

As I lay in bed between island chains, I worried about what exactly was out there. But still, Madeira was to the north and the Canaries were just two days to the south with both Europe and Africa to the east; my sense of safety zone was expanding with each voyage and I was as 'offshore' as most adventurous sailors ever get. But the Atlantic Ocean loomed in my mind; it was, to me, the greatest unknown.

In the Atlantic, there would be no land to offer even the falsest of reassurances. Out there was just wild ocean and endless skies. It was a huge void that I would be entering in less than two months and it was the void that frightened me the most. It would be unrelenting unfamiliarity where the rules of the world I grew up in did not apply. Where I was, quite literally, out of my element.

It amazes me now just how much of my time I spent worrying about all the trillions of things that could happen. I would lie in my bunk, half trying to sleep and half repeating the order of reefing, how I'd rescue Alex if he fell into the water and just how the electrical system worked. It was a fairly disastrous method of resting.

But after the waterspout, I lay through an inch of fibreglass and listened to the water whoosh past and felt a quiet sense of glee. After all, in two days we'd be in the Canaries and even I could see in my haze of worry and disbelief, that sailing to the Canaries was A Long Way.

That maybe, just maybe, I could actually do this.

Chapter 4

A Familiar Ocean

How inappropriate to call this planet Earth when it is quite clearly Ocean.
Arthur C. Clarke

Colours raged on the western horizon and it was my third night at sea. The wind had finally subsided and we could bring in the warps that we'd been trailing for the last few days. The rough and fraying ropes that had filled a cockpit locker for months had been tied together and hung off the transom in a fifty-metre loop to slow us down.

The acceleration zone that whips wind into a fierce funnel between the Canary Islands hadn't died offshore like we'd thought. Instead it plumed on out into the Atlantic.

Within twenty four hours of leaving Gran Canaria, it had become apparent that not only was the wind not going to subside, but also there was no way we could turn back. We had stepped onto the conveyor belt that was the mid-Atlantic trade winds and were well and truly on our way.

We had been managing just over a hundred miles a day and the three little crosses that marked our noon positions were heading further and further away from land. But even as these crosses travelled away from Africa, they weren't getting any closer to terra firma, it would be two full weeks before the distance from solid ground began ticking down again.

I immediately got into a routine that I would keep for the next month, a focus on getting through the voyage rather than appreciating it. We settled on three hour watches and I only thought of the next three hours at a time, unable to picture how I could keep it up for weeks. But my fears had been eased somewhat by the waves that had washed us westwards so far. They had been huge and yet we were fine. There was still a chance we would stay fine.

Because the Canary Islands are volcanic, it didn't take long for the depth to drop off the capability of the echo sounder. I could still practically touch the cliffs of Tenerife and be in depths of 400 m or more but the land was still right there; it wasn't until the ocean was stretching to every horizon that the sheer scale of our position was obvious to me.

The French for deep is 'profonde' and there is no better way to describe the feeling you get when you're floating above 4000 m of ocean. Four kilometres. The colour of the water had changed as well, no longer the slate grey Atlantic of my childhood, this was a blue I'd never even seen before. A blue of such clarity it seemed to belong in the sapphire of a Queen's ornate ring.

Where the Channel's water seems opaque and heavy, this felt pure and fresh, it was like the ocean had been Brita filtered. We had a small following of fish that used the boat as shelter and kept pace with us for days. Whether they swam at four metres or four centimetres below the surface, their images were crystal clear.

I would drop a bucket over the side and haul it into the cockpit when the dirty plates and cutlery had built up and it even felt clean to touch. I could spend hours just watching the sea slosh past, a blue that never ceased to amaze me. I really had thought that the whole Atlantic was grey.

The third night was the clearest yet and not a single cloud impinged my view. We were more than three hundred miles from Africa and the sea yawned peacefully, swell rolling under the stern, then bow and then continuing on its epic journey.

A sliver of moon, a fine cut in the fabric of the night allowed the stars their own celestial theatre and they roared with light. No patch of sky was truly dark, the Milky Way a haze smudged across the entire dome of the world I was now in.

There were constellations here too that I had only glimpsed before or not at all; each degree south we made brought new stars working their way across the horizon and the constellations of my youth were in positions I barely recognised. You don't realise how familiar the stars are until they are different.

My little ten-metre boat and the two lives it carried was the only solid thing for miles around. Nothing below us but water, nothing above us but starlight, nothing in any direction. It did feel profound; it felt like a huge, gaping abyss of incomprehensible magnitude.

The boat rolled gently from side to side under the twin headsails and I wedged my back against the cockpit combing and my feet against the far frame of the companionway hatch. From this position I could lean my head back to look along the starboard rail, see the AIS reader hanging inside above the chart table and look aft to watch for oncoming clouds. The combing was also at neck level in this position and I could easily tilt my head back and lean against it to look at the stars.

The switch panel glowed an eerie red in the darkness and it always made the night seem quieter somehow; the deeper colour, less harsh than white, had a way of dampening sound.

I'd settled into the motion surprisingly quickly and seasickness had abandoned me within the first 48 hours. Most of it was caused by anxiety, something which was fading after the first two days of high winds and doing four knots under bare poles. Compared to that, this was a breeze.

Anxiety was something that had saved itself up until I turned twenty-three and hit me smack in the face with very little warning. Well, very little obvious warning anyway. It had been there in the background, making itself known in sneaky, nefarious ways since I was 19.

Retrospectively, I can see it truly began when I suffered my first panic attack towards the end of my first year of university. I had no idea what it was when it was happening, I thought I was dying. I had a friend drive me home from the party I'd been at and laid in bed, staring at the wall and trying to slow my heart rate. I'd had too many plates spinning and, while I knew something would fall, I hadn't realised it would be me.

A year later I began grinding my teeth in my sleep or at least that was when I first discovered I was anyway. That lasted for many months before the grinding stopped and horrific nightmares began. I woke up screaming, crying, shouting. It became so bad that Alex had to sleep in a separate room just to get enough sleep every night.

I sat hunched and small on the chair in the doctor's office, legs tightly wound around each other and hands clasped and wringing. Even as I spoke I couldn't believe that I'd spent half my childhood on the stage, precocious and extroverted.

"I would say you are suffering from anxiety," he said kindly. "An element of social phobia and probably a little depression. I don't really want to prescribe you anti-depressants at this stage because I don't want you to get the impression that this is something that can be cured by drugs. Only you can cure this."

He was right. I had got myself there through a series of unfortunate events and it was only me that could get myself out again. He gave me a number to call and that in itself was a piece of medication, just that paper with that number.

Looking back over childhood diaries, I was horrified to discover that, actually, these dark episodes hadn't begun at university at all. They'd been there all along, I just couldn't remember. I had been a prolific diarist as a child, I even found diaries from 1995 when I was just seven years old. They were filled with worry and sadness.

Some years were inconsistently written, months of blank pages but some had tens of thousands of words of the rollercoaster that was childhood. I read an entire page before ripping it up into tiny pieces and then another and another. Some I couldn't read at all, their pain so visceral on the page. How could this have been? I was only twelve here but bent double in agony. Or thirteen there dealing with a relentless bully at school. Or fourteen there and there and there.

I spent hours ripping, literally, through diaries. I tore the endless paper until my fingers and thumbs were bruised from the effort. I was astounded and devastated for my younger self. It was almost incomprehensible that I could've been capable of such pain but, as I read, I remembered.

Some people live through horrific childhoods but I was never abused, I didn't come from a war-torn country and no one ever hurt me who I didn't first give permission to. But I was so painfully naive, so willing to give myself up to those who asked and even those who didn't.

As a teenager I shrugged off my parents' divorce of many years earlier, saying, 'they're much happier apart'. It sounded adult, I even believed it, after all it was true. But re-reading those stacks of diaries told a very different story, one that I shredded page by page with my hands rather than have the truth exist in the world I had created.

So, although my anxiety didn't start at university, it certainly reached a tipping point afterwards.

I didn't leave Plymouth, my university city, straight after graduation. Instead I found a room in a friend's house and a job in a bookshop. Because I had transferred to the university in my second year but into halls of residence, my housemates, although my age, all still had a year to go. I didn't want to return home to my parents – in fact, I never even entertained the idea. There was something about going back that would cut the independence I had so diligently created that I simply couldn't acknowledge the concept of returning.

I craved adventure though and found a way to get back to it.

In the summer of my second year of my degree, I had travelled across the USA for two months with my diminutive best friend Sophie. We'd volunteered on organic farms from Missouri to California and met a ragtag bunch of wonderful people on the way, including a nomadic rock climber called Ryan.

After meeting in a Denver hostel, Sophie and I hitched a seven hour lift up to Wyoming with Ryan to go to a climbing festival we'd never heard of. Both small and poor, Sophie and I hired a large sleeping bag between us at an outdoor shop and Ryan said we could use his tent, he'd sleep out under the summer stars.

Ryan, an excellent rock climber and an easy-going Texan, was not my type. A romantic to the core, he had an intensity and attitude that belonged more in a John Green novel than in the men in my life. But I liked him a lot and found him easy to get along with.

The climbing festival was only three days and we returned to Denver afterwards, hitching a lift from another climber who lived near our next volunteer farm. Over a year later, Ryan invited me back to the States to go climbing at the festival again, which he was now manager of.

I was a graduate working for a pittance in a bookshop I loved but was growing out of. I needed more adventure, I needed something. So I said yes. I planned to go for three months, climbing and living out of the back of Ryan's van and tent, embracing the climber-bum lifestyle that is so prevalent in certain regions of the USA. I'd read about it in books, idolised the men and women who spent years living like that and why not? I was 22, I'd just finished a dissertation on travel writing and this would be the perfect adventure. I booked my flight for May 2011.

"So when are you and Ryan getting married?" said the customs officer, staring at me with a critical expression.

"We're not getting married," I said for the eighth time.

"Why are you travelling to America?" he asked.

"To go rock climbing," I said.

"Not much rock climbing in Detroit," he said.

"I know. I have a flight to Denver tomorrow morning," I said. He raised his eyebrow in a way that I could only assume was practised, possibly even mandated.

I had moved out of my room in Plymouth only the week before and moved my belongings back to my father's house in Hampshire. I'd quit my job at the bookshop. Somehow, I had no idea that both these actions were in contravention of the visa waiver I was travelling on. All I knew was that you could be in the States for up to three months. That was fine, I had a flight booked home in 87 days' time, just to give myself a bit of leeway in case a flight was delayed. I thought I was being sensible.

"Do you have Ryan's number?" asked the man. He'd been questioning me for half an hour and it was becoming clear that I was not going to be spending the next three months living the Kerouac dream. I retrieved my phone and started scrolling through it. "Hey, can I see your phone?" the officer asked. I handed it over.

He told me to sit down against the wall which I did obediently. He called over another officer and asked him if he knew how the Blackberry worked. They proceeded to go through all my texts, laughing and looking up and me and then back down again.

I had met Alex ten days before. Ironically, we'd met at the leaving party my housemates had thrown for me, a pirate-themed murder mystery. Alex had been at university with them and had himself only just returned from a year of backpacking. The two of us had gotten very drunk and decided to drive to Amsterdam two days later. We spent a hilarious and glorious week adventuring, exploring and sleeping together. I was enamoured. But I had flights booked.

I knew that they were laughing at the texts Alex and I had sent to each other in the past few days. In any situation where ritual humiliation is being dished out to you in front of other people, I would've thought I would be crying. But I couldn't. I was drained. The eight hour flight had flown me back in time so while it was 8pm in Detroit, my body thought it was the small hours. After the endless questions and insinuations and outright accusations, I realised that it didn't matter what I said to these men, they wouldn't believe me anyway.

"Come here," said the officer. I got up from the waiting room chair and walked back over to the desk. "What's this?" He pointed at a text I'd sent to Alex at the airport.

Ryan said he had a friend who could get me a job at a cafe – I can save money for our South American adventure!

Oh. I thought. Shit.

Ryan had indeed said that, although I had in no way planned to take him up on it. Not because I was being diligent about US visa laws per se, just that I didn't want to work, I wanted to be a climber bum. My naivety was staggering but more than that, my wide-eyed optimism was staggering.

Not wanting to give up on each other after such a week, Alex and I had talked about going travelling to South America after I got back from the States. It was a pie-eyed dream that we concocted just to give each other a smidgen of hope that this wasn't the end. There wasn't a chance in hell I'd have the funds to go anywhere and besides, Alex was a carefree traveller: he wasn't going to wait three months for me to finish travelling with another man.

But the Americans had their proof. And although it took me a very long time to see it, they were right. They were doing their jobs.

"What happens now?" I asked.

"What happens now is that we're going to put you on a plane to London, that's what's gonna happen!"

"Tonight?" I asked.

"Yeah there's one in half an hour, we'll get your stuff and take you down there. Just some paperwork first," he said. I sagged with relief. I couldn't believe my luck. I had just watched a Mexican woman taken to overnight detention because the next plane back wasn't until the morning. I was going home.

As they fingerprinted each of my fingers and took my photograph against a height chart, I fixated on England. London. Heathrow. Never have I wanted to see Heathrow airport like I did then. I wanted to go home and never leave. I would never, ever try to leave again.

Two officers escorted me to my plane, one walked in front, one behind. When we reached a lift, they opened it and told me to stand in the corner, waiting for me to get in before following me.

"I know this feels awful, but it's not that bad. You haven't been deported, you've just been refused entry. It's different, it means you're allowed to come back," said one of my guards. I looked at him. I want to say I gave him a smile, to show I appreciated his kindness, but I think I just stared at him, unable to yet comprehend what was happening.

We arrived at the entrance to the plane, the passengers not yet onboard.

"This one's a refusal," said the guard to the steward and handed over my passport.

"Okay," said the steward. He showed me to my seat, a middle seat in the middle of a four-person row. I would never sleep. "I'll keep hold of this, so I know where to find you," he said, flourishing my passport with a smug smile.

I have never been without my passport. Not really. It hasn't always been on my person of course, but it's always been in my possession. The feeling of a stranger having possession of my passport made me feel completely cut off from my identity. I had no way of proving who I was without that. I was just a person. I had no way of proving to Britain that I was British, that I belonged, that I should be let in.

The plane filled up around me and I felt like I was holding my breath. I felt as though I would be holding my breath until touchdown. It was 2am in the UK and it would take another 8 hours to reach Heathrow. By the time we landed I would've been awake for almost 30 hours.

I still couldn't cry. I couldn't do anything because I was surrounded by normal people, excited Americans going to see London. I knew that if I cried I wouldn't stop. That I'd be comforted by the large ladies on either side. That I'd look crazy.

I watched films the whole way back although I have no recollection of what they were. They were just stopwatches to me, two hour sections of the flight. Once I'd watched three I'd be almost there.

As we landed at Heathrow I texted the only person I could face. Alex. How could I tell my friends and family that my momentous trip was cancelled? How could I see my dad and know that he'd take me home and make me a coffee and tell me that it would be okay? It wasn't okay. Nothing would ever be okay ever again.

So I texted Alex.

I've just landed at Heathrow. Can you come pick me up if you're not busy? Please don't call me, I'll start crying.

Alex, never one to take too much instruction at face value, called. I was still on the plane as it was taxiing and the second I heard his voice, I started crying. He said he was already in the car and that he'd be there in two hours.

The steward appeared as I wiped my face and handed me my passport without a word. I held onto it more tightly than I'd ever held onto anything before.

I wanted to kiss the immigration officer as he barely glanced at my passport and waved me through. I was home, I belonged to England and England belonged to me. It seemed incredible that I had only left 20 hours before and yet I looked at the airport branches of WHSmith and Boots as if they were long-lost friends.

I stared at myself in the mirror in the toilets, horrified by what I saw. My face was so pale and young and exhausted. I looked like an entirely different person. I looked ugly. I scrabbled in my backpack for mascara and ran my fingers through my hair. I felt filthy from all the time on the plane. I felt stagnant and empty.

I sat outside at the pick-up area for over an hour, receiving the odd garbled message from Alex as he updated me on his progress, texting at red lights. I sent a message to Sophie, asking her to email Ryan and tell him I wasn't coming, that I was never coming. I could've done it myself, but I couldn't. I wanted nothing to do with him or his country, I didn't even want to see his name.

When Alex pulled up I broke down with ten hours of built-up pure misery and hopelessness. He bundled me into his car and drove me back to his parents' empty house.

When Emma Bovary loses interest in the things that once charmed her, her doctor-husband prescribes her a change of air and they move towns. I'm not saying Flaubert's infamous novel is something to use as a regular source of advice but, after meeting with my doctor, I prescribed myself a change of air – Indonesian air.

The nightmares that had plagued me since the America incident 18 months before ended on a two-month trip to Bali where Alex and I spent our time meandering in the beautiful villages and forests of this enchanting island. With nothing to do except look and marvel and eat at night markets, I finally relaxed for the first time in years. It compounded what I already knew: my anxiety was something I created.

But upon my return from Bali and the last couple of months of rushing to get ready to set sail, the stress and anxiety came back. A soul-sucking constant: you can't do this, you'll fail.

The symptoms changed from nightmares to a physical one. Bizarrely, a runny nose. It plagued me for months on land and at anchor but, strangely enough, never at sea. Never while literally sailing. I couldn't work it out, this constantly evolving outlet for anxiety.

And yet the symptoms disappeared as soon as we set off from the Canaries. Or, at least, the crazy unexplainable ones disappeared. They were replaced with bouts of good old-fashioned worry. I could deal with that after two months of blowing my nose every five minutes. My incessant stress-induced nasal issues stopped with the suddenness of a light being turned off.

The hardest thing to do in sailing, maybe in all travel, is leaving. The act of last minutes, of saying final goodbyes, last emails and untying your lines is the hardest. So was it all anxiety tied up in that? One great big worry about crossing the Atlantic?

Because once I was out there, out of sight of the land, it was ocean. I was okay.

I spent hours and days picking apart what it was that changed inside me as I shifted from land or anchor to sailing mid-ocean. The fear was still there, the appropriate concern for the precariousness of my immediate situation. But it was so much more than that.

When I was at sea, it was as though nothing else mattered. As if the rest of the world paused to allow me to sail across this ocean whereupon it would start again. Like a stopping a film so you can go to the toilet or make a cup of tea.

Freud talks of an oceanic feeling in his works, although it wasn't him who coined the phrase. He explored the idea of this all-encompassing concept of the primitive ego, the pre-ego almost that we have before we understand what is us and what is other.

While a baby, he explains, has no concept of where it begins and ends as a creature, it has a sense of limitlessness – this oceanic feeling of being everything, or at least a part of everything. The baby has this sense of limitless being until it discovers that its mother is separate from it and then it learns it is an individual in a world of other individuals.

But there is a way to get back to that feeling, at least in some way. And intentionally or not, for me it was in the ocean. Out there, all the trivialness, the highly tuned ego and the painstakingly complex natures of humans and societies just… fell away. My body stopped trying to drive out its stress and anxiety through strange physical ailments and seemed to surrender to the environment, to the ocean.

Despite my reservations, my fears and my sometime discomfort, I felt at home on the Atlantic in a way that I had never felt anywhere before. Some part of me felt like I belonged there, with nothing to prove.

The feeling came and went with the hours. There would be moments of boredom and frustration and then, just an hour later, it would be as though I had suddenly plugged myself back into the world, and I felt the oneness again. Like a state of flow, the times it happened were euphoric. I felt as though I'd seen over the huge wall I'd built around myself.

Like I'd come home.

Chapter 5

Full Sea

At sea, I learned how little a person needs, not how much.
Robin Lee Graham

It was a hot and lazy afternoon on the 22nd December and it already seemed as though we'd been at sea for weeks. I found myself writing aimlessly in a notebook, lamenting that only six days had passed and we still seemed so distant from our goal.

We had finally crossed the Tropic of Capricorn the day before and, after spending months in the sub-tropics, had reached that invisible band around the planet that we'd been using as a target for so long. The tropics.

I'd remembered reading Ellen MacArthur's first book *Taking on the World* months before we left and only half believing her when she described the relentless heat of the tropical Atlantic. I'd spent every night watch through Atlantic Europe bundled in the warmest things I could find and still being cold but now a shift was taking place.

I often spent the nights in sailing salopettes but I wasn't cold anymore. As the voyage continued I would soon learn that she hadn't been exaggerating, the tropics had a whole world of heat in store for me.

I had begun reading her book, *Full Circle*, shortly after leaving the Canaries and it eradicated my fears on more than one occasion. To read about a woman no larger than I, battling with Southern Ocean swells and storms, alone, in a high-performance trimaran, made every squall and every four-metre wave we came across look like a spring day in the local park. I was only half a mind away from making a bracelet that said 'What Would Ellen Do?'

I had put my notebook away and was catching up with my British hero when the fishing line shrieked out of the spool and off behind us. Before I could so much as close my Kindle, Alex had shot out of the cabin, onto the stern seat and was grabbing the fishing rod. I had a feeling this is what he'd been waiting for.

The fish was strong and it took some time to reel it in. I hung onto the backstay and watched the water behind for any signs of what it was. Alex let it take some line, reeled it in a little and let it take some more. Impatient to find out what our first Atlantic-crossing catch would be, I stood up on the transom combing and searched the sea.

Mahi Mahi, Dorado, dolphin or dolphinfish are all names for this one, beautiful pelagic creature. Bright yellow and blue, these fish often followed us as we sailed, clearly visible a wave or two behind. Mahi Mahi is Hawaiian for 'very strong' and it was easy to see why; they run back and forth alongside the boat and, just when you think you've tired them out, they disappear off as long as the line will let them.

The effort is always worth it though and as we brought this one over the side I could see that it would feed us for days. Two-feet long and pure muscle, it flapped and crashed about the cockpit until I threw a towel over it and held it down. It took as much pressure as I had to give to hold it, leaning over and pushing my weight onto its firm body.

Mahi Mahi are strong, long distance swimmers and impressive predators. As a result they have firm, wonderful flesh but are also difficult to dispatch and deal with. Alex got his dive knife, a beast of a thing and forced it through the fish's thick skull. I held it down and looked away, hating the sound of metal on bone.

It had taken me a while to get used to catching our own fish and I'd been vegetarian for twenty years; the intimate and very real deaths I now witnessed caused conflict within me and on more than one occasion I'd removed a hook from the lip of a mackerel and released it.

But I knew that this was the best way to eat fish and, as the voyage around the Atlantic progressed, the only way I could conceive of in future. With no by-catch and no death by suffocation or crushing, the fish we caught were killed quickly and never wasted. When we fished inshore and caught optimistic young fish that were too small, they were released with no more than a tiny hole in their lip.

I could reconcile myself with a knife through the brain if it meant I was consuming fish as ecologically sound as when they consumed each other. The thing that really concerned me was whether we'd accidentally catch a genuine dolphin on one of the many occasions they turned up. It didn't take long to realise that it would never occur, they were simply too smart.

This was the fourth Mahi Mahi we'd ever caught and after the bloodbath of the first, Alex had come up with a solution.

Once the fish was dead and Alex had made several precision cuts, we tied a rope to its tail, its tail fin hard and powerful, and tied it off the back of the boat to allow the blood to drain out.

While this was a fast and effective way to get rid of the copious amounts of thick, bright red blood, I would've expected it to bring attention from sharks. The fact that I never saw evidence of one made me wonder just how vast and empty this ocean really was. Were we alone but for passing Mahi Mahi?

The fish weighed several kilograms and it took Alex a long time to fillet and box it up. This was the reason we had a fridge on board, to make the most of the fish we caught and not to let it go to waste. We chopped a small amount up, marinated it in lemon juice before eating it raw as ceviche; it was times like that which made me realise what a privilege it was to be out there on the ocean, eating the freshest fish and doing everything ourselves.

Before sailing, I had never eaten fresh fish. I mean truly fresh, as in within the hour of catching it, sometimes, within ten minutes if it was something like mackerel. It was a completely different taste to that which you buy at the fishmongers where the creatures have been on ice for days.

I couldn't believe I had been eating tinned tuna before, how could it ever be worth it when its by-catch was despicable, it was months old and it tasted so... so cardboardy. When we caught a bonito, a smaller relative of a tuna, in the Caribbean, it sunk in that the fish that reaches our supermarkets is really unrecognisable from what it is when its fresh.

The Mahi Mahi was transformed over the next three days into many different things and we ate it for lunch and dinner. Alex made a batch of fish cakes that were utterly delicious. Without a recipe book, I floundered in the kitchen but Alex repeatedly stunned me with not only rich and flavourful dishes from his imagination, but also that he could create and cook in the severe rolling conditions that we were experiencing. Occasionally I would consider boiling the kettle and making a cup-a-soup but even that I deemed too much effort.

It wasn't laziness, or though in retrospect I wonder if caffeine withdrawal had something to do with it, but across the Atlantic I could just about get from my bunk to the cockpit. I even put off using the bathroom until I had to because the motion was so difficult. So the idea of lifting up a bunk cushion, opening the storage locker beneath, finding a packet of cup-a-soup with my head now upside down in a rolling boat and then hanging onto the grab rail in the galley while the kettle boiled… it just wasn't going to happen.

In fact, I developed a way of knowing when I could find food for us in the lockers; after all, I was the one that knew where everything was, having stowed it meticulously in Gran Canaria. If I could open a locker, find it, give it to Alex and then get back into the cockpit all on one breath, I'd be okay. Seasickness could be tricked, I'd worked out. It didn't hit me if I completed tasks below at lightening speed.

Considering it was only two metres from the cockpit to even the furthest food locker below, I often made breath-hold locker searches in the dinner time hours. Little hunting forays into the depths of storage where my only danger was then being struck down by sickness and being unable to enjoy the dinner anyway.

"Didn't you used to eat fish finger sandwiches at university?" said Alex, teasing my poor choice of study food.

"Yeah yeah I know, it's not even fish," I said, stuffing my mouth with another chilli and curry paste fish cake.

"This is fish," he said. Fish fingers, incidentally, are delicious. As long as you don't compare them to actual fish.

Nine days had passed and we hadn't seen a single ship or had any hint of one out of sight on AIS. I felt truly isolated and it had been days since the catching of the Mahi Mahi. I was beginning to wonder whether we'd see anything at all now until we were much closer to the Caribbean.

The wind had all but dropped off and it was Christmas Eve. Through sheer, wondrous luck, we had discovered a minuscule branch of Marks and Spencers in Las Palmas and had spent thirty odd pounds on a Christmas pudding, a Christmas cake, chocolate truffles and a box of mince pies.

I'd felt a little ridiculous stood in this Spanish city buying as much British Christmas food as we could but, by the time we'd reached almost a thousand miles into the ocean, we were happier than children on Christmas morning.

We started the Christmas cake that evening and, as we sat in the cockpit catching raisins as they crumbled from our hands, Alex spotted our new companions.

A pod of dolphins were racing towards us at impossible speeds. They flung themselves from the water, high above the waves and dived back in again until they were surrounding the boat and matching their speed to ours.

There is nothing in the world that lifts the spirits like dolphins and they raced around in circles, three in formation at the back, following the motion of the Aries' wind vane with their noses as it merrily steered the boat downwind.

I went and sat on the bow, my legs dangling over, a position much more enjoyable now that I was just wearing shorts and a t-shirt and not bundled with layers. Dolphins dipped and dived, syncing themselves effortlessly with the up and down of the bow, jumping between it and the water seconds before it crashed down into the waves. They leaped and flipped as though their whole species' Olympic careers depended on it and it was plainly obvious that they were over the moon.

In all the times I'd seen dolphins, they'd always seemed to be at least as equally pleased to see us. They twisted and swam sideways, peering up through the clear water and looking straight into my eyes. They always gave the distinct impression that they were well aware we were separate entities from the boat.

As I went to bed for my three-hour nap that evening, I lay listening to the squeaks and pips of these ocean-going mammals as they escorted us across their domain.

The wind was gentle as I sat in the cockpit at 3am and we were doing four knots in a force 2. The wind had changed direction and we'd swapped the twin headsails for the main and genoa, reaching with a south easterly.

The dolphins had gone as far as I could tell and I was left with the occasional thwack of a flying fish mistiming its leap. I threw them overboard if they landed in the cockpit, careful not to damage their strange wings.

With nothing in particular to hit, night watches mid-Atlantic were easy if the weather was stable. Unless particularly squally, it was a serene and relaxing affair and on this night it was so quiet that I could daydream for half my watch.

A snort of air made me jump out of my skin and grab the cockpit combing behind me. I stared into the water and saw a faint green glittering plumage highlighting and following the outline of a dolphin like fairy dust. Another snort came from the other side of the cockpit and I peered over the edge. A handful of dolphins had returned and were quietly and steadily swimming alongside.

I settled down in the cockpit again with my head over the side, chin resting on my hands like a child on the bus. Dolphin escorts are comforting; I firmly felt that nothing bad could happen to us while these elegant creatures were with us.

The phosphorescence made them glow and sparkle and I wondered what the hull must look like underwater leaving huge, magnificent trails of the stuff behind it.

While we had gentle winds and a two-metre following swell for several days, by the 30th December the warps were out again and the force 6 north-east wind meant that we just had a scrap of jib and a heavily reefed mainsail. An unpleasant, but not unexpected, cross swell had picked up and the now four-metre waves had a distinctly confused edge to them, several breaking over the cockpit for the first time.

As the wind dropped slightly to a force 5 the following day, we brought the warps in again and cracked open the truffles to celebrate New Year's Eve.

As is the way of nature, it chose that evening to show that 2015 wasn't quite over and, lacking fireworks, it gave us its own show. I was down below, reading before dinner when Alex called me up on deck. I figured it was dolphins and happily hopped out into the cockpit.

A huge dorsal fin surfed down the face of the wave and dipped below the surface. The water was so clear that we could see its mammoth body glide and swoop below us, rolling under the keel and showing its long white stomach that matched ours. Something gripped my heart, adrenaline, fear, awe. I'd never seen any creature that big.

As it dived deep we searched the water for any signs and it reappeared behind me, ejecting air and spray with a sudden whoosh that made me spin around. It was as long as the boat. This was truly an ocean giant but its size made it, if anything, even more graceful. It moved slowly but carefully, the lazy elegance of something completely at home in its surroundings.

I was close to crying. Dolphins were happy, acrobatic and irrepressible, leaping and somersaulting and never for a minute pausing. The whale was so different, so curious and steady. It too, like the dolphins, rolled onto its side and looked at us as we leaned over the guard wire and peered back at it.

We were the only boat for a considerable distance and still hadn't seen another. The whale was solitary: how many things as big as us had it seen recently? Any? It stayed for an hour, during which we ignored everything around us and just followed its every movement. The sun was setting though and it was dark before we could be certain he'd left. He may've continued on with us for a lot longer than we'd known.

The weather had fallen into a predictable pattern, 15 knots in the morning with a large swell but not too much wind chop followed by 20 knots by 11am and rougher seas. The wind direction changed as we were 900 miles off Venezuela and it was time to lower the genoa and main and re-set the twin headsails.

I turned on the engine and, with Alex on the bow ready to drop the genoa, I turned the boat into the wind and swell. Going from downwind sailing to upwind motoring is always a shock to the system, even with the 3-4 m swell we'd been rolling along fairly gently. But now I was holding her into 3-4 m swells with just enough revs on to keep her into the wind: the motion was violent and obscene.

I watched Alex on the plunging bow, barely able to hold on as he dropped the genoa. The boat plummeted off the back of each wave and I was astounded that he could do anything up there. My whole body was filled with tension as I ran through man overboard procedures in my head, convinced he would be swept off the bow any second.

We'd done some man overboard practice when we'd first put the boat in the water, but in the Solent it may as well have been in a lifeguarded swimming pool. What a joke. The only way to survive falling overboard was not to fall overboard in my view.

Alex was much more adept at multitasking on a plunging bow than I'd given him credit for and, as he hoisted the twin headsails, I couldn't help thinking he should've been born into a Texas rodeo family. He would have dominated.

He ran the long headsail sheets back to the cockpit and I kept concentrating on keeping the boat into the wind and waves; if I let her pay off at all the motion would be even worse and it would take a huge rev of engine to get her back up into the wind. I wasn't even thinking about anything else as the headsails flapped and raged in the wind.

Alex furled the headsails and went back up to the bow to finish up and bring the genoa back aft. Despite my concentration on the wind direction, a slight alteration in the note of the engine sent me immediately for the throttle. I whacked the engine into neutral and hesitated – the boat would pay off, what if I was wrong?

"Alex!" I called, "Something's wrong with the engine!" I jumped forward and turned it off.

"What's wrong?" he shouted back, coming aft, hands stay to stay.

"It sounded wrong," I said as my eyes scanned for a truth I didn't want to think about. But Alex was coming down the starboard side and we both saw it at the same time. One of the unnecessarily lengthy sheets had whipped into the water and, judging by its tightness over the toe rail, had wrapped itself around the propeller.

I closed my eyes. How could I have let that happen? I knew to keep the sheets out of the water, I knew it. Alex gave another tug. Nope, it was well and truly stuck. We couldn't even use a different rope for the headsail because we couldn't reach the clew without half dropping the sails and we wouldn't be able to re-hoist them in such wind.

Alex dropped the headsails and took them and the genoa below deck. We continued sailing under the third-reefed main but with no headsail at all, we were down to just under three knots. I couldn't believe it. The relief I'd felt when he hoisted the twins without falling overboard and now we were practically wallowing in the ocean.

We stuck the GoPro over the side on a broom handle (honestly, why would you buy a selfie stick when you can just use a wooden pole?) and looked at the damage on my iPad. The last time we'd done this we'd been watching the whale, now we were looking at a nasty mess.

I'd put the throttle into neutral within around 2-3 seconds of the rope getting caught but at 2000 revolutions, there was a lot of rope twisted and wrapped around.

We checked that the propeller shaft wasn't leaking in the engine bay where it came into the boat in case the rope had yanked it outwards but it seemed to be fine. I repacked the grab bag again just in case, the improbable idea of the shaft falling out the back of the boat keeping me awake.

For two days we plodded along, cautious and dispirited. I chided myself for the mistake but mainly I thought over and over again how everything could go from good to bad in seconds. The ocean was a safe place in a good boat but became treacherous in a faulty one.

Finally, the sea was calm enough and Alex slipped into the sea to go beneath the boat and cut the propeller free.

"Watch out for sharks," he said before taking a deep breath and disappearing. I looked out around him but the morning sun glazed the water in its bright glow and I could see nothing below the surface.

"Sharks," I muttered, wondering if they'd still be following us even though the last time we caught a fish was four days before. If a shark ate Alex now then I'd have to sail under main for the nearest piece of land before having an inevitable breakdown. At three knots, a thousand miles would take a long time.

Alex surfaced with a handful of melted, fluffy rope and handed it to me before going down for more. I ran it through my hands and stared at it. It had melted with friction underwater.

He managed to cut the propeller free, most of the rope destroyed to the point he could rip it apart off the shaft. He climbed aboard and I was relieved, not having realised how much I was actually worried about shark attacks.

We stared at the rope, twisted and deformed.

"I've been meaning to shorten those sheets for ages," he said.

"Well now you don't need to," I said.

With the sea not yet affected by much wind chop, we turned into the swell and hoisted the twin headsails, me holding tightly onto the ends of the sheets. Down came the main and we were back to proper downwind sailing; I felt my muscles relax ever so slightly.

On the 11th January we were only five hundred miles from Grenada and it changed everything. I felt livelier than I had for the whole passage and sat merrily on the side deck showering with a bucket and shaving my legs – something I really had not bothered with at sea before then.

I no longer drifted around, my body was happy with its new found three-hour rhythm and I even cooked the odd dinner; "God, it's so rolly down here! The onion keeps falling off the board, how do you cook normally?!"

"With great difficulty," said Alex raising an eyebrow. He always did the cooking because he didn't get seasick below, which I did unless I was reading or sleeping or generally lying down. In fairness, I always did the washing up in a bucket in the cockpit.

Five hundred miles was something I could get a handle on, something I could picture. It was around the same distance as Falmouth to Spain's A Coruña, less than the trip from Portugal to Porto Santo and only two more days than Madeira to the Canaries.

We were no longer impossibly and preposterously far from land and the tension and anxiety drained from my body in one huge whoosh. I practically danced my way around the boat, cleaned the bathroom in a frenzy of productivity and stood on the transom, watching the flying fish scatter under the bow.

I was considerably better company and Alex no longer had to entertain himself while his un-nerved partner buried herself in a book to pretend there wasn't a squall squatting heavily on the horizon.

Only a few days to go and the weather changed. The wind blew stronger and veered, becoming southerly. It brought rain and created a confused and deeply ruffled sea. We put the hatch boards in and watched out the windows as the surface of the ocean turned into a blur in the downpours. We took turns running outside to reef or let out more sail and eyed our new course distastefully. We were now going north, not west.

We'd already changed to main and genoa after a different windshift and now we rode out this bizarre new weather, hoping it'd blow itself out and rumble on. The thing was, it didn't appear to be going much faster than us and we were concerned we were just sailing along with it as it rolled its way north.

I studied Hal Roth's *Handling Storms at Sea* and tried to work out if this was the edge of some huge depression and, if so, where exactly in it were we. We scratched our heads and decided that we had probably been run over by the Intertropical Convergence Zone – something unpredictable and not to be easily dodged.

We hadn't managed to pick up any SSB radio forecasts from the USA and instead sat out the depression, meandering about, heavily reefed, in whatever direction the wind was going.

It lasted for around 36 hours and then we were back on our way, decks nicely washed down by all the rain and several cloud-showers having been luxuriously taken. I could practically smell land.

We had, in general, been going as fast as was comfortably possible the entire passage but, as we came within 80 miles of Grenada, it became obvious that we were going to have to slow the hell down.

We had picked up a 2-knot west-going current and were doing a hefty 7.5 knots over the ground. That would get us in around midnight and a night entry into a reefy, tropical island did not feature in our plans at all.

We reefed down and cruised along at 4 knots. By 2am I had slowed the boat right down to 2.5 knots, the slowest we could go in the waves without the sails flapping and the motion being unbearable. Still, we would be lucky if we made it after sunrise.

A bird appeared on the guard wire where it met the pushpit in the cockpit, rocking back and forth to keep its balance. In the dark it looked a lot like a crow and certainly didn't look like a seabird. Seabirds have extraordinary ability to balance on moving objects and have always had a certain unflustered charm about them when they occasionally hitchhiked.

I didn't want to turn the torch on this tired bird in case it took offence and flew off into the dangers of the sea and so I couldn't get a particularly good look at what it was even though it was sat a metre away from me.

It was a black bird in a black night and we chatted idly as the boat lurched from side to side, wishing to go faster but halted by her blasted crew.

Having birds on board means not only not making any sudden movements, but also moving glacially when you need to do something. This applies to most birds anyway; we had a Brown Noddy later who was perfectly happy with us sloshing buckets of water over the solar panel where he was stood, to get rid of his abundant droppings.

For over an hour I moved about the cockpit, very aware that if we were going to see ships on this 3500-mile crossing then now was the time we would see them. I studied the horizon, the AIS and the chart, all in slow motion to avoid startling the bird.

In the end it was a wave that caught us on the aft quarter that rocked the boat enough for the bird to lose its footing. It flew up and again, it didn't fly like a seabird. It repeatedly tried to land again but the boat was rolling and lurching too much for it. It eventually got a hold on the solar panel but abruptly fell off and disappeared completely.

I always hated it when birds left the boat and wondered for hours what had become of them. Had they just needed a rest? We'd had a racing pigeon on board across Biscay and after 24 hours of snoozing in a shoe box he spied a fancier looking yacht and had flown off looking much refreshed.

It was a short-lived concern this time however, because at 3am Alex came to relieve me and I feel into a deep sleep until dawn and Grenada loomed ahead.

When I said that I could practically smell land, I hadn't actually realised that you could. Previously I'd never really been far enough from it to notice the difference, or at least not for long enough.

After weeks at sea though, the smell of Grenada hit me full in the face. It was like going from the cool English clarity of winter straight into the rainforest biome of Cornwall's Eden Project. The smell was tangible, thick and alive. It turns out that you can literally smell land.

A squall came and obscured our view, dowsing us in torrential rain as soon as we began motoring up to the entrance of Prickly Bay in the early morning light.

I was at the helm and almost blind in the furious rain while Alex put on a snorkelling mask and took photos of us making landfall in the Caribbean. There's a GoPro video of me shouting over the wind and rain, 'we have arrived! And it's awesome!' I'm yelling, sticking my thumb up and getting a face full of water.

Prickly Bay was full off boats and, as the squall sauntered off west, we wove our way through them right up close to the marina and the small beach. We anchored and turned off the engine, enthralled by our new reality. We had crossed the ocean.

After arriving on the tropical shores of a Caribbean island, you get the distinct impression that you've entered via the back door. It scarcely seems possible that you could've made your own way, by the power of wind alone, to such a distant place.

The Caribbean of my childhood was played out in the pages of holiday brochures furtively acquired from the local travel agency. The places within seemed unattainable, once-in-a-lifetime destinations requiring long flights, excess baggage and the sort of money that few people I knew could reasonably possess.

It never occurred to me that you could just go there yourself in a boat, a lengthier version of, say, walking to Wales from Southampton. The idea you could visit the Caribbean without inflating the wallets of luxury hotels, airlines and Thomson Holidays was non-existent.

But now I knew you could because I had. I kept meeting similarly bemused sailors, wandering around in the sort of eerie tranquillity of someone not quite sure if what they're experiencing is real.

We'd all set out on this borderline mythic voyage of 3500 miles with the intention of making landfall in the Caribbean; but now we had made it, it became clear that many hadn't actually expected to.

Despite the hundreds of yachts crossing the ocean from east to west each year, it's still a pretty marginal method of arrival. There may be endless flocks of charter yachts exercising their motors and occasionally stretching their wings but trans-Atlantic cruisers are still countable on one hand in most anchorages.

Once into the routine of life in Grenada, the twenty-eight days at sea began to seem unreal. While the days had stretched out under sail, they condensed at anchor; that month was a strange stasis, we were frozen in time and re-entered the world exactly a month later.

It almost felt like a tiny psychological experiment; relinquishing the internet, all forms of communication and becoming entirely self-sufficient. All for one month.

Imagine stocking your house with food but shutting off the freezer, filling your bath to the brim before turning off the mains, cutting the phone, TV and internet and setting up an 160 W solar panel on the roof. Now imagine not being able to leave the house for a month.

Admittedly this thought experiment doesn't work particularly well because your house is (hopefully) impervious to the fickle attitudes of the weather, springing a leak won't send you to your grave and you can get a full night's sleep instead of waking up every three hours for your watch.

But still, you get the gist.

When you re-enter the world one month after you withdrew from it, when you turn on the internet and buy fresh milk and fruit; the most disconcerting thing will be this – nothing changed.

The news is the same with some names changed; the social media train forgets itself as soon as it posts anyway; nobody died; your emails are all from companies you once bought something from and your friends have just had another month working and weekending.

You expect the world to have changed because you have. Every day a triumph of mileage, survival and dolphin spotting. Each three-hour nap a restorative achievement. Each meal a battle won against the continuous motion. You've experienced joy, fear, adrenaline, serenity, fresh fish, curious cetacean, brutal exhaustion and furious winds. The ocean has played with you across a vast football pitch, eventually called time and lobbed you to the safety of land.

You re-emerge into the world dusting yourself off, smoothing down your hair and saying, 'gosh, that was pretty wild', and the world glances up and says, 'whatever'. Unimpressed, it didn't even notice a tiny boat forging its way across the sea.

And then you realise something wonderful. You stepped out of the world and into the sea for a whole month and nothing changed. You could do this *all the time*.

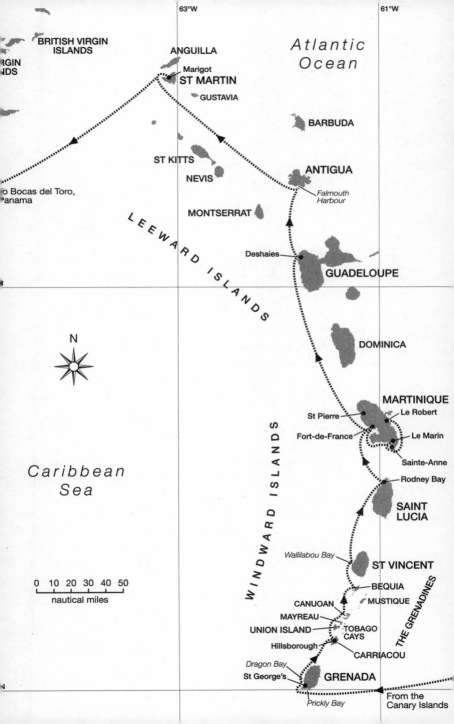

Chapter 6

Racing Grenada

A ship is always safe at shore but that is not what it's built for.

J. A. Shedd

"What's in your rigging?" called a South African voice. Alex was sat in the cockpit cleaning the genoa winches and I stood on the companionway steps and looked out into the anchorage.

A tanned and unkempt young man was, amazingly, rowing a Lymington Scow up to our stern, the golden curves of its classic panels glinting in the Caribbean sunshine.

"Baggywrinkle," said Alex, looking up at the fluffy, slightly ratty looking pompoms clinging to the rigging.

"What now?" said the South African, shipping his elegant oars and coming alongside.

"Baggywrinkle, they stop the sail rubbing on the stays when we're going downwind," said Alex.

We were the only fibreglass yacht I'd yet to see with baggywrinkle and the only other boat at all was an impressive wooden schooner with considerably more professional looking tufts than ours.

It was Alex's idea (I'd never even heard of them before) and, as a child brought up on *Swallows and Amazons*, I think he wanted them for tradition's sake as much as practicality. Incidentally, this is the same reason we ended up eating a disproportionate amount of steamed pudding (duff) and ham and pea soup (made with Spam which is, you'll be happy to know, available everywhere).

As a 20-year vegetarian only relatively recently turned to meat, I found Alex's fondness for corned beef and tinned ham took a bit of getting used to; especially as he eschewed all processed meats otherwise.

We had strung a piece of fishing line up across the cockpit from cleat to cleat back in the Spanish Rias and diligently spent hours tying cow hitch after cow hitch on using strands of an old three-strand rope. Eventually, if you tie enough of these along around a metre of line, you'll be able to tie it onto the shroud and wrap it around until it resembles a sloth with a perm.

I'm not sure you could get away with it on a new Beneteau but the four baggywrinkle we had, two on each aft-lower shrouds, had certainly caused their fair share of both amusement and appreciation in marinas and anchorages.

"Can you show me how to make them sometime?" asked the South African.

"Sure," Alex nodded, "which boat are you on?"

"I have the little Dufour 30 over there," he replied, pointing into the dense forest of masts in Prickly Bay, "but I'm working on *Coral*, you know, the big schooner?"

We couldn't not know the big schooner, she so dwarfed the rest of the yachts. We'd even rowed slowly past her, gawping at the extravagant beauty of her design.

"Actually,'" he said, "you wanna race in the regatta?" Alex shrugged and nodded, not sure how the subject had changed so wildly. "Richard, the skipper on *Coral*, is racing her but I think he needs an extra guy 'cause one of my guys dropped out," he looked thoughtful.

"Yeah that would be awesome," said Alex.

"Cool, cool, I'll check with him. They're going over to St George's tonight but you wanna come with me to meet him tomorrow? You too," he said nodding at me, his earnest face peering over the toe rail.

"I'm not sure I'm much of a racer," I said, my stomach tightening. There was no way in hell I was going to be racing on a yacht, just thinking of the angle racing boats heeled at was enough to make me want to get to dry land and never look back.

"Nah it's cool, you can still come and look around *Coral* though, she's beeaaauuutiful," he said. I nodded, the sincerity and assuredness in his voice something that, as I was to discover, no one could say no to.

"Sweet I'm going over there like, eleven tomorrow morning, I'll meet you guys at the bar?" he pushed the Scow off and put the oars in their wobbly rowlocks.

"Okay, sure," said Alex.

"Sweet," the South African said again, "I'm Shaun by the way!"

And that was Shaun, a 23-year-old South African who had a tendency to appear when you least expected him, make a ruckus and disappear before you knew what'd happened.

At midday the following day, we were nursing the very last of our lemonades when Shaun showed up, carrying a holdall and rucksack.

"Hey guys!"' he said, "sorry I got caught up on this other yacht I'm doing some work on," he noticed a sailor sat across the café and waved with a little called exchange before turning his attention back to us, "you ready to go?"

We walked up the marina's drive to the road that led to Sugar Mill and, eventually, St George's.

"Shall we catch the bus?" suggested Alex. It was a hot walk to Sugar Mill and an impossible one to St George's.

"Nah let's hitchhike, I don't have the money for a bus," said Shaun and slung his bag down at the end of the drive. "I always hitchhike from here although maybe it'll be harder with three eh?"

Sure enough, it didn't take long for a friendly Grenadian with a huge truck to stop and let us aboard. We were almost at the roundabout where the road split when Shaun seemed to change his mind.

"Actually guys, do you mind if I get out here? I need to go up to my friend's house to borrow some cash. I'll meet you at the marina in St George's yeah? At the bar there?" And he was gone within 30 seconds, practically leaping from the car but first having left us his holdall to look after.

We thanked the driver and got out at the Mill, catching a bus that was en route to St George's. It's not difficult to catch a bus in Grenada and there are no timetables or even really bus stops. Instead, a decrepit minivan would screech to a halt whenever it saw someone walking and holler at them, trying to persuade them to get on.

Pumping West Indian dance music at insatiable volumes, the Grenadian buses were usually packed full and there was always room for one more regardless of capacity.

The driver would be free and easy with both the accelerator and break with a guy in the first seat behind the front passenger who was in charge of the money and the sliding door.

All you had to do is show even the mildest of interest at an approaching bus and the door will slide open as it's still moving and you jump in, trying to squeeze around large ladies with their shopping bags and uniform-clad school children. The bus stops for the shortest amount of time, just enough for you to step on board before it hurls itself back into the traffic, the driver desperately looking for buses coming up from behind and pulling out before they can get past.

This is how the bus system works in Grenada; if there's a bus just in front, they'll get the passengers and the money. If a bus does nip past then you'll be hanging around on the roadside for a few minutes, giving prospective future passengers on the roads ahead the chance to accumulate again.

The stop-start deafening journey is completed at high speeds where, to stop, you bang your fist on the exposed shell of the minivan to let the driver know you want out. You pass your crumpled, sweaty dollars to the doorman, sometimes via the helpful hands of everyone in between should you need change, and jump out the van, which is gone before you can even check you have your bag.

The Grenadian free enterprise system has created this pace and the buses will get you to your destination faster than you could ever imagine. If you don't know where to get off, everyone is more than happy to help you and smack on the side to make the speeding vehicle stop. You never wait more than a minute for a bus on this island.

We got to St George's, the capital of Grenada and headed into the Camper Nicholson marina. Considering our boat is a Nicholson, I wondered if they'd give us a discount to moor up here but surveying the other yachts in the marina I thought, no, we are too short and not shiny enough. This was a superyacht marina.

The Grenada Sailing Week is the baby sister of the Antigua Classics and is also sponsored by Mount Gay Rum – which is as good a reason as any to be part of it. It started in two days' time and, as we walked along the basin edge to the bar, the pontoons were humming with activity.

The bar was full of classic racers, all wearing baseball caps, all in old regatta t-shirts and all wearing faded pink shorts – in deep discussion with each other.

We established ourselves at the bar and ordered pineapple juice as it's one of the few juices you can get that wasn't out of a long-life carton.

Opposite the bar were four ginormous motorboats that gleamed under the effort of tens of buffing hands. Almost barbaric in size, the merest fingerprint or raindrop stain is enough to tarnish these status symbols, boats designed to sit in marinas puffing their chests out rather than making bow waves anywhere.

I met a crew member on the pontoon later and asked about the job. She told me the fridges must always be full in case the owner flies in. When was the owner last on board? I asked. She shrugs, before her time and she'd been working for four months.

Shaun turned up after we'd been at the bar for an hour, visited the bakery and returned to the bar for a further twenty minutes. He was as energetic as he was when we first saw him that morning but now he'd got $100 in his pocket. He ordered a grilled chicken sandwich but with 'a decent portion of chicken and a little bit of lettuce and tomato on the side', he added, grinning at the waitress who giggled in return and flapped her hand at him.

"Sweet guys, look I just gotta get hold of a VHF and then we can get a lift to *Coral* okay?" and he was gone.

He returned five minutes later to say *Coral* wasn't responding but he'd convinced another sailor to run us all out to her at anchor in his dinghy. He glanced around at the bar.

"Okay quick let's go before they realise I haven't paid for the chicken

I ordered," he said and we speed walked from the bar. The pontoons were filled with sailors, boxes and sails laid out like wilted butterflies. Everything is being measured and traded and off-loaded for lightness.

We got to the dinghy dock inside the marina basin and shook hands with Dave, a crew member who'd be racing aboard the 72 ft classic yawl *Galatea*, a masterpiece of design from 1899. I slipped my flip-flops off and was about to get into the dinghy when another turns up.

"Ah shit, it's Richard," said Shaun.

"Shaun, how are you?" said Richard, a man with a tall and commanding stature who nonetheless gave off an aura of utter relaxation.

"Yeah good, I couldn't get hold of *Coral* on the radio," said Shaun.

"It's off while Charlie's fixing something," said Richard, tying off his dinghy and standing on the dock. "'You need a ride out there? I have to go to the skipper's meeting and god knows if that'll be on time but I should be done in an hour."

"Do you guys mind hanging out another hour?" said Shaun. I shrugged, what was another hour?

Poor Dave got thanked and relieved of his duty, the beer Shaun had bought him as a thank you was instead passed to Richard who drank it in three gulps while surveying the marina.

"Ah, and this is Alex and Kit," said Shaun, "I thought Alex could race on *Coral* and Kit's a sailing journalist," he added. I'd shared this piece of information with Shaun in the momentary car ride earlier and he'd cackled with his South African drawl.

"Man, Richard is going to be so happy with me for bringing a sailing journalist along! It's all good publicity eh? *Coral* is a charter boat too so media is perfect. Ha, am I gonna be in his good books!" he'd said.

"Ah, who do you write for?" said Richard.

"*Yachting Monthly*, although unfortunately they don't cover boats like *Coral*. But I also publish on *The Huffington Post*," I said. "I wondered if I could come on board and take some photographs."

"*Yachting Monthly*, ha," he laughed, "'absolutely, you're both welcome. Are you coming on board later with Shaun?" he asked.

"If that's okay," I said.

"Sure, sure. Well you guys entertain yourselves and I'll go listen to someone drone on for an hour," he said and left us on the dockside.

"I wonder if my chicken burger's ready," said Shaun.

The chicken burger had come and gone when the waitress realised it had been abandoned but with a wicked grin and a wink from Shaun, it was brought back in no time.

It was 5pm by the time I actually climbed aboard the 85 ft schooner *Coral of Cowes* and the near equatorial sun was making tracks south. It was literally a climb too, so high were her sides but old boats have a lot of trimmings to hang onto.

"That's Dexter up there, he's our bosun," said Richard, joining me on deck. Dexter raised his hand in greeting, "He's Grenadian, I've had him for two years on board *Coral*."

A young man emerged from the glass companionway and Shaun handed him the holdall.

"This is Tom, he's first mate," said Richard, "Tom, this is Alex and Kit, she's a journalist, be nice to her."

How did journalists act? I wondered. And how long would it be until everybody realised that I was just a fake? Should I be asking thoughtful questions? I suddenly had no idea what I was doing there, Alex was the one that would be crewing on this enormous boat, not me. I was just the girlfriend. I didn't even write for *Yachting Monthly* in a real sense, I was just a freelancer who happened to sell them a lot of articles. But I didn't write for anyone else, so was I even a journalist? What was a journalist? Suddenly I couldn't believe I'd never looked up the definition before.

"Let me show you around," said Tom. He was only my age, the typical age of yacht crew. How had I managed to make people believe I was a real person? With a profession?

Never having been on a classic schooner before, I understood little of what I saw. Alex seemed to understand everything in the same way he could tell me what make of car was driving towards us in the UK;

he just knew. I didn't really see *Coral* from a sailor's point of view. I saw her for what she was to me, a phenomenal piece of creation.

Everything was wood and rope. The mainmast and foremast were hollow pine and everything else was teak and oak and bronze and copper. She had sailed straight out of the distant past but glowed with love and attention. I had never seen anything like it.

Butterfly hatches had been opened on the raised skylights giving the deck an almost botanical feel with the classic glass, threaded bronze and teak construction. The end of the main boom was bronze capped with *Coral* embossed into it. The wheel was the kind of thing I'd only ever seen in museums, and *Pirates of the Caribbean*. It was stunning as was the aft deck immediately behind it, perfectly constructed for lounging on and yet without any gunwales or provisions to stop people from falling off. With a severe overhang, the stern made me feel almost vertiginous.

While modern superyachts are palatial inside, *Coral* had the narrow interior of a classic. Still, she was certainly palatial by my standards and the saloon was the size of a moderate sitting room but decorated like a stately home owned by a seafarer.

The galley was narrow but looked as though it should be in a country cottage rather than a yacht with its wooden counters, huge sink and wood and glass cupboards. I was soon to be spending more time in there than I imagined.

As it was the day before the racing began, the crew started making an enormous spaghetti bolognese, 'carb loading', they joked and Richard invited us to stay for dinner. Never ones to turn down a free meal, I found myself squeezed in around the saloon table surrounded by hungry men eating spaghetti like it was going out of fashion.

"So, are you going to race with us tomorrow?" asked Richard, topping up my wine glass.

"Oh, no thank you, I wouldn't know what I was doing," I demurred, genuinely having no idea how ancient wooden schooners worked or, even, exactly what a schooner was.

"Ah I'm sure you'd be fine," he said, "but please come anyway, just take photographs or watch from the stern, it'll do these boys good to have a girl on board, it'll make them work harder," he laughed. I agreed on the condition that I would only take photos and in no way have to do anything practical. As photographer, I had two jobs; firstly, take photographs and secondly, stay out of everyone's way. It suited me, I could hide my fear with a camera. I emphasised my utter hopelessness and general ignorance when it came to sailing.

In truth, the idea of racing scared me. Monohulls go faster when they are heeled over as speed is a function of their waterline length and that's longer when they are heeled. The problem is, I don't like sailing really heeled over... it makes me think the boat might, y'know, fall over.

Later that evening I asked Charlie, the 20-year-old deck hand, how much *Coral* heeled over when she was really pushing it. He looked thoughtful, "not a scary amount," he said. I would've felt more relieved if this hadn't come from someone who planned on rowing across the Atlantic the following year. His definition of scary probably differed from mine.

The next day we caught the bus over to St George's and met the rest of the crew who weren't living on *Coral* at the dinghy dock. Tom arrived and picked us up, roaring us out to the yacht at anchor. With a permanent crew of only four plus Richard, *Coral*'s racing crew needed a bit of bumping up and, in the end, with friends of friends turning up, she was fully laden with 16.

As the majority of the crew made themselves useful on deck, I found myself in the galley with a Brazilian lawyer called Adriana and a vast quantity of sliced bread, cheese, mayonnaise and approximately a thousand tins of tuna.

"We just have lots of tuna…." Tom had said, opening the cupboards and showing me where everything was. "We forgot to buy anything else. We sort of forgot that we needed food for the race. We got beer though!"

Phillipa popped downstairs while we were mayonnaising bread en masse and rolled her eyes, "they're all boys, they're bloody useless at shopping for food," she said. A Kiwi, Phillipa had been the cook on board *Coral* many times for the charter weeks and had sailed all over the world as a chef on yachts.

It was a race to make enough sandwiches to feed the soon-to-be-hungry crew before the race began and Adriana and I searched the kitchen and entertained ourselves with some creative sandwich fillings. We were just putting the last cling films over the sandwich plates when *Coral* began to move under our feet and Tom shouted downstairs that we were heading to the start line.

When a boat you've never been on begins sailing, it's always a challenge to work out how the downstairs stows. As I would soon find out, the young crew of *Coral* weren't always utterly comprehensive in the stowage and the kitchen didn't even seem like it was built by someone who knew what heeling was. Adriana and I did our best to secure the cupboards, drawers and make sure nothing looked like it would shift around during a tack and burst free from its confines. Over the three days of racing, our efforts weren't always spot on, but for that first day at least, nothing broke.

I headed up to the ladies' cabin, a bench just inside the glass companionway from where I could see everything that was going on but, crucially, be out of the way of the crew. Racing against other large and almost unreasonably aged yachts, *Coral* was still a giant amongst her competitors. But as a giant, she was less quick on her feet, especially through tacks.

Richard was at the helm, an extraordinarily commanding man who, despite the patchwork nature of his impromptu crew, continually assessed the ever-changing situation and gave commands easily, his powerful voice booming down the length of the ship.

With two masts, the capacity for seven sails up at once and a mesmerising amount of rope rigging, each member of the crew had a single job to do and no one was at a loss. The first course of 11 miles was two circuits of a four sided course and the strategic elements of yacht racing up close were amazing to watch.

With a spotter on the bowsprit, our good friend South African Shaun, Richard would have approaching wind shadows called out to him and be able to deal with them accordingly. To feel the 76-ton ship beneath us pick up speed and charge towards the next turning mark was a feeling utterly different from that of my own yacht.

As we approached the marker, bore away for speed and then performed a huge, shuddering tack around it, every square inch of heavy wood shifted its weight with the change in course and it was as though the great ship was as alive as the horse beneath the jockey. But *Coral* rarely lumbered, rather danced, as she was built to do, through the flat water and spritely wind. As she heeled over, and over... and over, it didn't feel as though I were standing on a precipice – it felt like the most natural thing in the world.

"Don't worry," shouted Richard, his eyes alive with the rush, "she's designed to do this."

And she was. That's the thing about classic yachts, they weren't designed just to be fast, or to be palatial to live on – they were designed to flow, to live, to sail. An enormous gaff-rigged schooner like *Coral* may look luxurious as she minces up the Solent on a sunny summer's day but give her a starting gun and an opponent and she's ferocious. She sails like a lady, if that lady were Catherine the Great.

With huge deck locker fridges filled with beer, the crew was contentedly chowing down on the sandwiches and celebrating the first half day of racing. *Coral* wasn't the fastest boat in the classics division but perhaps she was the most uproarious when it came to crew relations and morale.

I spent the races practically crawling about the deck taking photographs of the crew in action. There was something so utterly photogenic about a race onboard a classic yacht and by the end of the second day my camera had been dead for an hour. I can see why the record breaking multihulls of today are stunning, but surely there's something even more incredible about a 113-year-old yacht still thrashing the competition in the Caribbean?

We repeated the process for three days, arriving on board at 8am, Adriana and I making copious sandwiches with ever-more imaginative fillings while the crew sorted out the deck and then racing hard around two courses a day. With other classes racing at the same time on different but overlapping courses, we had some unbelievably close calls with lightweight modern racing yachts and even our own competitor, the 100+-year-old *Lily Maid* just inches away from touching our hull.

Due to our main competition pulling out to sail northwards for an imminent charter and *Galatea* breaking her topmast, as well as three days of excellent racing, *Coral* won the classics class for the Grenada Sailing Week and the celebrations were riotous. With a huge bottle of Mount Gay rum and an even bigger trophy, the whole crew was elated at the prize-giving ceremony and party at Prickly Bay Marina.

I was leaning on the bar, laughing at Charlie's collection of free sponsor-branded sunglasses tucked into his t-shirt when the navigator, a British man called Alex, turned around on his bench and asked me, "how fast does your yacht go to windward?"

I paused to think and, just as I opened my mouth, he said, 'that's when you sail into the wind', in the single most patronising voice anybody has ever used on me. I stared at him before doing what any spineless girl like me would in the situation, I laughed and said, "yeah I knoooow. About 6 knots."

But I felt as though I'd been smacked. Exactly as I had two years before when the lawyer at my firm had laughed off my sailing plans, saying I'd probably never sailed across the Channel. It was the derision, the eye-rolling 'she's an idiot' that some men had down to a fine art. And every time it knocked me for six.

But why had he assumed I wouldn't know what 'windward' meant? I couldn't imagine him saying that to any of the other women that had raced on *Coral* despite their relative inexperience with hands-on sailing. So it wasn't a gender thing, or at least, it wasn't just a gender thing. I couldn't imagine him saying it to a man at all.

The comment rankled me for days. Years actually, considering I'm writing about it now. But the more I thought about what had prompted him to say it, the more I realised it was down to two factors. The first being that he was the kind of person who enjoyed undermining others and the second, and most important, was that I had given him permission. In fact, by continually undermining myself before and during races, explaining away my photographic and non-sailing role with 'I would just do it wrong and get in the way', I had announced to everyone that I had managed to sail across an entire ocean and still didn't know how to sail. I'd told the whole crew that I was an idiot.

Even though I wasn't. Even though I did know how to sail. I did know what to do on *Coral*, I was just too afraid that I might not do it well enough. I had been broadcasting my totally imagined failures on all frequencies and was it really anyone else's fault that they believed me?

When people say that you are your own worst enemy, I was consistently seeing that, in my case, it was true. I happily went around telling people I was awful at things, incapable, ignorant and an appalling learner simply to avoid being in any situation that might test me in any way. I was bowing out of so many things and letting people think I was genuinely stupid. Did I really want to be seen as that just to avoid the embarrassment of not trimming a sail perfectly?

I left the closing race party with a sense that I had a serious issue with not underselling myself, but negatively selling myself. For all the confidence in my endurance and abilities sailing across the Atlantic had given me, I was still hugely failing to respect myself when it came to talking to other people. And as the old adage goes, how will others respect you if you don't respect yourself?

A week after Grenada Sailing Week, we left Prickly Bay for good and headed north for the tiny Grenadian island of Carriacou. We'd been in Grenada for almost a month, far longer than we had intended, it was definitely time to be moving on before we strayed deeper into the semi-permanent cruising community that lived there. First though, there was something I had been meaning to see.

There was an odd sensation of suspense as I finned gently north of the red buoy marked on my biro scrawled map. Needless to say, I did not bring it with me. Instead, I tried to imprint it on my brain.

The visibility wasn't bad, maybe ten metres, but there were occasional clouds that brought a deep gloom to this underwater world as they passed over the sun. Still, when I abruptly saw the first sculpture it was arresting.

Twenty or so children stood in a circle facing out, gripping each other's hands as they peered into the blue. Coral and seaweed hung off their lips as parrotfish nibbled their knees. A sea urchin had glued itself to the side of a child's head like a grotesque tumour. They stood, lifeless but enchanting, as part of this microcosm reef but simultaneously alien to it.

The Circle of Children is around five metres deep and it was easy for me to free dive down and fin around them – their resident fish completely unperturbed. I was amazed that there was no one else there, no swathes of tourists, no other cruisers, no one.

I didn't want to leave them for a reason I cannot explain but there were others that I wanted seek out. Soon I came upon The Last Correspondent in his lonely office. He sat hunched over his typewriter at his desk, angelfish inspecting his eyes. He was hairy with weed and didn't look up as I swam over him. Set on a patch of sand, he was surrounded on all sides by high reef.

Christ of the Deep stood in his own hollow nearby and held his arms out and up, imploring those above. His face was clear and easy to read but showed no emotion. I left him gladly, feeling his presence fade away as I swam.

Serena appeared after minutes of reef and empty sand, kneeling at depth and praying with her hands pressed together. Three puffer fish were browsing the reef beside her and she had a haunting manner. As though someone promised they would return for her and never did.

I came across the Circle of Adults soon after and found a huge parrotfish in perfect azure feeding from a hand. The circle felt different from the children although it looked very similar. While the children seemed content, the adults looked as though they were prisoners. It reminded me of something, viscerally, but I couldn't grasp what it was.

When I found the Naked Ladies it was like stumbling upon an open grave. First I saw just two, lying close to each other on their backs. As my eyes adjusted to the difference between rock, reef, sand and sculpture, I saw more. I thought there were only four but more and more appeared, some face down in the sand, some face up. It looked like a neatly arranged slaughter. A mass suicide. Like they just laid down and never got up again. I didn't stay for long – I didn't even count them.

Over a bank of reef and I was back in the Circle of Children, a shoal of yellow and black striped fish greeted me and escorted me through the scene. I felt their eyes watching me as they must have done to so many other swimmers. I didn't want to look back in case the Children had turned their heads. A cold shiver scuttled along my back. I made the swim back to the boat moored in the next bay with difficulty, a strong counter-current having formed. It felt like I was abandoning the eerie community, fleeing the scene.

The water temperature in the West Indies was deliciously warm and the temperature would only increase as the year progressed. Finally I could absorb myself in a world I had only seen a few times before except now I lived in it. Instead of going for a walk like I would in the UK, I could just hop over the side and be amongst the fish and the corals in a moment.

As we sailed north into the island chain of St Vincent and the Grenadines, more and more I found myself at anchor with no other boats in sight and a rich world beneath me. Having trained in free diving in Bali several years before, I had become more at home underwater than I ever had been in the past.

The simple pleasure of swimming along the sand, metres beneath the surface, and being followed by curious fish never wore off. I felt no self-consciousness beneath the water, no judgement, no frustration and no need to be or do anything other than just drift along with the fish. With no sudden movements, I was simply another member of this aquatic community and accepted readily.

No struggle, no fighting, no apparatus to force my way into this world, just a deep breath and open eyes. And it was to get even better.

Chapter 7

Tropical France

Travel can be one of the most rewarding forms of introspection.
Lawrence Durrell

"I found a lobster 'otel!" said Eric in his thick Brittany accent, eyes wide and hands apart, gesticulating with excitement.

"In Martinique?" I said.

"Yes," he nodded. "The east coast has no boats, just reefs. And lobster." He grinned and jigged absentmindedly, his tiny son bobbing up and down on his back.

Over his shoulder, I could see two West Indian women in bejewelled bikinis grinding unabashedly against a man in orange tartan. Eric and I were shouting at each other, trying to be heard above the pumping bass of stacked speakers, four high, strapped onto the back of a pickup truck.

The women were shaking every ounce of fat they had, their enormous breasts all but overflowing from their Rio-esque costumes. As the procession inched its way down the street, dozens more glittering girls and women danced in their underwear, gyrating distractedly as they gazed at the sky, drank from beer bottles or, somehow, continued conversations on their mobiles.

We were at Carriacou carnival, a truly extraordinary event absolutely sure to damage an entire generation's eardrums in just one day. This tiny island, part of Grenada, was a world unto itself and its mixture of Scottish and Caribbean celebration was overwhelming.

"Whereabouts on the east coast were you?" I shouted, the music vibrating my ribs and the sun streaming into my eyes.

"Ah," said Eric with a smile, "we go back so I don't tell you in case find my lobster apartment!" I laughed, this had been going on for a while now.

We had met thousands of miles before in the miniature Portuguese island of Porto Santo and had run into Eric and his little French family in the Canary Islands as well. Each of us were always spearfishing and comparing our catches.

Over the next six weeks we made our way through the Grenadines, an island chain belonging to the biggest island, St Vincent. Each island was tiny, with a smattering of people and a few boats in the anchorages.

The one I had really wanted to get to was Mayreau, a minuscule island with a lookout area from its highest point. We walked up the winding, pot-holed road, goats bleating and running in front of us as we passed.

It took us a while to find it and we walked back and forth along the top road a couple of times. Well, top section of the road at any rate considering the island only had one road.

"Maybe it's in the churchyard," I pointed out, remembering the Swedish sailors we spoke to three islands before and their description of the find.

We walked into the church's tiny patio and there I saw a small wooden sign with an arrow, 'Tobago Cays'. We darted around the side of the building and emerged onto a sort of stone terrace.

The island dropped away beneath it and the cays stretched out, luminous in their azure blue water, reefs swirling and encasing them. It was silencing.

From our vantage point, we could see every tiny palm tree cay, every anchored yacht, every deep section and shallow section. We could see the two entrances, the south – risky and the north – clearer. I tried to stamp the image into my mind because it would look a lot different as we negotiated the reefy entrance. Or maybe I just wanted the image to keep forever; my camera couldn't pick up exactly what I saw. Not really.

The next day we upped anchor in Mayreau and tacked off up around the top end of the island, into the wind. We'd left at mid-morning to give us good visibility with which to see the reef and Alex stood on the bow, running back only to tack the genoa.

The labyrinth of reefs, islets and pure sand cays make this place the stuff of postcards and Microsoft wallpapers. Even a scene or two from *Pirates of the Caribbean* was filmed here. While Tobago Cays has an impressive reputation, its survival is really down to one thing – it can only be reached by boat and has no cars, no roads, no houses. It's loved and cherished and looked after.

As we finally switched the engine on and nosed our way into an anchorage, I could barely keep my focus. My eyes were darting everywhere looking for those aged leviathans, those serene creatures, those stone-like wanderers. Tobago Cays wasn't just a piece of idealism; it was a sea turtle sanctuary.

We dropped the anchor in just three metres of water and imagined the keel almost brushing the sand. The water was so clear it might as well have not been there at all. I wanted to cry at its blue; its perfect, crystalline blue. It was the blue that dreams are made of.

Within five minutes I was immersed in a sea of obscene clarity. I swam down to the keel bottom and checked the depth, planting myself beneath the boat and peering upwards. I loved her for bringing me here and gave her lead-filled underside a hug.

Immediately past the boat was water too shallow for anchoring and so it was an easy swim to the first outcrops of reef. As a nature reserve, no spearfishing, Hawaiian slings or indeed fishing of any kind could take place and the fish are surprisingly friendly. I swam straight through a shoal of sergeant major fish and they wove and bloomed around my yellow fins, one taking the time to tap on my mask and say hello. I was in love.

Coral of every shape, size and colour formed the outcrops that sprung from the flat white sand bottom as suddenly as the New York skyline springs from the Atlantic. Partially hidden around the coral fringes lay huge lobsters, unthreatened by humans and laying low for passing food. Their long feelers poked out from under the rock and gave them away. Troops of electric blue fish, no bigger than my thumb, nibbled on invisible things and rainbow coloured parrotfish eyed me curiously. Trumpet fish, with their slimline bodies and trumpet mouths, drifted on unseen currents with barely a flick a fin.

As I cruised along the reefs I kept my eyes peeled for signs of turtles and tried not to be disappointed when I saw none. There were so many anchored boats there, perhaps the whole idea of an anchorage in a turtle watching area was ironic – surely the turtles avoided it like the plague. I finned around the bay in a big circle and contented myself with the extraordinary reef fish and the occasional conch crawling laboriously along the seabed.

It was getting into afternoon and my stomach called me back to the boat. I swam warily, looking out for dinghies and their treacherous outboards. With my head mostly above the water through the anchorage to check for those dangerous monsters, I almost missed the fellow dreamily swimming below me. So lazy was his stroke that I barely noticed him, despite his size. But I caught myself and dived beneath.

The turtle half swam, half drifted along the seabed, pausing to gulp a string of eelgrass. He looked at me casually and continued his slow pace through the water, unperturbed by my presence. I forgot oxygen, I forgot dinghies, I forgot lunch. I drifted along with him, keeping my distance but keeping pace. He was nature slowed right d o w n . . . He even blinked in slow motion.

Eventually my lungs cramped for air and I allowed myself to rise the short two metres to the surface. I swam slowly back to the boat and watched the turtle gliding below. I look at people chatting on their yachts, drinking their beers and laughing with their friends and wondered if they realised they were only metres away from one of the world's most majestic animals.

It broke my heart to leave the turtle and I vowed to return to the water later that day. The Caribbean was a big place and these pockets of extreme postcard idealism were not as abundant as you would think when looking at the brochures. But the places they do exist in are as painful as a broken heart; you know that you cannot stay there, that the beauty, at least for you, is temporary.

We sailed from Mayreau to Bequia after exhausting ourselves with turtles and fish but found ourselves stranded by strong winds and steep waves. We were determined to make Martinique in one hop though, shirking the islands of St Vincent and St Lucia – we couldn't stop everywhere and we'd heard that the islands were less laid back than most.

It took us two attempts to leave Bequia, once thwarted by short, sharp 3-metre waves on the nose. But eventually we crossed the channel between St Vincent and St Lucia and nipped into St Lucia's Rodney Bay at night for a rest.

Sneaking out of Rodney Bay at 7am was slightly pointless given that the border patrol, armed with sub-machine guns, were already out chasing a speedboat off the harbour limits at full speed. They clearly had more important things on their plate than an errant yacht slipping in and out of the country.

At the very north-western extreme of St Lucia, it doesn't take long once you're out of Rodney Bay for you to hit strong trade winds. Within a mile, the sea had turned to hideous short, two-metre chop, hitting us directly abeam. The wind was 15-20 knots and there wasn't a chance I was going to let the wind vane steer, as capable and uncomplaining as she was.

White knuckled, I steered across the twenty-mile channel between St Lucia and Martinique, turning up into the larger waves so they didn't roll the boat enough to get her boom underwater.

I had developed a technique for this type of sailing, the kind where I was wearing a corset of tension. One wave at a time. One squall at a time. One gust at a time.

Naturally, being the type of person that thinks through every outcome, pointlessly far ahead, reigning in my subsequent anxieties was hard. But I was learning, one passage at a time, that the wind and waves would look at your plans and chortle.

Despite the swell, we reached the south-western point of Martinique within four hours and its southern peninsula had blocked the worst of the swell. As we sailed on into Martinique's wind shadow, switching between light winds and 17 knot squalls, the boat heeled right over, racing across the now flat water.

Martinique's capital, Fort-de-France, is deep into a huge bay that looks like a giant has taken a bite out of the island's side. As we rounded the hill before the bay, we were blasted with a wind straight from the direction of the anchorage.

Out of the swell, I don't mind strong gusts, even if we had shaken the reefs out. I developed my taste for flat water beating near St Michael's Mount in Cornwall and there's rarely a time when the boat goes faster.

Now we had seven miles to tack up to Fort-de-France and I was in heaven racing along, knowing that within the day I would be in a French supermarché.

French supermarkets mean more to me than the average supermarket does; they're settled deep within my psyche and have been since I was very young.

Born to parents who counted their bicycles as extra limbs, I'd visited France on numerous occasions by bike. As we rolled down the ramp of the cross-Channel ferry (in front of all the impatient cars), the first thing on my young mind was where is the nearest supermarché?

My sister and I found French supermarkets the utmost in holiday entertainment. Bigger than any shop we'd ever been into, SuperU, E. Leclerc, Champion and Carrefour were names filled with possibility and excitement.

Other children would hop in the car and go to Alton Towers; we hopped on our bikes and pedalled through French countryside until we got to a supermarché. Or better yet, a hypermarché.

The experience would start with the then novel custom of needing a coin to put into the trolley to release it. At that age, a coin deposit was especially exciting because there was always a chance a parent would let you keep it at the end and the French francs were so foreign to me that I loved to inspect them in detail.

As my sister and I stood, eyes wide, in the doorway of the monstrous warehouse, we were overwhelmed by the possibilities within. Almost no recognisable brands could ever be found in these palaces of food and that was the thrill; everything was new.

Our next entertainment, after the little spark of putting the coin in the trolley, was the fresh produce section. Unlike back home, you had to weigh your own fruit and veg, press the corresponding button, remove the sticker and affix it to your bag of whatever.

As our parents ummed and ahhed in the apple department, my sister and I would merrily press our palms onto the scale, press the funniest looking picture button or the one with the weirdest name and take the stickers.

Honestly, if schools want their children to take more of an interest in French class, they should just run trips to a Carrefour in Calais and have them play with the sticker machines. By the age of ten I was more or less fluent in the names of French vegetables.

The stickers weren't wasted and we never went overboard. Instead we'd get one or two from each supermarket, carry them carefully through the shopping process like sticky butterflies and then press them neatly onto the frames of our bikes.

After a two-week holiday we'd have:

Carrefour
Rennes – Centre Ville
Poivre rouge
0.043kg
F7.32

SuperU
Z.A. Maritime – Vannes
Fraises
0.500kg
F13.00

Champion
S.A. Bordeaux Ouest
Champignons
0.081kg
F5.42

E. Leclerc
S.A. Fontainebleau Nord
Pomme de Terre
1.128kg
F21.37

Not to mention the stickers from every apple we ate while abroad. Our bicycles were the culinary scrapbooks of our supermarket forays. The stickers even had the store's town or city printed on them so we'd know where we'd rested our chins on the scale and hit 'cerises'.

Picking from the endless cheese counter, sticking our noses into piles of warm, crusty baguettes and paper, scissors, rock deciding between boxes of cereal bars, French supermarkets were singly responsible for me understanding implicitly that Britain was just Britain, that only 70 miles from my house in a straight line was the beginning of an entirely different world.

"It's not actually going to be like France you know," said Alex matter-of-factly. "It's just going to be the same as the other islands with a different language. Don't get excited about cheese." I pulled a face.

"They have multiple flights a day to Paris, there'll be French supermarkets. You know the French, they can't live without good food, even in the Caribbean," I said pointedly. Alex shrugged, unwilling to argue with me about something neither of us knew.

I was feeling a little deflated by the time we'd thrashed upwind and dropped our anchor in the lee of the castle. He was probably right, there'd be more terrible Caribbean supermarkets with mice hopping around the floors and junk food imported from America. If I hoped for street cafes and espressos then I was going to be sorely disappointed.

But when we tied our dinghy to the well-maintained dinghy dock alongside a pretty park promenade, my excitement was beginning to brew again.

The road along the waterfront had slightly rundown shops on one side and the concrete mess of a cruise ship dock and long term parking on the other. We shuffled to the back of the chandlery and used the computer to check in.

The shop assistant give our printed form a once over and scribbled their name, charging us €5 for the clearance. Compared to the hours of disinterested immigration and customs officers on the previous islands, we were amazed to be out within a few minutes.

It was then that it happened. Amongst the pedestrians traversing the pavements and weaving their way between the traffic across the road, was a woman carrying a Carrefour bag.

It didn't take us long to track it down, all things in France eventually lead to a Carrefour and this one was part of a shopping mall in the dead centre of town. A little plaza with a crêpe stand stood outside where you could get a crêpe with endless toppings and a little bottle of Heineken. The small collection of metal tables and chairs filled me with joy, what better way to be in the French Caribbean than to eat a Nutella-filled crepe and sip une petite biere?

We descended into Carrefour and Alex was no longer a sceptical Brit. Being an exquisite cook, I realised that he was probably more excited than I was, finally having access to quality ingredients.

We searched the aisles like ten years olds, picking up everything and shoving it under each other's noses to smell or look or read.

"Cumin gouda!" I said.

"Fresh steak!" said Alex, reading a label, "from France!"

Almost everything had been flown from France, as fresh as it would in the St Malo supermarchés. With multiple flights per day, even the yoghurt was as fresh as if it had just walked out of a dairy.

As well stocked as any Carrefour, this shop occupied us for far longer than seemed possible, even for me. We left with heavy bags of wine, cheese, chorizo, steak, vegetables, Nutella, baguettes and a few bars of Milka.

We dropped the shopping off at the boat and returned to town to sit in the open terrace of a tiny hotel, refresh ourselves with a malty beer and read a two-day-old copy of Le Monde. Afterwards we roamed around and enjoyed the atmosphere.

While Chris Doyle, author of the famous *Doyle Guides to the Caribbean*, says that Fort-de-France is full of shops boasting 'Paris fashions', he may actually only be correct if he's talking about Parisian brothel fashions.

A baffling amount of shops sold Lycra dresses, crotchless underwear and clothes with more cut-outs than a bikini. The array of crude and hilarious remarks printed on the backs of pants and stretchy jeans was so outrageous I was tempted to buy a range and send them home.

Considering the locals were dressed in normal clothes – jeans and t-shirts – I failed to see who these endless stores of Lycra were aimed at. Not once did I see anyone dressed as though they'd wandered out of a particularly low-end strip club.

If they were for the benefit of the twice weekly cruise ship passengers then they were targeting the wrong age range by generations.

But Fort-de-France wasn't all hooker shops and patisseries, there was a semi-hidden history that permeated the streets like it does in Europe; mostly unseen, but when you look hard enough, it's everywhere.

Not something you'd notice until you walked right past it, the Schoelcher Library is light years away from anything you'd expect to see in the West Indies. And it's breath-taking.

Before I visited the Schoelcher Library, I didn't know that buildings could be moved. Not buildings like this at any rate and certainly not at the distances that this one had travelled.

As I read into the history of the library, I discovered that it had first been constructed for the Paris Exposition of 1889. An extraordinary iron and glass construction, it wasn't until I looked at it, really looked at it, that I stopped and realised the scale of what I was seeing. I walked past it twice without paying much attention until the third time when some tiny detail caught my eye and I was gobsmacked that I could have missed this building.

But the builder had always meant for it to reside eventually in Fort-de-France, to house the thousands of books donated to the island by French abolitionist Victor Schoelcher. After the Exposition in mainland France, the building was deconstructed, shipped thousands of miles across the Atlantic and rebuilt where it stood in front of me.

I made my way inside and found the very top of the ceiling was lined with the names of great French writers, philosophers and social reformers, the words overseeing the visitors like long-dead curators. J.J. Rousseau, La Bruyere, La Fontaine. The same continued on the outer north wall, Isambert Perrinon, Allen Benezet, La Rochefoucauld-Liancourt.

The library is a shrine not just to literature, but also to the accessibility of literature to all people from all races. Victor Schoelcher had a strong belief in racial equality and was determined, above all, to wipe out illiteracy. Alex had to drag me away.

Fort-de-France's busyness, the noise and water quality soon drove us across the huge bay to L'Anse Matin on the opposite side. With strong easterlies, we tucked ourselves in amongst the many anchored yachts in front of two hotels and headed for shore.

A luxury hotel, with ground level mini-apartments, held the foreshore with a manmade breakwater to create a little tropical paradise pool complete with swim-up bar. The narrow peninsula had a marina within two minute's walk and a tiny, tourist town complete with bikini shops and patisseries.

The town was excellent for a real croissant and a baguette but it wasn't that that stole our attention. Jutting out of the palm tree fringes and overshadowing the luxury resort below, was an enormous, seven story hotel that had long been abandoned and left to the elements.

A vague fence had been erected to give visitors the impression of a restricted area but the gate was wide open and the fence was mostly overgrown. We nipped through and, within two minutes, were taking tentative steps towards the lobby of the hotel.

I could still hear splashes and shrieks from the beach as bikini-clad tourists enjoyed the tropical sun but we were suddenly light years away from them. Vines and rubble disrupted the path up the steps and into the hotel. Where once cars would've pulled up to the front doors, now broken glass and graffiti lay in the shade of the concrete cover. Palm trees had grown taller than the monstrous building, desperate for a new view.

Lobby pillars, walls and stairs had become the canvases of artists dedicated to spray painting and angry words. An elaborate painted hibiscus roamed across the doors of a lift.

Everywhere the outside world was trying to get in. The glass and window frames had long been stripped and creepers curled their way in across the walls. There was no outside or inside there though. They had merged into a hybrid, the green and luscious plants hugged and blended with the concrete until they were inseparable.

The building was room after room of hanging, strangled fittings and the detritus of mankind. The grounds drowned in weeds and vines. In front of this veiled monstrosity was the tropical white beach with honeymooners bathing and the bar suspended above postcard water. So close, yet there was no one else there in the hotel. No one ventured through the creepers to the ghost of tourism.

It was distinctly Ballardian to the point that I wondered if he too had come across this marooned wreck but in fact it had only been abandoned since 2008 and it was the jungle and sea air that had done their best to destroy it.

The local town considered it a blight and an embarrassment and the building does not hide its dilapidated state. Numerous demolition plans had been put forward and after years of delay there was finally a firm goal that would see its total destruction set for November 2015. Eventually, demolition begun in May 2016 and the eerie hotel is now nothing more than a memory. Soon a shiny new hotel will stand on its grave.

As I ran my hands along its crumbling walls, I was sad to think that it would disappear and be replaced by another luxury resort. There was something undeniably fascinating about its state of entropy and its ability to stand proudly in its withered beauty, jutting its wind battered chin out over the holiday brochure paradise below.

With calmer weather approaching, we took the opportunity a few days later to sail back around the south-western corner of the island and beat up to Ste Anne and Le Marin; the true sailor towns of this French department.

Tucked into the lee of fairly desolate peninsula, Sainte Anne was a small fishing village with a large open anchorage and as many small French yachts as you'd find in a Brittany cove. We stayed for a night before motor sailing up the Le Marin Channel.

We'd accidentally chosen an inopportune moment to begin our journey of five miles into the well-protected bay of Le Marin. While we'd seen a host of brightly colour dinghies just off the coast, we hadn't realised that they were on their way back in and that, in fact, they were racing.

The channel was narrow and flanked by shallow sandbanks and within ten minutes we were in the middle of a fleet of Martinique Yoles, long wooden open boats with huge, fluorescent square sails.

With around ten crew each, tightly packed and hiked out on the windward side of the hull, the Yole racing was clearly a serious business and a smattering of motorboats and RIBs were following closely behind, watching the action.

I found myself performing an odd sort of jerky motion with the boat as I slowed her down to allow a Yole to pass across her bow and then speeded up to nip in front of another and so on and so forth until the first one tacked back again. It wasn't too dissimilar from dealing with the immense Saturday traffic of Southampton Water but the Yole crews were cheerful and waving as they passed, enjoying the challenge of a yacht in their midst.

Le Marin was a small paradise for the weary cruisers, at least those who hailed from Europe. The more I cruised in the Caribbean the more it seemed that certain nationalities stuck to certain places and none were as notable as the French and Americans.

Very few Americans could be found in Martinique and those we spoke to months later found the place unfriendly and unhelpful. Expressing indignation that many menus were solely in French and most residents spoke little to no English (or had any interest in revealing that they did), American cruisers in general seemed to harbour a mild irritation for the place.

The French protectiveness over their language wasn't exactly new and I had grown up with France as my neighbour so to me the French were just... well, French.

I actually found the inhabitants of Martinique incredibly friendly and many patrons listened patiently at my mispronounced attempts at their language, a language I love but struggle with. I could conduct my café forays in French without receiving much more than a smirk of comprehension and the efficiency and availability of things were refreshing beyond belief.

Le Marin was a mishmash of Europeans and I couldn't have been happier; finally others to share my homesickness for my continent with and the culture shock of the eastern Caribbean.

We met Florian and Julia after having been in Le Marin for a few days and were pleased to find at least one boat with people our age on it. While we'd come across crew working on boats who were in their twenties, we had yet to find any cruising on their own boat this side of the Caribbean.

Florian and Julia were hovering just below thirty and had sailed from Croatia in their Oceanis 37, an ex-Sunsail charter yacht. Bavarians, they had broken free from their fairly landlocked lives post-university and decided to spend two years sailing around the Caribbean.

Animated and bristling with intelligence, our new German friends rekindled our belief that we couldn't be the only 'young people' cruising. We shared dinner on each other's boats and shared our knowledge of the lobster 'otels that our French sailor friend Eric had told us of two months before.

Florian, enthusiastic about fishing, was all for concocting a plan to explore the reef-strewn east coast and spend a few days gorging on seafood. Watching him and Alex discuss fishing lures as though they were talking of rare treasures was as hilarious as it was contagious.

After anchoring off Sainte Anne again when the swell forecast dropped off, both our boats set sail at 8am one morning and began the lengthy tack east around the Sainte Anne peninsula. The wind was fifteen knots and the journey was fast despite the beat at the beginning. Soon we were close reaching northeast up Martinique's treacherous coastline.

This coast was not in the guidebooks and, in fact, where it is mentioned, the advice was to avoid it altogether. The reefs were to leeward of any passage and so numerous that an overcast day would add more danger than it was worth. Nevertheless, we had picked some good conditions and were up in the anchorage before evening.

Alex and I were rowers. Or rather, Alex liked to row and I like to perch on the back and admire the view. We didn't have an outboard or even a dinghy with a hard transom and instead we rowed a forty-year-old Avon inflatable dinghy around whatever the weather.

Since Eric had told us that the lobster 'otels were right out in the middle reefs at depth – 'aah but I won't tell you anything more' – Florian and Julia suggested that we all go in their dinghy and motor up.

The wind the next morning wasn't particularly strong but with four of us and a 3 hp outboard, we shipped more water than we crossed in the Germans' little dinghy. With 27°C water though we hardly cared and anchored next to a lively looking reef after a lengthy motor.

What surprised me about Martinique's eastern coastline was that the two bays with good shelter for anchoring actually housed tiny fishing towns and sheltered inlets with moored local boats. Because of the fishing here, the channels into these safe harbours were actually well buoyed and perfectly navigable for the average cruiser.

If you chose to risk the journey in reasonable swells or dangerously high winds then, of course, you stood a chance of making landfall on a reef but that level of poor decision-making was likely to land you in trouble anywhere.

I began to suspect that the writer of the famous guidebooks in this area had either never ventured here himself, or that he was cleverly keeping an untouched cruising ground empty for his own pleasure.

Either reason was as likely as the other and the absence of cruising notes in the guidebook was working wonders – we didn't see a single other visiting yacht on the entire coastline.

We had anchored the dinghy near the Le Francois Bay channel markers where we'd spotted a good looking reef on the way in and flopped into the water with all the elegance of baby elephant seals.

The water was amazingly clear considering the murkiness of where we'd anchored the boats and purple sea fans wafted gently in the current. Butterfly fish, angel fish, rainbow parrot fish and yellow grunts streamed through the nooks and crannies of the extensive reef and barely gave me a second glance.

In places the coral seabed was just two or three metres deep and in others the coral reef was more like ten or deeper. Lobster traps were marked with algae-filled Coke bottles, tied to manky string and each housed several lobsters as well as a small, depressed community of reef fish.

The trapped lobsters proved that the there were more around and Florian and Alex set about peering in every crevice and overhang they could find.

I wasn't really looking for lobster and let the boys spend their time hunting, I was more interested in gliding above the reef and watching the millions of brightly coloured fish move about their garden landscape. I did, however, spot a conch.

In the West Indies, conch is often called lambi and it features in curries and rotis – soft, pastry-like things. While I'm sure it has a unique flavour to itself, I'd only ever had it covered in some kind of spicy sauce or rolled into hot lambi fritters. So when I discovered one ambling across the seabed, I was pretty excited.

Seeing a conch move at all was actually a first for me and I wouldn't have spotted it if it hadn't been moving. Conch shells may look beautiful in the shops, polished and impossibly evolved with pearly pink interiors but in reality, when they're alive, their shells are almost furry with weed and blend perfectly with their surroundings.

This one, however, was moving at quite an impressive pace considering it was essentially a big shell and a muscular snail. I called over to Alex, who had the catch bag and gloves and he scooped it up from the bottom. Lobster or no lobster, at least we'd get to try some conch that night.

We reconvened at the dinghy, bobbing much further away than I thought I'd swam, and inspected our catches. We had three reasonably sized lobster and two... well... sort of crab-like things, long with orange-peel hard shells.

That night we went to *Tun*, Florian and Julia's Oceanis and stretched out in their wide and comfortable saloon. Every time I went on boats like that I was in awe, even though it was only 2 ft longer and 4 ft wider, there was just so much space – it felt like a proper living room.

I perused the cookery bookshelf before realising that even Ottolenghi's *Plenty* was in German and eventually found an English fishing book. We took a look at the unidentified creatures, a matching pair.

"I think they're lobster," said Florian. I flicked through the index to 'L' and found what I was looking for: slipper lobster.

The poor black and white photo in the book showed just what we had, a pair of slipper lobsters. Good eating, normally found walking around. This is exactly how Florian had found them, following each other across the sand and coral. Unlike the Caribbean spiny lobsters we normally caught, these ones hung out in broad daylight.

"What is a slipper?" asked Florian.

"It's like, you know," I said, thinking of how to describe it, "a soft shoe for inside, to keep your feet warm." Florian ahhhed and nodded. You never realise how much you take language for granted until you have to describe a noun. After all, what's a dressing gown? An indoor coat made of towel? Sounds ridiculous.

We had a small Magma barbecue attached to our stern rail and, while Julia and I picked apart our languages and practised rolling our 'r's, the boys dinghied over to our boat to barbecue the lobster and deal with the conch.

When they came back they were giddy with the feast they'd personally hunted and the slight guilt about the fact they'd apparently destroyed a wooden chopping board while they tried to violently crack open the conch.

The conch got its revenge. Shapeless and tough, it was covered in some strange and sickening kind of goo, even after cooking. The goo was so sticky that it was simply impossible to separate from the flesh and the idea of it dampened my enjoyment of the meal considerably.

There's something inherently unappetising about a snot-like membrane on your plate. It made oysters look as normal as carrots. I nibbled some slipper lobster, which was indeed excellent, but mainly concentrated on Julia's incredible coconut rice and let the others devour the seafood feast.

I vowed never to catch a conch again, not least because I'd just been reading the guidebook and realised, too late, that you weren't actually allowed to catch conch in Martinique.

We talked for hours after dinner, mutual outpourings of university, work, life and sailing, things that we just couldn't talk about with 99% of the sailors we met. All four of us were exploring the Atlantic by boat at the same age, the age where everything is ahead of you.

Our wonder for our way of life was not lost on each other and yet we all had so much more to talk about. Florian, with a PhD in robotics, was bursting with ideas for businesses and projects he could start when he and Julia returned to their native Munich.

And that is what we missed, and what we found in our new friends; the endless possibilities of our lives. This was only the beginning: we weren't going to cruise forever, there was simply so many other things we wanted to do and achieve.

To say that to other cruisers, even some our own age who were using boats as accommodation rather than transport, we were just met with blankness – why would you want to stop cruising? We didn't, yet. But we would and we knew it.

I had struggled so much in Europe, in the first half of the trip, with worrying constantly if I was risking some unknown great career by stepping out of the world for a year or two. At a time when all my friends were getting their feet on the corporate ladder, qualifying as solicitors, doctors, junior executives, managers, I was sauntering off abroad on a boat, achieving what?

For a while I had comforted myself with thinking of the 'proper' jobs I could get when I got back, I found myself almost wishing that I was back already and starting one, working towards a career. What career? Who knew? I just knew that you should have a career.

Meeting Florian and Julia helped alleviate my concerns because they were so self-assured, this adventure was a firm part of their life plans and would make them better, more experienced people. It would add to their lives, not postpone it.

Slowly I realised that I was learning more, achieving more and experiencing more in each single week onboard the boat than I would have in an office in England with an imaginary career. All I really wanted to do was write anyway and I certainly didn't need middle management, staff perks and 9-5 job for that. I needed life.

It took me months and months to realise that I wasn't stepping out of the world at all; I was stepping into it.

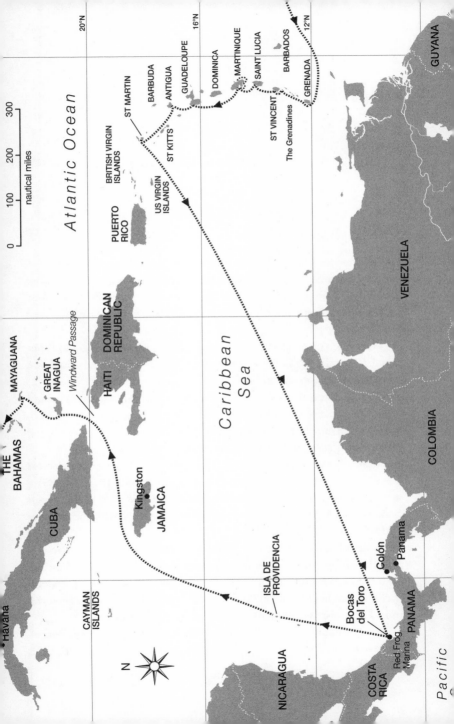

Chapter 8

A Caribbean Crossing

Wherever you go, you take yourself with you.

Neil Gaiman

The North Atlantic was a mess and Saint Martin was a stewing pot of sailors refreshing the weather forecast every hour and grumbling about provisions. This European island has the strange political geography of being half French and half Dutch, quite literally, with a line down the centre.

The Dutch side uses US dollars and the French side uses the Euro, which, in mid-2015, were worryingly almost equal in value and exchanged one for one on buses.

After the ruggedness of the West Indies, I was very taken with Saint Martin – the French side. Along the shore in Marigot Bay was not only an Auchan French supermarket but also Serafina's, possibly the greatest patisserie in the world, including Parisian ones.

Serafina's was a true chocolate box type place, all pastel colours and glistening counter tops. Its seating area was large with rattan furniture and glass-top tables, open to the Caribbean sky. The thing about Serafina's though, was the extraordinary array of cakes and quiches and breads and chocolates.

In an island chain where 'bakery' meant one person out in the suburbs with an oven who might occasionally produce a sugary loaf of bread once in a while, even the existence of a modest French patisserie was an incredible concept. And indeed, Saint Martin wasn't even the most French island out there, compared to, say, Martinique.

But Serafina's defied the culture and eschewed the non-baked-goods-eating peoples of the West Indies and instead produced, on a daily basis, a spread that wouldn't look out of place at one of Marie Antoinette's decadent parties.

Behind domed glass cabinets lay pastel macaroons, éclairs, miniature crème brûlées, profiterole pyramids, a deep amber tart tatin and endless squadrons of petit fours, each in lines of its own kind with every colour and flavour under the rainbow. Nuggets of fruit were everywhere, jellied, crystallised, glazed, all peering out from the tops of cream swirls and gelatinous layers upon biscuit. Puff pastries bursting with chocolate lay next to madeleines as meringues lounged in their paper bowls.

By nine each morning, a line of wondrous residents gazed into the cabinets until called upon by the blank-faced servers, unimpressed by the glory they worked in. Behind them was the real call for the early morning customers though. Almost vertical baskets were laden with baguettes and loaves of every flour and flavour. From traditionale to rustique and most of the line leaves with at least two tucked under an arm.

I was there for something else. Le croissant aux amandes. Stored in their own separate cabinet, the pile of almond croissants sat heavy and dense waiting for me each morning and only occasionally did I stray to the other choices of pain au chocolate and butter croissants. I was obsessed.

Serafina's wasn't my only reason for loving Saint Martin though. All non-European West Indian islands resolutely had tiny supermarkets stocked with ageing, faded tins and packets of imported foodstuffs usually heavily processed. Endless tins of spaghetti and meatballs and boxes of Smash and pancake mix.

So when I discovered that Saint Martin had a huge SuperU, I was beyond ecstatic. After all, there is only so much breadfruit a girl can eat before she needs, say, some camembert and bread that will go stale if you don't eat it the same day. I was European and no matter how far I travelled, I needed not just the delicious tastes of the continent, but I needed the essence of it.

I had never realised how strong my ties to Europe were or how fierce my love for it was until I left. It wasn't just the underlying

125

European-ness I craved, but I could see now how lucky I was to have grown up in such a wealthy continent. Many of the West Indian islands existed with such little infrastructure and such little variation of food and goods, that I couldn't even see how they could function. The further up the chain I travelled, the more I realised that it wasn't that these islands struggled to function, it was that they simply didn't function in the way I was used to.

Again and again I saw the same thing: strong communities relying on each other, on the land and on the sea. Even the children were out fishing, learning the tricks, shooting about in boats far more capable than I was with an outboard.

It took a long time for me to stop comparing countries to my own and see that comparing a minute Caribbean country with the machine that is the UK would be like comparing a robin to an ostrich. You simply can't, the differences are too… different.

The simple act of visiting an EU island within the Caribbean was the same as going home and I revelled in it, not having ever for a moment admitted to myself that I was homesick. After all, I didn't have a home in the traditional sense. No house full of my belongings, no address, no geolocation that I could claim as where I belonged. I hadn't lived with my parents for seven years and my post was all sent to my sister's house for her to judge storable or chuckable on my behalf.

The closest I had to a home was the UK in general and, failing that, Europe. But after months of ocean and island life, the cheerful French I heard on the streets of Saint Martin was the quintessential feeling of home to me. And the almond croissants were the cherries on the top.

The water in Marigot Bay was the clearest I'd seen, my hand casting a perfect shadow on the sandy bottom as I held it out over the side of the boat. I donned my mask and snorkel and went overboard with a scrubbing brush. Weed and algae growth on the hull could slow us down by a knot and was surprisingly easy to feel while sailing, even minimal amounts. After a while it was like driving with a flat tyre.

I scrubbed off the hull, watching the clouds of algae float off with the current. I didn't feel too anxious about the imminent voyage, by now I could put journeys into perspective. If you look at the Caribbean Sea on a map of the world, it just doesn't look that big and it's so utterly encircled by land that it seems, in comparison to the Atlantic, pretty cosy.

The main reason why I wasn't stressing out though was because the voyage would be downwind the whole way and by now I knew what that meant out here. It meant warmth and sunny days and no drama. Protected from the swell by the fragmented West Indies, the Caribbean doesn't have a fetch like the Atlantic. Big waves can develop, it's still 1000 miles across, but it feels more confined, like sailing across an enormous pond.

Whether it seems nonsensical or not, this was the idea that kept me calm and untroubled as we checked out of Saint Martin and set our sails for the shores of Panama.

We hadn't intended on going to Panama, we hadn't intended on going further west. Or rather, we had and we hadn't. When we arrived in Antigua for the sailing week, we'd been set on continuing up to Saint Martin and re-provisioning for the return journey to the UK. After all, we had been gone almost a year and the typical Atlantic circuit is completed within a year, it made sense.

But at the same time, we'd come all this way. Neither of us had been to Central America before except for Alex dipping a toe across the US/ Mexican border once years before. Now we were in the Caribbean, Central and South America were right there. Could we really just turn back?

Even more than the pull of new lands, we were stumped when it came to knowing what exactly we'd be going back to. We had no home in the UK, our home was here, under our feet, floating in clear Caribbean waters. Our friends had scattered, living in different cities in new jobs, even in different countries, starting new families. There was no single place we could identify as where we belonged.

A large part of me wanted to return to Europe. I missed the ease of life there, the people, the civilisation, the shops, the convenience and the fast-pace of self-imposed hectic life that we all tuck ourselves into in the wealthy countries of the north. My bikinis were fraying and coming apart from the relentless UV and daily use and yet I was in a place where I'd have to wait three islands just to find a shop that might sell them. It was frustrating for me, knowing that this island didn't have something I needed but a few hundred miles north I might find an island that did. After growing up in a society that increasingly had everything you needed (and everything you didn't) on tap, the Caribbean was often difficult in that it had such limited supplies of anything.

But when I arrived in the European / Caribbean mash-up of Saint Martin, satisfied my need for western products, huge well-stocked supermarkets and the ready availability of everything from French chocolate to board shorts, I realised that I didn't really need that much after all. I just needed to know it was there.

In fact, when I really sat down to think about it, the endless buying, the circular earn-more-buy-more way of life in the UK, I actively wanted to go further into the Americas. I wanted to carry on, get more lost in this new world of living that much closer to the natural world.

We made the decision in Antigua but it was cemented in Saint Martin; we would go to Panama. Hurricane season was due to start in two months, which would mean that, once we were in Panama, we wouldn't be able to leave again for at least four months unless we carried on through the Canal. It meant adding another year onto our voyage, our voyage which didn't have a timescale anyway, so why not?

Provisionally, we even toyed with the idea of continuing on through the Canal down to Easter Island and down to Chile and Patagonia. The isolation and extremity of Patagonia appealed to me in principle. Down there we'd be truly alone, out of contact and out of reach for months at a time. With towering mountains, fierce and fast extremes of weather and the prospect of living at the very edge of the world made Patagonia an enchanting destination.

We talked about it with light in our eyes, working out how we could insulate the boat against the cold in Puerto Montt after the two month sail out from Panama and down in a huge semi-circle. We'd go all the

Crossing the Bay of Biscay for the first time. (Alex)

Arrived safely in Northern Spain having crossed the Bay of Biscay. (Kitiara)

Setting out from the Canaries to cross the Atlantic. (Kitiara)

It wasn't the only storm we faced crossing the Atlantic. (Alex)

But it was peaceful when we arrived in Grenada. (Kitiara)

Although a bit hectic when we raced onboard the big schooner, Coral. (Kitiara)

But we had to move on − here sailing towards St Lucia.   (Alex)

We enjoyed watching the traditional boat racing in Martinique.   (Kitiara)

One of the Caribbean's many beautiful beaches, this time on Guadaloupe. (Alex)

Falmouth Harbour in Antigua. (Kitiara)

Finally, in Panama — we had made it to Central America. (Alex)

What a place to anchor — Isla Providencia. (Kitiara)

Sailing through the Bahamas. (Kitiara)

Meeting the wildlife in the Bahamas. (Alex)

Going back across the Atlantic. (Alex)

Safely across and in the Azores where bulls on rope were a major form of entertainment. (Kitiara)

way out west to the Gambias so we could avoid the counter-current that sweeps north up the Chilean and Peruvian coastline. I hadn't felt the cold for so long, I couldn't even remember what it was like to be truly cold. The last time had been briefly the November before, standing on the roadside near the top of Tenerife's El Teide volcano with its snow-capped peak. But it had been a quick shock of cold that passed as we descended by car to the heat of sea level.

Whatever we would end up doing though, first we were going to Panama.

I always create images of what I think a place will be like before I go there. Probably because I worry and try to plan for all eventualities which is a) impossible and b) preposterous. It's further challenged by the fact that it's difficult to plan for much of anything if you don't know a place at all, geographically or otherwise.

And I didn't know Panama. But usually my imagined version of a place is overwritten by reality as soon as I arrive and so I forget my expectations or can only sense the slight ghost of them. With Panama, for whatever reason, I can remember.

Possibly because what I imagined of Panama and what it was like were so completely different, my brain couldn't even reconcile the two. Or perhaps it was that I stayed for 6 months in the end and got to know the area on a different level. Either way, I had a comically naive vision of Panama before I got there and my ability to compare it to reality showed me exactly how much my impression of new places is influenced by my societal prejudices.

Panama to me had been Panama City. Or at least my imagined version of Panama City. I'm not sure I'd ever heard anybody talk about the Panama outside of Panama City and so I'd never thought about what it might look like. While I knew where Panama was (that thin bit of land linking North America to South), I didn't know what countries it shared a border with. I think I had even believed, some time in the past, that neighbouring Costa Rica was an island. Which, admittedly, I may have been getting confused with Puerto Rico.

Before we'd decided on Panama as a destination, I'd imagined it in hazy sepia. The sort of image of Mexico you get in American cop dramas, where at any time a ball of tumbleweed might roll across, distorted by the immense heat rising up from the ground. I know, it's laughable. But that's what I thought of when I thought of Panama.

Heat hazed streets, huge skyscrapers in the city and wallowing ghettos in the suburbs. Everything I'd heard about Panama could be summed up in these two sentences; 'Never walk around in Panama City, always take a taxi,' and, 'Offshore banking.'

Of course, my other piece of knowledge about Panama was that there was a canal cut through the middle, forever changing the flow of shipping around the world. Even this was somewhat of a poor piece of knowledge as I'd assumed the Canal was complete from Caribbean to Pacific but it's not. Instead, the centre is two huge lakes and the canal structure is just the final stretches to either coastline.

The day before we set sail from Saint Martin, I'd bought an old Panamanian pilot book from a second-hand chandlery. It was full of aerial photographs and that was when I truly realised that I wasn't going to a hazy desert but a vibrant jungle. We'd booked in online to a marina in the Bocas Del Toro region, right next to the Costa Rican border. Over a hundred miles north of the Canal entrance, the Bocas archipelago was not only hundreds and hundreds of miles from Panama City, it was on the opposite coastline. It was nowhere I'd heard of and nowhere I could've imagined. I felt a vibration of excitement: we were jungle-bound.

But first the Caribbean Sea with its host of difficulties.

When I'd been in England before I set sail, I'd imagined that the sea was always cold. Yes I'd been in warm oceans but only on the fringes, the beaches, the shores. Mid-ocean? Surely it was cold? My greatest reluctance for sailing always stemmed from the discomfort of cold sea breezes, cold water sloshing about the cockpit and having to wear layers upon layers just to keep it out.

By the time I turned away from the West Indies, those islands we think of when we think 'Caribbean', I'd learnt that sailing could be wonderfully warm where the biggest problem was which bikini to wear. Even beating up between tropical islands was warm, where waves over the side brought refreshing relief from the sun. But the West Indies bathed in the trade winds, a constant breeze to alleviate the harsh sunshine.

The voyage south west was very different.

There's a reason why ships traditionally sailed a particular route across the Atlantic and even around the world. The bands of trade winds are called that because they pushed the trading ships to where they wanted to go. Huge square-rigged ships were specifically designed to sail downwind and it was this that I'd done across the Atlantic.

But the Caribbean was a whole step up into the tropics and every day en route from Saint Martin to Panama was that much hotter. Sailing downwind robs you of the breeze that's crucial to keep you cool. Travelling with the wind means that you can no longer feel it and I was soon exhausted by the building heat.

I began to dread my watches where only after 4pm would the sprayhood be between the sun and me, offering blissful protection. The majority of the day was delirious, the burning sun making metal too hot to touch and drying seawater to a crisp within moments, the cockpit covered in the oily crunch of salt crystals.

The weather was easy on the sailing though, with few adjustments needed at all. With the twin headsails up and the boat merrily looking after herself, there was little for me to do but battle with the sun for ownership of my own skin. It changes all the time, all excesses are wiped away, turned into energy to survive in this climate. I'm proud of my legs, their ability to adapt, to balance on this rolling ride and their deepening colour despite their determined ignorance of the word 'tan'.

There is no relief below. There is one small fan over Alex's bunk but it doesn't reach me and, even if it did, it's not powerful enough to cool. It simply moves hot air around. The rolling of the boat means I'm trapped in the tightness of my lee clothed-bunk but it's so hot that

I can't sleep. I'm naked except for bikini bottoms when below and the tightness of my rash vest only makes me hotter when outside.

35 degrees eating through my body. 15 degrees north and decreasing. 66 degrees west and pulling further, flowing further towards the sun. The sun. It's everything; it consumes and guides and hurts. Every day we get flying fish onboard but they die within minutes – crisped and crunchy – with no time for me to rescue them from the sun's burning gaze. They are punished for their daring evolution but the seabirds are happy.

Simply put, I am not designed for this place. I can feel the UV digging its claws into my skin and I worry. What danger am I putting myself in here? No amount of suncream can defend me from this light surely? I sweat it off and my rash vest is starting to breakdown, I can see the fabric beginning to crumble under the pressure of its job. How often do we ever see fabric fail, how often do we keep our clothing for long enough or use it enough for it to reach its limit?

I stalk the cockpit on tip toes. I rock with the boat, undulating downwind on the backs of ocean swells. My hands go from rope to rope, boom to stay, wire to grab rail. Always hold on, always hold on, always hold on. I hold onto the boat as she holds onto the ocean as the ocean holds onto the earth, never have I felt so a part of the world around me. Never has it felt so easy to travel with the wind and the waves. The relentless heat aside, crossing the Caribbean from east to west is easy.

Seabirds visit, circle, leave. They are using the boat as a fishing device as usual but their curious faces show their keen intelligence. I wonder where they sleep. Puerto Rico? Haiti? Venezuela? The sea? Do they take quick naps, a minute here, a minute there? I know how that feels.

The sea is endlessly moving, ceaselessly travelling waves of energy going going going where? We all just keep moving. I'm following the wind, the birds are following the fish, some follow the sun, some follow the moon. Some people say follow your heart.

Dolphins come at night, at dusk, whenever they feel like it. They hurl themselves under the bow in threes – baby tucked in behind mother's fin. How do they synchronise so perfectly? How do people walk in groups on the pavement? True. Good point.

They squeak, it always gets me. I can hear them talking. I love them with my whole heart. I love their joy, their energy, their restless fun seeking. They are the ocean's children in the world's greatest playground. Why do they do backflips alongside us? Why wouldn't they? I would.

But the ease passes and turns into frustration. The Caribbean is a swirling mass of sargassum, a heavy sort of seaweed that rafts up and covers the water's surface. It trails lazily hundreds of miles in orange ribbons in an endless tropical search. For what? It hosts millions of tiny creatures, infants born in the protection of this floating jungle. Eels are born in sargassum and drift eastwards on the north Atlantic gulf stream to the UK. But this sargassum here in the Caribbean is surely hemmed in, destined to circulate this sea forever.

But it's killing me, it really is. It twists and curls around the Caribbean like a conga line, in search of vanes and propellers to foul. Our Aries self-steering works with a vane to catch the wind and another vane underwater to alter our direction as the wind changes. Steering to the course we've set on the wind, this system means the sails stay filled although with a large wind change we may well find we're going in the wrong direction. Once, the Aries followed the wind around a full 360 degrees, a small balletic turn with an errant breeze.

So when the sails suddenly start flapping one day I know something is wrong. The first time, it takes me a while to work it out and it's only on a shout from below that I thought to check the Aries' underwater vane. Wrapped around its entire metre long length is a huge mat of sargassum. Alex and I get the boat hook and I lean over the aft transom to push the weed down and off the bottom as Alex reefs the headsails. We are doing 5 knots and the drag is enormous, I worry for the vane, strong as it is. Once the weed is gone, Alex goes back down for a nap and I continue my day-dreaming. And then the sails start flapping.

Repeatedly for the next few days, sargassum would wrap itself around the Aries' vane, slewing it to one side. Throughout night watches I'd go aft with my head torch to check, invariably finding single strands or more stable swathes of the stuff causing drag and weighing on the vane.

The aft transom is very narrow at just one metre and affixed to the top bar is our smallest solar panel. Directly in between me and the top of the wind vane, the solar panel loomed with its sharp corners and potential fragility. Every time the weed caught I had to lean over the solar panel, concaving my stomach so it wouldn't put weight onto the panel. But I was too short to reach the weed, even with the boat hook at full extension, without leaning on the corner of the panel with its sharp metal.

After just one night watch, my stomach looked as though it had been attacked by hungry claws, numerous tiny red Vs embossed into my skin from the corner. After the hundredth time, I was reduced to irritated tears and wanted to scream out at the treacherous weed.

The next day, Alex filed the corner of the solar panel to a more rounded edge, but my body was bruised in the exact place where I had to lean over the back in order to push the weed off. It hurt for days after the rafts disappeared on the horizon.

I was cheating the days as I followed the sun west. Every day we'd be a hundred miles closer to where we were going, a hundred miles further away from where we'd been. Each evening I'd eek out the dusk light for as long as I could before my little boat inevitably lost and the king sun left us behind.

With a new moon, I find myself absorbed into the depths of the night. It's far more pleasant than the day, especially as the Caribbean Sea's infamous squalls seem to be having their fun elsewhere. The night watches, without sargassum, are stunning movies of shooting stars and infinite pinpricks. Without a moon to outshine the stars, the sky is a perfect 180 degree map of time. So rare is this moment in our lives, when we can see stars from horizon to horizon, the horizons as far away as they can be, out here on the great flat sea.

I'm in an orb of night, the darkness cosying up to me, snaking around my shoulders like a boa. I stand on the aft locker and hold onto the backstay and breathe in the rich night sky. There are more stars than I've ever seen, so many that I have to choose a place to watch for meteors. There isn't even a shower, a misting of meteors, this is just a regular night. But meteors there are, with surprising regularity. I can't wish on them all and besides, that would surely be cheating with such rich pickings. I wish on one per watch, that seems fair. It's always the same wish; it's for me, it's for Alex and it's for our boat, our home; please let us stay safe.

On the 8th night there's a light, a moon reborn, a tiny orange cut in the sky. The ocean whispers on.

As we near Panama, shipping traffic increases. After days without seeing another ship, suddenly we have enormous container ships, fully loaded going to and coming from the Canal. I read their names on AIS and wonder where these ocean giants have been and where they're going. Without a transmitting AIS, we can see them but they can't see us.

There's logic behind this that goes further than the desire to save a few hundred pounds. Yachts transmitting their positions via AIS transmit on AIS B and often container ships don't look for these signals. Also, in the inevitable situation where you find yourself on a collision course with a 290 m long ship, it's always best to be the one making the move to get out of the way. After all, a yacht changing course is obvious, a container ship changing course is like watching a heavily sedated rhino consider its options.

Further to that, in any kind of waves we're immediately obscured from view and our AIS aerial would also be obscured. So instead we keep a good look out and take a turn around a circle if it looks like a ship will get too close. Occasionally we'd call them up on VHF and give our position to the watchman.

"So you see," said Alex, "we'll be quite close." He'd just read out our latitude and longitude as we were heavily reefed under twin headsails and changing course would've been challenging.

"'Ah," said the accented, disembodied voice over the radio, "yes, I see that. Hmmm."

Container ships aren't keen on altering course. Undermanned and over-pressured to meet their tight schedules, every course change is monitored and logged and must be explained. On the other hand, we got the impression that talking to us on VHF was sometimes the highlight on their dull nights ploughing along the dark ocean.

"I will alter course 3 degrees and we will be fine I think," said the watchman.

"Thank you very much," replied Alex, "have a good night."

"Yes, you too. Standing by on channel 16," replied the watchman.

These occasional conversations in the smallest hours of the night made us both smile. There was something exhilarating and companionable about talking to others in such a lonely place. Just the quick exchange of positions and headings with other souls out in the middle of this great sea filled me with love for my fellow man. There was a tiny human connection, we were not alone.

We updated the logbook every three hours while on passage. Some entries would be sparse, noting the course and wind. Some rambled on for lines and some, often the closest ones to 4am, showed the depths of exhaustion with spelling errors and almost unreadable writing. Sometimes I'd write the names of the ships that passed us, writing them down carefully as though pinning a butterfly to a board. You were there, I saw you, proof that I was there too.

Now, as I write this, I have the benefit of an internet connection which means that I can look these ships up, over a year later and see where they are right now. Right this moment I can see where that affable ship is.

Cape Tavor: Bulk Carrier. 289m x 45m. Gross Tonnage 87363. En Route from China to South Africa.

A few days before we make landfall, the line whizzes out the back of the boat. There is very little in this world that will get Alex out of bed faster than the sound of a fishing line going taut and he's in the cockpit before I even have time to register the situation. I reef the sails to slow us down and turn to look back just as a huge marlin hurls itself out of the water.

The blue giant with its long spike is frozen in mid-air in my head. Its silver shock catches the sun as it crashes back down into the water. The line is jerked and goes slack. Alex looks at me. We bring the line in, its lure long gone. I've never seen such a fish and as much as I would've loved to see it closer up, I'm glad it broke free.

We do, however, catch a bonito soon after. Torpedo shaped and strong, the tuna-like bonito raged and fought below the surface, running with the line before begrudgingly being pulled towards the boat, having recovered somewhat it would run again.

There is nothing in world like killing a fish this size. There is no escape from the reality of what you are doing, no knocking it on the head like a mackerel, no forgetting what it is, wrapped in plastic in the supermarket. Bonito are small compared to full grown tuna but they're solid, with large eyes and gasping gills. I hold the rod when the fish has exhausted itself and lies alongside the hull. Alex gaffs its hefty body because I am a coward, unable to be the one who penetrates its heavy flesh with a massive hook even though I will eat as much as he will.

We bring it into the cockpit and I weigh it down. It takes all my weight and still it's stronger than I am. I cover it with a towel to get a better grip and Alex takes a huge dive knife and pushes it, crunching, into the bonito's skull. There is blood everywhere. Tuna, bonito and Mahi Mahi have litres of thick, dark red blood and it sloshes about the cockpit. Bloody smears adorn the gel coat, the escaped mainsheet end and our skin. It's brutal and it looks like a murder has taken place. After all, it has.

The bonito lasts us for days and we eat it for every meal in every different way. No fish tastes as good as a fish fresh from the sea, a fish caught and killed right here. I know that this will change who I am, I feel as though I am taking responsibility for the things I take from the ocean even if I cannot bring myself to kill them. Yet.

I feel better for the fish, bored of lentils and onion. Fresh food doesn't keep this far into a passage and the succulent nutrients of the bonito invigorates us both. It's like a celebration, successfully living off the ocean, drinking the rain and eating raw fish with a squeeze of lemon. It's death but it's a strange death that made me feel even more connected to my surroundings, a true part of the complex ecosystem I live in. I wasn't separated by one degree, I was right in the midst – full ocean.

Chapter 9

Sloth Hunting

Animals are born who they are, accept it, and that is that. They live with greater peace than people do.

Gregory Maguire

The jungle was deafening. Invisible insects produced a riotous sound from every branch, leaf and tree. Tropical birds shrieked and called from deep in the green and when I looked up through a space in the canopy I could see enormous vultures circling endlessly above. If they ever flapped, I'd never seen it.

This was the kind of jungle children begin imagining after they watch *Hook*. Each leaf improbably large and each branch harbouring inch-long spikes seating fat, furry caterpillars.

All at once, the insects ceased and it was like someone had switched off my hearing, so sudden and complete was their silence. As suddenly as they stopped, they started up again.

It was impossible to be alone in the jungle and I always felt like I was trespassing. It was like a humid labyrinth with rules that were being held close to the chest. Everything was oversized, over-equipped and had at least one attribute that suggested it might be poisonous. It probably wasn't, but who was I to say? The closest I'd previously gotten to a jungle like this was the *Jungle Book* and the jungles of Bali which were staid and polite by contrast.

The insects turned it up a notch. It was a clicking, vibrating sound so fast it was only milliseconds from being one continuous note. It was like playing cards in bicycle spokes. Like something broken deep within a dashboard. Like crickets on amphetamines. It was extreme and yet oddly delicate. It's hard to explain – at any rate, it was all encompassing. The jungle was very much alive.

I was sloth hunting. Rather, I was hunting for sloths, not hunting them. It wouldn't be fair game if your quarry were perpetually snoozing.

Since arriving on Panama's leafy shores two weeks before, I had traipsed the jungle every day on my way to the sweet relief of the beach. Panama was not in the trade winds; in fact it didn't seem to be in any winds. The mangroves and jungles were undisturbed by breeze and only the squalls brought a slight temperature drop.

When I had considered the climate of Central America I hadn't been far wrong but I had only imagined it before, never experienced it. The humidity was suffocating. The air wasn't only thick with water and insects but also with a heaviness that sat in your lungs and weighed you down. It was exhausting.

We kept the boat in a marina tucked on the south side of a large, jungle island. The dense and impenetrable forest stopped any and all whispers of wind from touching anything other than the northern tree line and even then, the wind usually ground to a halt thirty miles off the coast. The distressing thing about marinas was that, for all the ease of walking, water and electricity, you cannot simply jump off the boat and into the water. Or at least you certainly wouldn't want to.

The mangroves prevented any stirring in the brackish, stagnant water and even the swarms of jellyfish seemed to be pulsating through mud. The marina basin was not somewhere I would've dipped a toe for the entire world.

By 3pm everyday the still air was unbearable and I'd take off into the jungle paths to seek out the beach. The sides of Bastimentos Island were almost unrecognisable from one another. Where the marina sat in dour, silent mangroves, mud and silt sluggishly forming the vague separation between water and land; the north beach was long and white and picture perfect, palm trees stretching over it like they'd wandered out of a waiting room poster.

The waves were large enough to wash you around and cool you down and the currents were strong enough to keep you on your toes.

The tree-line hummed with life and crab holes littered the beach, the intrepid creatures relentlessly casting out loose sand that some passing human had knocked down.

The jungle was wild and untameable despite a bizarre and eerie resort built into sections of it. Where paths had been cut through and villas built, within metres the intensity of the rainforest wilderness sat and sung, biding its time for the developers to give up their futile reclamation of land and relinquish it to the forest.

Corporate humanity jarred with the jungle and the villas were built in the style of ugly Floridian boxes with no kind of inspiration taken from the local style or surroundings. While houses made from wood and stilts peered out of the trees on other islands, this almost deserted resort had stamped its foot and demanded North American styling.

Everyone could see it was wrong, the jungle surely more than anyone else. But despite the resort's relatively large area, it was sometimes difficult to find and easy to forget. The rainforest was so unflustered, so vivid and strong, that it just absorbed the resort and continued regardless.

Every day since I had arrived I had been looking for the creature that defined the Panama of my imagination. That little smiling face that peered from guidebooks and advertising. An evolutionary wonder that seemed preposterous by its very existence.

The obvious problem with hunting for sloths was that, stationary in dense forests, they didn't exactly catch your eye. So inactive were they that I'd heard mould grows on their fur. So I peered into the endless lush vegetation and zoned out from the shouting insects.

Isla Bastimentos was trail after trail and not a soul around. The resort guests used golf carts to get from villa to sand and any tourists who arrived for the day by panga just accumulated on Red Frog beach. So I was always alone in the trails while Alex surfed the beach break.

I stood still every few hundred metres and studied the trees but all the branches I could see were empty, only unseen birds shook the leaves and unbalanced beetles.

The afternoon air was stifling in the forest and the humidity was a heavy, damp blanket; my lungs struggled to find air. There were birds everywhere but I couldn't see them. Some sounded so odd I wondered if they were birds at all. Cracking and crying in the canopy, they sounded like tools, metal on metal, a welder's workshop.

I walked trails hidden deep in the undergrowth and took care to step over the leaf-cutter ant highways, each tiny creature diligently carrying his huge section of leaf above his head like a green Mohawk.

Crabs scuttled in and out of rotting tree trunks and occasionally waved a little claw at me if I looked too closely. Strawberry poison-dart frogs sat on fallen leaves, the extreme contrast between the greenery and their vivid red bodies was arresting in its sartorial perfection.

Botany was one of the most popular of scientific studies during the Victorian period with almost anybody able to partake. But with the mass adoration of studying plants, serious collectors went further and further in search of previously undiscovered species with which to fill their newly dedicated botanical hothouses, one being Kew Gardens.

Their searching took them far and wide and in Panama rare orchids, ferns and all manner of exotic plants were discovered and sent back to the larger and larger glasshouses of Victorian England.

It was easy to see why the Victorians had been so taken with the exotic offerings of these far away places. Two hundred years ago these acutely evolved plants and animals would've been almost futuristic. They still are. Evolution showing off the full range of her artistic skill set.

So busy was I watching the forest floor, my step and the armies of ants, that I doubted I'd find a sloth at all. Unless one had fallen from a tree miraculously onto my path, the trails were far too rugged to be gazing skywards. Hot, sweat soaked and in need of a cold drink, I returned back to the main gravel path and meandered back to the boat.

Sloths weren't the only creatures supposedly living free in the jungle; a troop of capuchin monkeys also inhabited the island although it seemed like blind luck or immense patience was required to see them.

I sat sometimes in the resort's welcome centre, surreptitiously using the excellent wi-fi there after screaming with frustration at the unusable nature of that belonging to the marina. The thing that never failed to amaze me about rural Panama was that very little actually ever seemed to work. Be it bureaucracy, sanitation, postal systems or food logistics. The most frustrating part was that no one seemed to mind.

I was mulling over the wording of an email when an American woman made her way to the reception desk and began quizzing the Panamanian behind it. The resort had a zip line course set into the jungle behind the villas and it was one of the major adverts for the island.

I'd discovered the zip line course myself as Alex and I had gone exploring with a machete and we'd climbed to the first platform. Suspended high up in the canopy, I had been on the lookout for sloths but they had once again defeated me with their sleepy stealth.

Slippery, green moss covered the wire and wood bridge from the ground to the first platform and required serious concentration lest you miss your footing. The zip line didn't have much of an angle to it and I could see those on the lighter end of the spectrum having trouble getting to the end but still, it looked intriguing.

"And are we guaranteed to see monkeys yes?" asked the woman as though she was booking a pod on the London Eye – are we guaranteed to see the Queen?

I could hear the receptionist weighing up the options in her mind. The woman was so matter-of-fact as though anything in the jungle responded to a schedule.

"It's likely you will see some monkeys, but sometimes they are elsewhere on the island," said the receptionist evenly.

"Okay" said the woman, nodding with pursed lips. "But we'll definitely see sloths right?"

The receptionist nodded as though she was struggling to stay awake, "yes the instructors will point out the sloths to you." The woman nodded her acceptance, satisfied that the jungle was guaranteed to produce at least some quantifiable entertainment for her family; they will have seen a sloth.

I had long suspected that the jungle was indeed teeming with perezosos, 'lazy bears' in Spanish, but it was their inactivity that prevented my eyes from picking them out. I put away my tablet, closed my notebook and put them back in my bag. I slid off the chair and left the welcome centre, determined to find a lazy bear of my own.

When we originally planned to go sailing, one of things that really drew me to the idea was the flora and fauna of other countries. The backpacking and cycle touring I'd done in the past had shown me many countries and not an unreasonable amount of intriguing animals but sailing was such a slower way to travel, it gave me time to seek out these exotic creatures.

From the dolphins of Biscay and the puffins of Porto Santo to the lobsters of Martinique and the iguanas of Saint Martin, I had been repeatedly enamoured with the offerings nature provided the curious sailor.

Sea turtles in the boat's slipstream, tired seabirds on the transom, geckos in the cockpit and metallic orchid bees inspecting our supplies, I had been closer to wild animals than I ever had before on a regular basis. If anything, local creatures seemed to assume the boat was merely an extension of their existing territory. And, really, it was.

I was mesmerised by the great travel writers who connected with foreign peoples on multiple levels and brought them back to life on the page. But I struggled with it, the confidence to approach strangers, finding the questions that I wanted to ask but couldn't verbalise.

But there had always been something about the plants and animals of abroad that fascinated me. People are, often, just people. Animals and their habitats however could be utterly different, implausible and captivating.

And it was in the birds and animals of different countries that evolution seemed to really go wild. Evolution can be seen in people but not in the same way as say, the locking function of a sloth's claws so that it can sleep without effort as it hangs. Or the beak of the parrot fish as it crunches coral with no table manners, the loudest sound as I snorkelled over a reef. I could hear them munching.

And it wasn't just animals either, the plants in Panama were drunk on sunshine and water. The jungle was on a permanent, giddy trip.

We snorkelled everyday in Panama but it wasn't necessarily for the sights. With 35-degree air temperature and the incessant humidity, the only place to stay even close to cool was in the water. Bocas' underwater world was an intriguing place to explore thanks to its silty murk. Being a mangrove labyrinth, the seabed was thick mud and sediment hung freely, making visibility poor between the islands.

As we swam, all sorts of interesting creatures appeared out of the gloom. Baby barracuda, only 20 cm long would drift around the submerged roots of the mangroves, waiting to pounce. When a shoal of baitfish flitted past in their silvery clouds, the tiny barracuda would flash out and snatch one, the death almost too quick to see.

Caribbean reef squid infants used the seagrass for shelter, hanging out in little troops of five just above the gently waving blades. As I meandered along above them, they'd turn in unison, watching me for danger. Near invisible jellyfish wafted past too, sometimes the first I'd know about them was their hair-like tentacles pulling along my mask.

It was easy to get creeped out in these sediment-rich waters, not just because of the jellyfish and ethereal quality of my surrounding; but because you never knew what was just a few metres away.

Alex and I were snorkelling between Bastimentos and Isla Solarte one morning. We had puttered out from the marina in our increasingly soggy dinghy. An array of continuously repaired holes meant that we needed to take the pump everywhere we went. We had anchored it near a mangrove cluster and I had swum quite far, surveying the murky reef in an idle reverie. It was overcast as usual, but I could still feel the tropical sun heavy on my back as I swam.

I tread water and looked around, keeping a constant ear and eye out for the pangas that would roar past as 30 knots. I was looking over at the dinghy, searching for signs of Alex when I saw him splashing in the water on his back.

He had been spearfishing, hunting for our dinner and I was intrigued – what kind of big fish had he caught now?

"What have you got?" I yelled across the water. He was far, probably too far, to hear me given the ferocious splashing. I carried on watching then put my mask back on and started swimming over to him.

It was bizarre. I hadn't seen anything bigger than king mackerel here and sure, they were strong, but I doubted he had speared one. We had only caught one before, and that was trolling from the boat. I stopped again as he kicked up turbulence with his huge free diving fins.

"Did you catch a fish?" I shouted.

"It's a shark!" he yelled, finning furiously to the dinghy and heaving himself in. My exhilaration was gone. I was treading water in the middle of the lagoon with nowhere to go. The mangrove clusters aren't land, you can't exactly climb onto them and the dinghy was where the shark was.

"What?!" I shouted. I looked underwater, there was nothing but the dusky green hue. He pulled up the anchor and started the engine, making his way back over to me.

"I was attacked by a shark!" he said, as I hauled myself into the dinghy a little faster than usual.

"What kind of shark?"

"A huge nurse shark. I turned around and there it was right behind me, snapping at my fins!"

"Shit! How big?"

"Huge! I jabbed it in the face with the spear but it didn't seem to care. It just turned away for a second and then came at me again! Gnashing at my fins." He said, bowled over by the experience.

I looked at his catch bag, which he hung from his dive belt to store fish that he'd caught. He had been carrying three, each with blood oozing out forming a little red pool in the bottom of the dinghy.

"Well… you were carrying shark snacks."

"Yeah, good eh? Check these out," he said with a grin.

We had decided on this part of Panama for not just convenience, but a family connection. Alex had grown up sailing on a Moody 34 and that very same boat was now languishing in the marina with us; complete with Alex's parents.

Having taken early retirement, Mike and Jane had locked up the house and taken off on a voyage that was more than a trip. It was a continuation of a dream they had been living for their entire adults lives. What started off as dinghy sailing in youth turned into small yacht cruising with infants along the British south coast.

Mike had been an engineer at Fawley Power Station, the chimney of which had served as a waypoint for thousands of sailors over the decades. Alex's grandfather had been the power station manager and, a sailor himself, had chosen the job thanks to its sailing club. A small community of yachts had been moored just off the power station in the gloopy mud that furred up hulls and swallowed anchors for breakfast.

The mooring dues were £2 a year. It made owning a boat affordable to the workers and for Mike and Jane it meant they could keep a boat at a fraction of the usual cost. And so it was in the opacity of Southampton Water that they spent their weekends sailing in every type of weather imaginable and from where they had set sail when the power station closed down and the sailing club with it.

They had made their way more than once to the Atlantic Islands and the Caribbean and so it was with their recommendation that we chose Bastimentos to moor up for hurricane season. When we arrived they were in England, a sojourn to see friends and family and Alex spent a day washing the green algae and aspiring mould from the decks of their boat, *Isabella*.

After a year it was strange to see such a familiar creature in such a foreign place, like seeing someone you knew in school decades later in a different setting. More so, it was strange seeing *Isabella* and *Berwick Maid* alongside one another again, having graced the same moorings for twenty years. They were sisters almost, sturdy and capable boats, entirely dwarfed by the much large American, Dutch and German yachts nearby.

I knew that Alex was looking forward to his parents arrival and I wondered about my own. Thousands of miles away. I had missed things that were important. I hadn't been there when my stepmother's much loved mother had died. I hadn't been there to offer my support through the quagmire of grief that I knew they would be absorbed in.

I had missed the death of my own grandfather and not been there at the funeral when my dad had to say goodbye to his last parent. I had missed the birth of my friend's daughter and the horrendous weeks that followed when newborn Safi was fighting off a virus too cruel to afflict an infant.

There is a great admiration for travel and everything it gives you. There is something about it that stops you from being able to justify any frustrations or obstacles. You're travelling, what could possibly be bad? But, with everything, there is sacrifice. There is compromise. In order to do something, you must give up something else, even if only for a while. But a lot can happen in 'a while'. Lives can change, end, begin. And when I left England I didn't realise what it meant to be away. I thought I was escaping, not sacrificing. I was absent through a lot of events which I can never get back. Where I simply wasn't there.

We had been well and truly swallowed by the Bocas del Toro region of Panama by the time we'd been there two months. The archipelagic nature of the mangroves and islands there had meant that we'd yet to even reach the mainland and instead found ourselves drifting alone between the labyrinthine isles.

At the centre of the region was Bocas town, an almost floating community with cafes and bars stretching out into the water on stilts. The wooden buildings were painted in bright colours and the area attracted travellers from all over the world.

The Panamanians themselves were a mix of races and for every native Spanish speaker there was a West Indian who would respond to my broken Spanish in flawless Caribbean English.

A country only 100 years old, Panama was a mixing pot of tribal

Indians, Colombians and more recent immigrants. The Chinese ran all the supermarkets and bric-a-brac shops in the town with as many as four generations of each family being on the shop floor at once. Grandmother serving and great-grandchild munching plantain in her mother's arms.

The supermarkets themselves were a crash-course in classic equatorial experiences with filthy kittens peering out from under shelves, mice performing acrobatics across the pasta packets and parrots hooting and cackling from the rafters.

It was a place where I would settle for packaged food that had expired only within the last year, raw chicken sweated idly on the back of open trucks and weevils swarmed in rice bags. It taught me about not just the realities of the tropics, but also the realities of the luxury I experienced back home.

When I walked into a branch of Tesco, had I ever stopped to think whether the fresh meat had been continuously refrigerated? Had I ever spent five whole minutes scrutinising the cornflakes, rice and flour for signs of insects? Had I ever even checked to see if something was within its use-by date?

I didn't touch meat for the duration of my life in Panama and dairy was similarly dubious or, most often, non-existent. Food had to travel for hours over rough roads just to reach the ferry that would bring it to Bocas town and inland roads were often closed or impassable.

When food did reach the island, theoretically every Friday, it sat piled high in trucks for hours while being unloaded. The Chinese filled their supermarkets high with American products, ingredients lists as long as my arm and most food was processed, packaged, tinned and still out of date. But the most surprising thing was that, in a place where the wage is $2 an hour, these foods were expensive.

It was a testament to how many Americans were coming in and buying up homes, plots of land and even entire islands. Having raised the living costs of Costa Rica tenfold, Panama was the next cheap retirement destination.

And what of the locals, many of which lived in small communities deep in the jungles? Well it was simple, they lived how they'd always lived, off the land.

On an island near Bastimentos, a community of Kuna Indians still farmed the jungle in the traditional way, planting trees seemingly at random and harvesting the fruits. But it was nowhere near as random as it looked and instead they planted trees to live in symbiosis with others of different species, just as they would naturally.

No endless rows of banana palms there; no flawless lines of pineapple bushes. Instead the produce grew semi-wild and highly fruitful with breadfruit trees hanging heavy with their bounty alongside spindly papayas with their umbrella-like flare of leaves.

The result? Bananas cost us just two cents each and an entire bag full of fruits and unrecognisable vegetables would cost a dollar at most. In a land where you could eat fresh fruit and vegetables every day for a pittance and get extra crunch from the beetles in your sack of rice, why did you need anything with Kraft Foods or Nestle written down the side? This was a place where when you ordered a pineapple juice, the bar girl just put a pineapple in a blender and charged you 50 cents for the privilege of ice and a glass.

And that brings me to pineapples and a glance at my naivety. Because I thought, I think I thought, that pineapples grew on trees.

It's easy to scowl at reports of British children not knowing where potatoes come from or thinking that meat and milk come from supermarkets, not animals, but what did I know? I certainly didn't know how pineapples grew. Or, for that matter, peanuts, which I consumed in great amounts while sailing thanks to their energy levels and chuck-them-in-your-mouth ease.

Once I really started thinking about it, there were plenty of things that were difficult to place. Chickpeas for instance, or sugar. I always knew that bananas grew on palms but I didn't know that they grew upwards and not downwards. Until we anchored in Bayona in Spain, I didn't realise that kiwis grew on vines.

But the biggest ignorance was with the pineapple. Because when Alex pointed out a pineapple growing quite innocuously by the side of the path to the toilet block, I was absolutely astounded. Not only do pineapples most definitely not grow dangling from trees, they grow from stalks.

The path to the marina toilets did not just harbour an innocent pineapple bush though, and instead was itself another part of human construction that was being busily reclaimed by the jungle.

As I moseyed up the path one day, eyeing up the overhanging trees for sloths, I almost stepped right onto the middle section of an amazingly long snake.

Jet black and skinny, it had stretched itself across two thirds of the path, resting in the sunshine. The end of its tail was invisible, hidden in a bush from where it had, presumably, come from.

My brain initially registered it as a stick and everyone knows how enjoyable it is to crack a stick in half with your foot. So I took no action until I had already lifted my foot to land on it.

The slight lift of a tiny head and a flick of a tongue was enough to send me lurching forward to extend my stride, my down-coming foot missing the slick body by inches. I landed and jumped again, stifling a yelp and turning around to look at it.

It had not moved. It flicked its tongue once more and scowled at me before resting its head back onto the warm paving. There went my belief that snakes got out of your way if they heard you coming. This one evidently was not in a rush to relinquish its sunbed.

I crouched down and marvelled at it for a while, wondering if it was poisonous and just how often had I been missing snakes by inches.

'Ah you found the snake!' said a long-term resident of the marina. His algae-greened yacht sat glumly just a few boats along from mine.

"Yeah! I almost stepped on it," I said. He laughed.

"He lives here, I see him a lot relaxing in the sun."

When I walked back to the boat the snake was gone, but I was always watching out for him from then on, which is how I saw the next curious creature of that path.

The path was elevated slightly through a mangrove swamp and clear water hovered over sludge on the left side. This time though it wasn't a snake sunning itself, but a small purple octopus pulsing from rock to rock, enveloping unseen snacks and moving on.

With a head the size of my fist and eight almost jelly-like tentacles, it was in no way disturbed by me sitting on the edge of the path just half a metre away.

It would gather itself together before suddenly expanding outwards and streaming along the bottom, catching onto a rock and covering it entirely like a catcher's mitt on a baseball before springing outwards and gliding onwards. Back and forth it went over the mud, eating whatever it found and continually changing colour between pink and purple.

Glimmering and sweeping, the flesh between each tentacle was near translucent as it stretched out to poke something here and there. It was extraordinary.

I'd seen octopus in aquariums before but they've always seemed so solid and sulky. This was hungrily dancing in its territory leaving no area unexplored. Animals are so much more alive in the wild. So much... well... wilder.

My mind wandered as I walked up to the last jungle corner before getting into the marina and I was still alone on the path when I saw a large bundle hanging from an incredibly thin branch right above the path ahead. I stopped dead in my tracks and could barely breathe.

It was a sloth. He hung from one foot and one hand, from a branch so slim it seemed improbable that it wasn't bowing more. With his free hand he scratched his rear with a ferocious effort – or a sloth's version of a ferocious effort anyway.

He turned his little round face towards me and watched me watch him. He looked heavy, twice the size of a large cat and yet he hung with the most casual air. After a few minutes of heavy scratching he reached up with his free hand and turned away from me – becoming still. Within seconds he was completely inanimate, ready for another hour or so of daydreaming.

I was charmed beyond measure and when I returned the next day I found him in a neighbouring tree, hugging the trunk and resting in the nook of a branch. In the pose, he looked like a very furry child. Even though I stood below his tree, he only regarded me very slowly before turning his head and inspecting some crevice in the bark. I was elated.

Chapter 10

Beating Through Rainbows To Paradise

Make voyages. Attempt them. There's nothing else.
Tennessee Williams

"Why are you sailing without nav lights?" the American officer shouted over the wind and waves. Considering that the coastguard RIB appeared out of nowhere, they were hardly ones to be asking this question.

"To save power," Alex yelled back.

"He says to save power," the American said into his walkie-talkie.

We were sailing close-hauled across the Nicaraguan bank and the sun had gone down an hour or so before. The shallow depths had made the sea lumpy, but to avoid the bank we'd have had to spend at least a day tacking east. Protected by the sprayhood and the deep cockpit, we were dry in our bemusement while the American RIB, thrashing into the chop, was getting drenched.

"Where have you come from?" he yelled.

"Isla Providencia," Alex replied.

"Do you have proof? Exit papers?"

"Yes!"

There was more walkie-talkie discussions and the bright lights were making me feel a little queasy. It was all too strong, too in-your-face.

We were asked many questions about our ages, who we were, why we were sailing and how much food and water we had on board. Different men shouted the same questions at intervals but with different wording. Yes, we were still 27 and 30 years old, that hadn't changed in the last ten minutes.

The original man asked us if we'd ever been to America. Since the unspoken rule was that Alex only would speak – nothing's more confusing that two shouting voices – I didn't even bother to reply. Alex shouted across the pounding water that yes, he went to the States about ten years ago.

"And why are you sailing?" yelled a different American again.

"For adventure!" said Alex.

"America doesn't have enough adventure for you?" yelled the man. Considering Alex's distant holiday to America and our current sailing were as unconnected as lobster bisque and tea bags, this seemed like a redundant question.

Alex shrugged and I wondered if the question was actually, 'if you want to go on holiday, why wouldn't you just go to America… y'know, the centre of the world?'

Eventually they got to the point, around the same time we picked out the twinkling lights of a ship about five miles behind.

"Do you have any narcotics onboard?" shouted the main man, his pale, youthful face in a stern expression that almost made it look like this was a training exercise. Obviously, the answer to this question was, 'who says yes to that?!' but Alex had a better one.

"No!"

"Not even for personal use?" came the reply. I was careful to keep my expression neutral, bordering on weary because a) I was and b) while I was in the dark, I wouldn't have been surprised if they were watching us on infrared and misunderstood my would-be snort of laughter. Because what I was saying inside was, 'well there's a leading question if I ever heard one'.

"No," replied Alex. And the thing is, we didn't. I didn't even let a friend onboard with his hash-pipe in Tenerife because the boat was my home and, from what I'd gathered, if customs decided to take a walk on your boat with a sniffer dog and it smelt the old scent of a casually dropped iota of cannabis, they'd cheerfully tear the boat apart.

The mainsail still bore the boat's old race sail number and we were flying the British ensign despite it being pitch black. Our lack of suspicious signs and possibly the long-term standing of our trip eventually seemed to make them believe us and their tone changed ever so slightly to a hint of friendliness.

"Are you aware that you're travelling on a known drug-smuggling route?" shouted the marine. It's a known cruising route too, I thought.

"Not really," said Alex with a shrug.

They lost interest and fell back a little, saying they'd be back in a minute. They sat ten metres behind our stern but the floodlights were still very much on us. I could hear the marine shouting into his walkie-talkie but I couldn't hear what he's saying.

Really, all they needed to do is Google the boat's name with my name. It wouldn't take long to find articles and websites corroborating our story. Perhaps that's what they did because they returned shortly after.

"Okay that's all. Thanks for your co-operation," shouted the American.

"Are those your friends?" asked Alex, shooting a thumb back towards the lights on the horizon. The marine laughed.

"Yeah," he said, "they're ours." The other men, now soaked to the bone, waved us cheerfully goodbye and the RIB hauled itself around and sped off back to the ship.

"Well," I said.

"Yeah," said Alex.

We basked in the new dark of the night, stars visible once more now that the aggressive lights of the U.S. Coastguard RIB had gone.

"Fancy a honk on the crack pipe?" I asked.

The wind showed no sign of returning to its supposedly easterly prevailing habits and instead remained resolutely north easterly. We headed up to the Cayman Islands, but, not wanting to stop in such an expensive place, we continued on in Cuba's direction.

While long distance sailing is, fundamentally, extremely cheap, some countries charge exorbitant amounts just to check-in with customs and immigration. There was no real rhyme or reason to it either, with Grenada charging $50, Panama charging $300 and Guadeloupe

156

charging €5. It wouldn't have been a problem were we travelling even slower, but to pay hundreds to check into a small island where we'd stay only a week would soon become unmanageable.

Not only were the Cayman Islands pricey to check into, but food was also supposedly very expensive along with fuel and freshwater. I wanted to go, if just to see a British Overseas Territory, to touch some historic piece of home, but reason prevailed and we left the islands to the north.

Tropical sailing without a bimini is a tortuous activity. Large canvas covers fixed by poles to the cockpit, these glorious sunshades do little for your aerodynamics but plenty for your morale. With a small cockpit and an intrusive backstay, we simply didn't have room for a bimini.

Open to the skies, the cockpit felt like a sun catch and I found myself envying the simple luxury of other boats. Nothing I'd experienced before setting sail had prepared me for the reality of the baking tropical sun. The Christmas before the voyage began I'd flown out to Bali, my first time south of the equator and my first time in the tropics at all. But even Bali, with its punishing temperatures didn't prepare me for sailing in that harshness. It is the land of jungle, Coke Cola sponsored umbrellas and shade.

Multi-hour-long tacks upwind for days at a time was killing us both. The frustration of watching Cuba's southern coastline creep by while criss-crossing almost all the way south to Jamaica and back was unbearable. The few pelagic fish we caught only elated us temporarily before we'd fall back into our terse, overheated exhaustion.

It was too hot to sleep well and too hot to cook. We saw other yachts motoring close inshore, determinedly fighting the wind and powering to the next harbour. But without an electrically powered autopilot we'd have to hand steer for hours and, without much insulation, on our small boat the engine would only add to the already searing temperatures.

I had mixed feelings about seeing other yachts laden with fuel cans strapped on deck, resolutely pushing dead into the wind. On one hand, I was jealous, wanting the ease of just sticking on the engine and knowing I was making progress. But progress towards what? We were sailing, not driving. The idea of punching to windward with the engine, going against the wind rather than working with it, seemed far worse than the time-consuming long tacks up the sea towards Haiti.

I yearned for landfall but if I'd have had more than the 60 litres of fuel I possessed and an autopilot, would I have motored for two days into the wind to reach it? No, I don't think so. Engines are useful and there will always be times when it's preferable to motor for an hour to reach a reefy anchorage before sundown but you had to be careful to avoid the temptation of just driving a boat from place to place.

But it got me thinking about the reasons people sail. I was the most reluctant sailor when I began, I still am if the temperature starts dropping and if I can see my breath there'd better be a pot of gold at the end of the voyage. The most amazing experiences I'd had while voyaging though hadn't been tropical countries or hot beaches or rum cocktails on bamboo terraces; they'd been in sudden moments of utter clarity, hundreds of miles from land, with perfect wind, roaring waves and an almost indescribable sense of freedom.

My first moment of realising that this was what sailing was about was in the throes of Biscay, with stars above and dolphins below. It was cold and I was wearing a least five layers, dressed up as some sort of ocean-going sumo wrestler, but I could feel everything around me; the wind, the waves, the boat and even the thousands of glittering lights billions of miles away, all contributing to this moment.

It often happened at night but mainly at times of imperfection, when I was wishing that I was somewhere more comfortable, or more social or more... something. Then a bird would circle the yacht, or the wind would pick up just a fraction and the sails would reach their best performance or a squall would pass in the distance or dolphins would turn up under the arch of a rainbow, ridiculous creatures that they are. These things would jolt me out of my negatively and distraction, like being punched in the face by nature – look at what's here, look at what's around you.

And that is sailing to me. When you're travelling by the power of the wind alone, you're as much a part of the world around you as the whale rolling along beside or the seabird surveying the water for food. You're as much a part of the ocean as the seaweed that drifts perpetually, after all, the water supports you too and the wind helps you along as it helps the birds and creates the currents that move the seaweed.

In this way, the engine has no place on voyages. Instead it serves a necessary function of more easily manoeuvring in anchorages or marinas and enabled me to escape dangerous situations or rescue others. The engine is not there to power my fridge or drive me from one tropical cay to the next. But this is very much my ideal of sailing as it is to many others. In fact, I met several yachts without engines at all, having removed them to make way for more food or water storage. These intrepid sailors were destined for the farthest shores of the Earth, places where, if engines break, they're just dead weight. Far better to have more freshwater.

It stuns me to prefer difficult sailing to motoring. Back in the sheltered waters of the Solent, two years before, I would've given anything to just stick the engine on and go to an anchorage or better, home. I saw the engine as comfort, trustworthy, like walking for 15 miles and then seeing the car shining in the car park.

But it just isn't like that on our yacht. The engine doesn't make things more comfortable, it just changes the conducive environment to a jarring one. I can sail, I thought as we slopped around in the heat off Cuba. I am a sailor.

It was 3am and the bright lights of Guantanamo were blooming on the horizon. There's a 5 mile exclusion zone from the shore, annoying as we'd been tacking up fairly close but still, there was something eerie there that made me glad to be well over 10 miles off.

The chart showed a mesh of red lines with the phrases like, 'Airspace Warning Area', 'Major Operating Area', and, 'Explosives Dumping Ground'. At first I thought it was US warnings but eventually I spotted the phrase, 'Cuba Air Defence Identification Area'. In fact, it looked as though Cuba had created a voluminous military operating area just metres away from where the US Naval Base perimeters ended.

The chart indicated that the airspace above Guantanamo is restricted to 50,000 ft. Which, when I thought about it, was extraordinary when you consider that the average passenger jet cruises between 30,000 and 40,000 ft. And how can you own airspace anyway? What rights do we have to the sky, especially the rights to the sky above other peoples' countries.

As any offshore sailor will confirm, night watches can get strange. Out in the darkness alone, with just your thoughts and the strange sounds around you, it doesn't take much for your imagination to get out of hand. Often I'd hear voices and only sometimes could I firmly place them on the slight squeaking of the Aries vane when she needed oiling.

Night makes your brain attach meaning to everything it doesn't understand. That odd noise? That was voice. That light? Well…

I had been gazing at Guantanamo for a while in the balmy night. By some miracle the wind had gone more southerly, allowing us to make our way past the American base in just one large tack but it didn't take long for my mind to start wondering if, while I was gazing at Guantanamo, Guantanamo was gazing back.

After the bizarre and affronting oceanic interrogation we'd received off the coast of Nicaragua, I had little doubt that the mighty forces behind this American facility were aware of our presence. After all, we were sailing right past them, the RIB off Nicaragua must've picked us up on radar and then followed us for miles.

As 3am turned to 4am, I started getting the creeps. Just what was going on over there? And why was it happening? And were the British any better?

Suddenly, a flash went off above the boat and my eyes took a second to adjust. I stared up at the air above but I couldn't see anything except stars. It was a clear night and I knew lightning, that wasn't lightning. What it looked like, was a camera flash.

Then I started to get really suspicious. Did a drone just take a photograph of us? Did it fly ten miles offshore? Was that even possible? Of course it was possible, I thought to myself, haven't you seen the *X-Files*? By this time I was convinced that somehow, something had just flown over to the boat and photographed us. I imagined what my face would look like, exhausted, make-up free and surprised in the flash. Bastards, I thought, just buzz us on VHF like a gentleman and ask where we're going.

When Alex and I swapped over at 6am, I recounted the story to him.

"It was just lightning," he said.

"It wasn't lightning, I know lightning. It was just a single flash, way nearer than lighting would've been. And it was a clear sky," I said.

"So, what are you saying. You think a spy plane took a photo of us?" he said in a tone that said have you got out your tin foil hat yet?

"No," I said, "Of course not." Thinking, yes absolutely, you've seen *Homeland*!

I went to sleep, relieved that we were past the base. The sun was stretching out its arms, always the worst time to try to fall asleep, just as dawn begins to wake up your brain. As the morning light filtered through the boat, it did start to sound pretty silly in my head. After all, surely the Guantanamo Bay base had better things to do than photograph every passing vessel...

I often found myself making wishes on the voyage from Isla Providencia to the Bahamas. All in all, it hadn't been a particularly positive trip. I'd always imagined it as a struggle and I think, despite his protestations, Alex had as well. Sailing from Panama north east was never going to be favourable, the best we could've hoped for was flukily workable.

But it had instead been a battle. Not against nasty weather and waves, but against the determined easterly winds. I hated fighting the weather, no one won. The endless tacking had been interspersed with calms and most nights I'd spend my watch hours staring at the sails, praying they would stay filled enough, the slightest slam of windless fabric ricocheting down the keel-stepped mast and waking Alex.

"What's happening?" he would call, already irritated.

"Wind's gone," I would say, knowing what this meant. The sails would have to come down and then we'd just roll pitifully in the slight swell until it returned. In general, too much wind was more desirable than too little. We kept up a nice three knots across the Atlantic from Europe with no sail up and warps out the back, the wind pushing us along by the modest size of the hull alone. But no wind? The motion was terrible and the still air would cause the thermometer to rise even more.

I never felt more crushed than I did on the voyage along Cuba's south coast when the wind would die. Both exhausted and both without the ability to magic wind up, we descended into a terse and prickly state where everything was a disaster.

So I sat in the cockpit, day in, day out, wishing. Just let us get to the Windward Passage quickly and I'll never complain again, I'd say to the sky. Just let us get to Great Inagua and everything will be good from there. Just pick up another five knots, I'd say to the wind, and the sails will be filled just enough to not slam with errant waves.

I was bargaining. I craved sleep not so much for a chance to rest, but for the three hours in which I wouldn't have to think about how long it was going to take us or how slow we were going. The Atlantic crossing had been four times longer, but we were always moving, always making progress, never becalmed and rarely tacking. We'd just stepped onto the great mid-Atlantic conveyor belt and hung on for the duration.

By the time we reached the Windward Passage, the wind had spent the last two days howling down it. The waves in this confined channel were high and short, coming from all directions at once. The Windward Passage is notoriously rough as wind funnels through it in either direction. Separating the two vast islands of Hispaniola and Cuba, it also serves as a busy shipping channel with freighters taking the short cut from the USA to the Panama Canal and vice versa.

The shipping channel cuts close to Cuba and we wanted to hug the coast, getting through the Passage on the inside of the channel. But the wind had other ideas and we found ourselves forced into the port lane, doing the largest tacks possible before a ship would appear on the horizon, its lights bearing down upon us at great speeds.

The sea was the roughest I'd been in, or rather, our direction of travel was the most inconvenient for the sea state. At least in the large waves of the Atlantic we'd been going with them, here it was like taking constant punches with your hands behind your back.

I felt so vulnerable and small, the boat improbably tiny compared to the commercial giants that steamed passed. They wouldn't even be able to see us in these waves, no matter how close they were. At points during the night all I could feel was hate. I hated the waves, the ships, even my own boat as the boom slammed again and again. I would slip in the cockpit and the motion would hurl me into the sides, eliciting a scream of anger and frustration. I wanted to kick and punch and yell. Why was I sailing? This was awful. Why would anyone want to do this?!

The Windward Passage shipping lanes are only 18 nautical miles long but it took us all night to get up to the top. Battling upwind was treacherous, the deep second reef not doing anything for our windward performance and instead we were making more sideways progress than forward. Exhausted, miserable and afraid, I went to bed at 6am and curled up into the foetal position, jamming myself into my bunk to brace against the horrific motion. Alex was outside, doing what he did best: handling unholy situations with grace and calm.

My skin was covered in salt and it felt as though the dampness would never get off as it clung to my hair. The motion was too rough to spend time washing my face in the bathroom and besides, we were rationing freshwater as we always did on longer passages. I closed my eyes and wished again.

When I awoke a few hours later the sea state had calmed considerably. We were over ten miles north of the Passage and the localised sloshing effect was in our wake. Alex had cooked a delicious brunch in the miraculous way that he could achieve while I was asleep and I lazed around the cockpit in the sunshine as he rested.

Finally, Great Inagua, the first Bahamian island through the Passage, was within reach. Just another fifteen miles and we would be there. I felt the weight lifted off as I always did in the day we'd reach landfall. The wind was dropping however, the front had passed through the night before and now we were in danger of being left becalmed in the waves, hungover from the riotous night.

The day wound on and we waited until we were five miles from the still invisible island before switching on the engine. By this point I wasn't fussed about seamanship or the beautiful process of using the wind to move – I just wanted to anchor.

I went below for my off-watch time and dozed for an hour before Alex called me.

"Land ho!" he shouted, hand steering under the engine which had been busily roaring in my ear.

And sure enough, as I stepped outside, there was a flat strip of hazy land. Most islands can be spotted much further away but the Bahamas are as flat as Kansas and only visible at the last moment.

Through the binoculars I could make out the scrubby plants on the beach and a couple of palms drooping their frond-covered heads as they are prone to doing. The sand was white and not in the way that people refer to golden sand as, but truly white. The kind of white that only islands made of centuries old coral can be.

There was also, like the reefy Providencia, a defined line where the deep ocean blue ended and the clear turquoise began. Those colours, so perfectly delineated, pull you in even more than the lazy palms. The desire to jump in the water was overwhelming. I wanted to tear off my salty, sweaty rash vest and dive in, washing the weariness and the filth of long voyages off my skin.

It's difficult to get fully clean while physically sailing. The easiest method is to go naked up on deck and get a bucket of water from over the side, pouring it on yourself and soaping up. But with any wind, even in the tropics, this made me feel slightly chilled and uncomfortable. Alex, however, did this daily, sometimes twice daily and always with glee whatever the weather. He also loved showering in squalls.

But with my long hair it was a nightmare washing thoroughly on the move and I desperately wanted to swim and be comforted by the clear water.

As we motored slowly over the ridge, the deep blue gave way in a moment and suddenly I could see every grain of fine sand and every starfish below the boat. Despite the five-metre depth, it felt as though we were skimming the bottom, so clear was the water.

There were two other boats in the main anchorage but we continued a further half mile up the west coast to find utterly flat water. I'd known that there was a chance we'd have to leave immediately for Mayaguana, another hundred miles away, if a well enough sheltered anchorage couldn't be found. Thankfully though we nestled into a beach with just half a metre under the keel and, when the anchor was down and the engine off, we looked at each other and broke into broad grins.

I got my wish of swimming as Alex dinghied ashore with the ship's papers and passports to check into the country. Often, only the captain is allowed ashore until immigration is complete and I enjoyed the hour or so I had at every new country, alone to reflect on the voyage and relax into new surroundings.

The idea of dealing with the emotionless authorities filled me with dread and I was always happy for Alex to go and deal with the official side of things. The few times I was present in immigration offices, I was always nervous, believing they'd turn us away for the slightest reason.

I found the border authorities bizarre and unsettling. In Grenada the man hadn't said a word until the end of the paperwork where he'd asked for fifty US dollars. Instead he'd stared at us impassively as we explained we'd arrived from Europe and needed to check-in. Then he just sat in silence until he lumbered up out of his chair and fetched us a form as though it was located at Everest Base Camp.

In almost every West Indian country we checked into, we'd been made to feel as though we were seriously inconveniencing the officers by wanting to check-in. I was elated upon arriving in Martinique, where the check-in was a do-it-yourself affair with a computer in the corner of a chandlery. The same went for Guadeloupe but the computer was in a gift shop.

Panama was the strangest. Six officials turned up on a panga, five women with dangerously long fake nails and one man in a hard hat who said nothing the entire time. Unused to being on small yachts, the officials climbed over our guard wires with serious difficulty and then all squeezed downstairs into our saloon which, under no circumstances, is designed to house eight people at once.

They were cheery though, the women spending an inordinate amount of time giggling over their iPhones and occasionally filling out a piece of paper. Strangely, they had never heard of St Martin, where we'd come from and this caused an extra two days of paperwork as the immigration officer needed to check us in manually with passport photographs, fingerprints and the words St Martin, written in our own handwriting as if we needed to take responsibility for the island's existence.

With bureaucracy and stern officials putting me on edge, I was always relieved when Alex seemed happy to go ashore by himself. As yet, nothing had ever gone very wrong when checking in, but I could never shake the feeling that something would.

Most of my time while Alex was doing official business involved turning the saloon from bunks back into a saloon again and the forepeak from a messy storage area back into our double bed we slept in at anchor. The saloon always looked, as people said before the War on Terror began, like a bomb had hit it. It was difficult to clear because, without a guaranteed freshwater supply, I still couldn't wash any salty clothes. Instead I would hang them out in the sun, crisping gently, until the time came to either wash them or wear them again.

I'd become somewhat spritely at doing this, fast-tracking everything to its 'anchor place', so I could jump freely into the water and enjoy the phenomenal surroundings within fifteen minutes.

And Great Inagua's water was truly phenomenal. Below the surface I could see *Berwick Maid*'s keel, moving gently in the whisper of swell. It was as though she was floating in thin air and although this wasn't the first time I'd seen her in such waters, it never failed to amaze me. Looking at her like this didn't seem to reconcile with physics.

She was so sturdy, I knew that because I'd crashed through many waves in her, and yet suspended here in such clarity seemed utterly improbable. How could such a creature be held so easily by such delicate and moveable water?

I felt such love for her then, swimming about her, running my hands along her smooth curves, feeling and looking for any scars, any damage she may have sustained. She wasn't just a boat, she was a living, breathing thing that kept us safe as we kept her safe.

Having brushed her down well before leaving Providencia, there was no growth whatsoever below the waterline. Just a soft green flourish here and there near the comparatively nutrient rich sink outflows. She looked good, her six-month-old anti-fouling had barely a mark in it, meaning that we hadn't hit anything on the journey north.

I dived down and swam along the seafloor, running my hands through the soft, white coral sand. There was almost nothing on the bottom at all, no fish, no conch, nothing. I swam on to a dark expanse behind the boat, relaxing into the breath hold and feeling my untied hair billowing out behind – a feeling of true paradise after the damp, salty knotted mess that it had been before.

A coral head came into view, I'd seen it from the boat as we'd eased into the anchorage. Here was the life, fan corals wafting so gently it was like they were breathing. Electric blue fish, curious sergeant majors and sedate, cautious angels. As you swim around underwater near coral heads you can hear the fish eating. Parrot fish are the best to eavesdrop on; with their powerful coral crunching teeth, you can hear each bite.

I made my way back to the boat and wash my hair in the sea, reaching up to the scuppers of our low-sided boat for my shampoo and conditioner. It might sound bad, to use such harsh chemicals as shampoo directly in the sea, but in general I put it in perspective. After all, the amount of chemicals I used compared to the average homeowner is absurdly small and the amount of pollution is a dent in what we would be emitting on land.

When I washed my hair in the marina showers in Panama where was the grey water going there? Straight out into the mangroves. Most of the Bahamas rely on rainwater for drinking, there is no water treatment plant for a house's water supply, it comes straight from the sky. There simply isn't the infrastructure to support extensive water treatment.

Still, it's easy to wash your chemicals down the drain and never think about where they go. As demonstrated by the recent banning of microplastics, those nifty exfoliating plastics that give us smooth skin but end up in the stomachs of fish. And that's just in the UK's plumbing system.

Washing in the sea, I could see the small cloud of conditioner that I rinsed from my hair drift away and begin to dissipate. I could see my pollution and it did bother me. We are so blind to this back home, or rather, it's so well hidden.

I take small comfort in knowing that the sea will flush well here, this island out on its own, surrounding by currents. It's in places where many boats lie at anchor for months with liveaboards in mostly enclosed lagoons that the pollution can take hold of the area, turning the water from clear to polluted.

The ocean and the slow destruction of its ecosystems seems like just a newspaper story, something that we hear about in televised charity pleas or Greenpeace bulletins, its reality overwhelmed by everything else that's going on in the world. But for sailors it's unavoidable and it breeds unease. Swathes of dead coral, endless floating plastic debris and the strange things that cruising biologists find in their samples means there's no easy way to push it aside.

We are damaging this place, no matter how harmoniously we try to live. The materials the boat is made from alone are the results of horrendous processes. The problem seems unanswerable on some days but on others I feel a little pride that we are at least doing a little to limit our destruction on the planet.

I got into the cockpit and towelled down before the salt could dry on my skin and in my hair.

I often got asked how I could wash in salt water, didn't that just replace dirt and sweat with salt? The answer is, predominantly, no. So long as I towelled off while still wet, the salt was gone. My hair was living its own sorry story, but there was little I could do about that.

I watched as Alex pulled the dinghy down the beach and began rowing back to the boat. There was always a moment of apprehension at this point, where I was yet to find out how easy our lives would be in one country or another. After all, customs and immigration staff hold your fate in their fickle and bureaucratic hands.

"All sorted?" I asked, taking the document folder from him as he came alongside.

"Yeah no problem, we can stay for three months."

Three months in the Bahamas, I thought: that was something I would never have imagined happening. The Bahamas were some far-off tropical paradise that Americans frequented in films, I hadn't even known where they were exactly until the previous year.

I sat in the cockpit with an icy beer and opened up the chartbook for the Outer Bahamas, the ones farthest from the USA (and almost devoid of yachts) and conveniently exactly where we were.

The endless islands stretched out before me on paper as the sun warmed me through the cockpit tent we'd put up.

It was the 16th January 2016 and we'd sailed 1103 nautical miles in 10 days.

Chapter 11

The Sky, The Sea And The Wind

Sunshine is delicious, rain is refreshing, wind braces us up, snow is exhilarating; there is really no such thing as bad weather, only different kinds of good weather.

John Ruskin

I changed course to go around squall. Isn't it mad that you can do that, to change course for rain?

Before I went sailing I never imagined that you could change course for weather, I thought it was something unavoidable, something that loomed on the horizon and would hit whatever you did. Weather was something that happened to you. But now I'm discovering that that only applies to immovable things like houses, roads and other constructs that anchor us, pardon the pun, to the earth.

If my childhood taught me anything, it's that 'weather' chose the time, the place and the strength with which it hit. As we doggedly walked up Welsh mountains and through Lake District valleys, rain would be a given. Clouds would squat, fat and frumpy, on top of the hills and wait to envelope you as you ascended – there was no avoiding it; you can't out-walk a raincloud.

And so I went through life, seeing clouds dimly through gaps in buildings and above the trees but never giving them too much thought because, on land, there's not much you can do except zip-up your coat and unfurl your umbrella. Whole cities sprouting multi-coloured mushrooms, each with ten prongs and an ergonomic handle.

But it's different at sea; the squalls have nowhere to hide, no forests from which to pounce from, no cities to obscure their approach. There is nothing they can use to conceal the edges and there's another thing

I didn't really know. They do have edges, real ones. Finite ones. Some squalls really are just black and white.

While there are plenty of times, most in fact, that it's not possible or practical or purposeful enough to change course for a squall, I find it incredible that I can at all. These bubbling, deep grey clouds, heavy and bloated with rain and of a magnitude impossible to quantify; sometimes labouring across the sky, sometimes marching in droves. Sometimes I can just bear off a touch and know that in the four or so miles I have left, I might be able to just slink past it, maybe catch a light misting or skirt it altogether.

This is the phenomenal thing about sailing: these clouds, these squalls, these heavy thundering skies that shout and howl, they're not malicious. They're just going on their merry way, sometimes slowly, sometimes quickly but almost always in a straight line. They were there first. You can, sometimes, just step to one side.

The Bahamas has a particular type of weather that I'd heard about long before we arrived. The problem was, the only people who had told me about it were the kinds to exaggerate. So I hadn't expected them to not only be in the right ball park, but spot on.

Every year the UK suffers winter storms that have roared across the Atlantic and pummelled into Ireland and Britain as a whole. I'd endured many of these, marvelled at the energy with which the pounded the shores of the South West and stared at the bright high wind colours on the Scottish forecasts. But I'd never considered where they'd come from. I discovered it quickly.

The disturbances that evolve into the UK's winter storms begin around Texas and the Gulf of Mexico. They head east thanks to the Coriolis effect and roll over Florida, out into the Atlantic. The Bahamas sit on the southern edge of these lows but, before they leave the North American coast entirely, they deposit trailing fronts that drag along behind, whipping the entire Bahamian archipelago.

The fronts follow the same rotational pattern but lazily swing on behind, turning the wind 360 degrees throughout the Bahamian islands. The cruisers down there call it 'clocking round' and are constantly on the look out for these fronts as few anchorages are suitable for every wind direction.

Instead, the sailors must up anchor and follow the wind around: one of the main reasons why they collect in Georgetown, Great Exuma. This cruiser-friendly town is in the middle of a giant lagoon, protected from the east by the long, thin Elizabeth Island.

The clocking begins like this: the wind first strengthens from the south-east, the prevailing wind direction. Then it moves south and south-west. During this time, most yachts previously sheltered from prevailing winds have to move to get westerly protection.

Depending on the strength of the cold front, the westerly component might bring heavy squalls and gusts that make you look at the wind instruments with a raised eyebrow. Once the westerlies have had their fun, the wind continues to clock round to the north-west and then north-east, when all the yachts must move back to an anchorage sheltered from easterlies.

These fronts go through every week during the winter months and are the only break from the relentlessly good weather that the Bahamas benefits from. Sometimes a front could pass in a day but often it would take a full 48 hours for the wind to return to its starting point.

Weather had taken on the role of a third crew member within weeks of sailing away from England. Every daytime would be dedicated to studying surface pressure charts and other forecasts. Deep consultations would be had about the possibilities of wind direction and strength and often I'd be checking up on the weather before I'd even woken Alex up.

I knew the weather better than anything else, I tracked it's hourly fickleness, saw how the pressure systems moved across the globe. It was as though I'd only ever been looking through a pinhole my entire life, and now the board had been taken away and I could see the whole picture.

Even in the Canaries, just 6 months into the multi-year trip, I'd be sat in Sailor's Bar, refreshing the wind forecast for the Atlantic, looking for any tiny deviations that would bring undesirable weather. Was that strong wind sustained or just the island effect as it funnelled through the Spanish islands? Were those waves going to continue at 3 metres or would they calm as they travelled further west?

No longer was it enough to look at a localised forecast, in preparation for multi-day or multi-week voyages, I'd be looking at weather thousands of miles away because now I knew how it travelled, I knew that a depression wouldn't stay thousands of miles away, it would in fact, be coming straight for us.

As the cold fronts from the southern USA dragged their tendrils across the Bahamas, the temperature would drop within hours. As the wintery air was sucked into the lows and spat out, we'd suddenly have to pull out a jumper while the day before had been too hot to move.

And with greater understanding came greater appreciation. No longer was bad weather irritating: how could it be when I knew where it came from, why it was there? I realised that it was the apparent randomness of it that had annoyed me before. If I woke up to rain it had seemed spontaneous and deliberate. Inconvenience with no excuse.

But as I watched the rain coming in from hundreds of miles away on the satellite charts, there was a deep understanding, even affection, as it turned up on my horizon. Sort of like, hello, I've been expecting you. I could see how far it'd come, the distant places it'd seen on its way. Like a letter from the other side of the world, the systems, the wind and the rain, they'd all travelled too, specifically, for a reason.

We were forced to leave Great Inagua just two days after we'd arrived. Protected only from the east, we would have been anchored on a dangerous lee shore in the coming westerlies.

Instead, we left as the winds began the clocking round and sailed 110 nautical miles downwind to Mayaguana, another, even more remote, outer island. With an exceptionally shallow but well-protected lagoon, we knew we could see out not just this front, but the much stronger one following it.

While the Bahamas is susceptible to cold fronts all year round, they predominantly affect the sprawling archipelago between November and April. From June the islands run the risk of hurricanes coming up from the mid-Atlantic or from the Gulf of Mexico to the west. But while these low-lying islands have their fair share of savage weather, it's not bad news for many communities.

By the time we arrived in Mayaguana we hadn't filled up our water tank since Providencia. With no reverse osmosis plant on the island to turn saltwater into fresh, the Providencians collected rain water in huge tanks below their houses or water butts that caught run-off from their roofs.

We had filled our tank to the brim with water we ferried in jugs and buckets from the tank of a generous local. He said that there'd been a drought when he was a boy and the water on the island became perilously hard to get. From then he'd sworn that when he grew up he would never run out of water. He had the largest tanks on the island below his house, and gave water freely to others when they were in need.

"My mother said that the water came from God and so it's his to give, not mine to sell," he told us. "Take as much as you need, even when I am out fishing, just come and help yourselves."

But Providencia could have rain showers that were more akin to short-lived monsoons and even during the relatively dry season, sunny weeks would end in an hour-long drenching, topping up the tanks. The Bahamas experience far less rain.

We had been careful with our freshwater during the sail north from Providencia. Even though the voyage only took 10 days, we had no idea when we'd next be able to fill up the tank and we'd experienced no rain showers in which to collect our own water. By Mayaguana, we were getting worried.

A desolate and sparsely populated island, Mayaguana sits on the very outer reaches of the southern Bahamas. Yachts occasionally stop off for a night at anchor as they travel to or from the Turks and Caicos islands but, with nowhere to really buy food ashore, they rarely stay.

The Mayaguanans are friendly, welcoming to everyone who ventures out to their island and, while they have very little, they'd give you world. We found a gentleman with vast underground rainwater tanks and, as we were struggling back along the road with 40 litres, a car stopped alongside us having come from the direction we were walking.

"You guys need a ride? You going to the dock?" A lady leaned out and told us to get in, driving us to the concrete fishing harbour. "You on a boat out there?"

"Yeah, we sailed from Great Inagua," I said.

"Ah huh. Where did you come from before?" she said.

"England, originally."

"But you didn't sail from England," she said, looking at us in the rearview, her young daughter sat in the front passenger seat but facing us with her wide, curious eyes.

"Uh, yeah we did but it's taken us almost two years," said Alex. Two years? I thought. Have we not been home in two years? The passing of time was impossible to comprehend.

The woman whistled in disbelief and parked on the harbour edge. We got our cans out and thanked her but she waved us away and wished us good luck.

The water smelt slightly of bleach but it tasted good. I was relieved that we'd found some, 40 litres is a lot of water when you're rationing it. I knew first-hand how it felt to be running low on water and the idea of living on an island that relied only on rainwater made me feel claustrophobic. Tropical Providencia was one thing, but Mayaguana saw little rain and rarely sustained.

With a weekly mail-ship, the isolation of these islands was acutely apparent. They relied on the rain as much as they relied on that weekly ship. Mayaguana has a tiny population and no industry at all except for community fishing.

When you think of the Bahamas, it's not Mayaguana and Great Inagua that you might picture. 600 miles north, just a day sail from the Florida coast, are the classic Bahamas. With big hotels, resorts and endless bars, those Bahamas are the white sand, rum cocktail paradise of marketing dreams. But the outer islands? They're the Bahamas without the tourist industry.

Once I had become inextricably bound to the weather, other things started to unravel before my eyes. I saw islands shaped by prevailing winds, whole landscapes defined by what the weather brought and where stumpy trees grew. I saw the scars of hurricanes past.

The people had different attitudes too, living out there. On the brink of massive tropical storms, they weren't party to the scare-mongering and ignorance of the media-frenzied countries further north.

"I spent a summer in Louisiana a while back," said a young woman on Eleuthera. "They had a hurricane forecast and my God, it was crazy. Everyone was panic buying, terrified, blockading themselves in their houses. When a hurricane hits the Bahamas? We're on the beach watching it come. Life just carries on, it has to."

But the Bahamas have a different infrastructure to the USA. Squat houses, endless straight roads, few cars and nothing much else. Compared to America there's simply less for the hurricanes to destroy. The Bahamians expect hurricanes and build accordingly. Their islands are kept in a way that is in tune with nature, in a way that allows hurricanes to roll right on over.

Bahamian roof tiles are felt, easy to replace. Their houses are low and made of concrete. We saw numerous semi-subterranean buildings too. We had arrived less than 6 months after a major hurricane. In November 2015, Category 5 Joaquin had approached the Bahamas from the south east and sat on top Long Island for two days. The destruction was still apparent when we arrived in February 2016. Neighbouring Rum had its coconut palms wrenched from the earth, an important crop for the islanders. Cruisers from Georgetown were ferrying young coconut plants from the Exumas to the worst affected islands, already starting the replanting.

The hurricane had dealt a severe blow to several inhabited islands but the buildings were still standing and the people carried on. They fixed the things they needed to, they drove a little further because their local shop had been damaged and there were a lot of roofs that needed re-felting. But the damage compared to that of an American city was nothing, the Bahamians live with the understanding that nature isn't so much a part of their lives, it is their lives.

The damage dealt by major hurricanes that make it to the States is evident by their longevity in our memories. Who can't remember Hurricane Katrina, whether it affected them or not? The destruction isn't marked by the force of the hurricane, after all, the same category hurricanes hit other places with less destruction (and less news reporting). Instead it's marked by how much was destroyed, infrastructure that was never built with hurricanes in mind despite being in a hurricane zone.

Who wants low concrete buildings and felt tiles in the land of freedom and plenty? But a nation's wealth can't protect against the forces of nature. Building regardless and hoping that natural phenomena won't happen is surely a recipe for disaster.

On the days it got too hot and too sticky, I'd crave the cold fronts, watching them peel out over the northern islands. They'd clear the air within hours and suddenly there'd be a luxurious coolness in the air making it warmer in the water than out of it.

Panama had been the hottest. A full year into the voyage and I was deep in the jungle experiencing the kind of muggy heat that I'd only felt before in steam rooms. Wind was rare but the rain could be heard coming for miles across the dense forest.

It was when the thermometer was pushing 35 degrees and the water around the mangroves was 31 that it became almost unbearable. Without a breath of wind, even the simplest tasks were exhausting and rage inducing.

The sun was barely subdued through the cloud cover, the light giving an intensity that felt like being cooked in a microwave. I could take cold showers but it didn't matter, the second I stepped out I would just start sweating again.

It was always difficult to convey the special type of misery one experiences when suffering this kind of heat. The beach on the other side of the island had such a flawless curve, such pure sand and so many iconic palms that any mention of negativity would only generate scathing tones.

I was in paradise, wasn't I?

But while the West Indies had the same beaches along with easterly trades, Panama had stagnation with its postcard views. It was the kind of place I'd buy a Coke just to press it against my skin rather than to drink it.

All of the Americans in the marina there had air conditioning: something that I hadn't even had in my car back home, let alone the boat. Any issue, any breakages, any disagreements were amplified by the intensity of the heat. Jumping into the water did little to alleviate the stresses with its own high temperatures, poor visibility and abundance of jellyfish.

I felt stuck in these instances, did I really want to be the person who complained about the cold and the hot? How could I ever tell people that sure, the beach was nice but man, it was just too sunny.

But it was relentless. The locals only fished towards dusk and lived in wooden houses built well under the forest canopy. Even those in Bastimentos town, working hard to meet the expectations of the tourists, stayed under shelter. Everyone was covered up, relaxing under the shade of shop fronts and working slowly in the liquid heaviness of the heat.

Only the tourists were out in the sun at any time of the day, spread out over bar terraces, lying on the beach and paddle boarding in bikinis. Even the local Panamanian boys wore rash vests in the water.

It was Panama that really made me worry about my skin. It had a special kind of intensity that I could feel on my skin during all daylight hours from 6am onwards. The days were often utterly overcast but the UV index would still be 11+. No cloud could keep this equatorial sun out.

But hats made my head hot and rash vests felt sweaty and hot. Insects would stick to my skin and sometimes I wanted to scream with discomfort. I couldn't live in the jungle, it was too much.

When I got to the Azores around a year later, I finally discovered what I'd been looking for, the ideal balance of temperatures. With their sub-tropical location, their mid-ocean fresh air and their lush green mountains, the Azores were warm, clear and refreshingly European. It could reach 26 degrees happily on a summer's day and drop to a comforting 24 overnight. Even when the clouds descended, as they often did, it was still only light jumper weather and in winter never dropped below 10 degrees.

Weather, as Clive Owen's character said of time in *Closer*, 'is a tricky fucker'. Alex is a naturally hot person and I'm a naturally cold one. Together we can always be guaranteed to have some level of dissatisfaction when it comes to temperature, with me wearing three jumpers and hopping from foot to foot and Alex wafting his t-shirt to cool down.

The Azores however, were the one place where we both drifted around in a state of abject bliss, neither one too hot or too cold. Even on the days of light drizzle in Flores, which could be called the mistiest island, we were warm and even reinvigorated. My adoration of Flores was heavily biased by the sheer relief of arriving there after a long ocean passage but still, its Welsh dampness and sub-tropical comfort was a great celebration.

I learnt more about weather than I did about anything else during the two and a half years away. It was a constant yet changeable presence, always evolving and devolving, always something I needed to watch. The clouds took on new meanings for me, I could see in their streaks the strong winds that were still hours, even a day, away.

I learnt friendly clouds, unfriendly clouds, clouds that would rain soon, clouds that would rain after they'd passed us. I could smell the incoming weather on the wind, I could taste it in the air. The colours of the sky mean different things in different places, the rhyme, 'Red Sky at Night…' only works for England with its prevailing south-westerlies.

In each new place I would work out what the smear of reds, purples and oranges on the horizon would mean. I would watch the barometer, judging the speed of its fall, the slowness of its rise. Weather was far more intricate than I had ever realised before but, for all its whimsical mystery, it was also far more logical than I had ever realised. Forecasts aren't particularly accurate and yet the sailor-forecaster stood on deck and, watching the conditions for days on end, noting the clouds and the wind speeds and direction… well they could be much better.

Weather is inherently difficult to read but, when I started to live and breathe it, it took on a much different role in my life. It was no longer the untameable beast that dictated my days, but instead a gruff companion who could sometimes, just sometimes, be lulled into telling you their secrets.

Chapter 12

Northern Bahamas

If you go anywhere, even paradise, you will miss your home.
Malala Yousafzai

We'd left the boat anchored alone in a mirror sheen of afternoon sunlight. She sat suspended in a clarity known only to these islands and I could trace her chain all the way to the anchor as we rowed to shore.

Halfway up Eleuthera's western crook, I was amazed to find stable light easterlies and we'd stopped in the bay on our leisurely journey north. Once more we'd given into the temptation despite our previous failures; we were going to find a cave to find.

This one had co-ordinates and, while I didn't have a GPS with me, the instructions were fairly basic. Walk north along the road behind the beach until you reach a road sign, then take a west-going track. On an island with scarcely more than one road, this cave was going to be an easy one to find.

The road had the same name as all the other main roads on every Bahamian island I'd yet come across: the Queen's Highway. So consistent was the naming of each island's single main road that I wondered if there was only actually one Queen's Highway and the seas in between were merely large, oceanic fords.

Looking behind, the road stretched out with Roman straightness and up ahead was the cusp of a modest hill and the road bore off to the right.

"That's it, up there," said Alex. Sure enough there was a sign, although it was an arrow pointing west and hanging from a white frame. The track it points down is like a Devon country path; tyre tracks down either side and tufty grass and stones along the middle.

We took it, albeit with a reasonable dose of suspicion. Could the cave really be down such a well-preserved track? With an actual sign that looked, well, nice? And, after a hundred metres the path did curve south then west then north then south then…

"This is definitely going to take us back to the beach," I said. But the problem with winding paths with uncertain endings is this: you simply cannot abandon the path until you know where it ends, or, at the very least, until you know it's categorically not the one you want to take. When you say, let's just see what's 'round this corner', you have to keep going, even if around that corner is another corner.

Why? Because if you turn back and, by some unimaginable miracle, it turns out to have actually been the path you wanted, then you'll have to walk it all over again. It's better to follow a moderately obviously incorrect path to its bitter end than it is to turn back half way on a hunch.

This thinking got us all the way to the end, which did happen to be around 50 metres along the beach from where we'd left the dinghy. Definitely not the cave path.

We retraced our steps to the arguably endless Queen's Highway and carried on, the 3pm sun digging under our skin and attaching itself. Eleuthera is scrubland, like the rest of the Bahamas, and the trees are wiry, short and savagely dry. Walking any further than half a mile becomes a serious undertaking requiring something bordering on a rehydration plan.

What I at first found strange in the Bahamas – that the houses were crumbling and the supermarkets non-existent but thirty-grand cars are everywhere – now made sense. No one really walked. Anywhere. In fact, every time we'd walked anywhere at all we'd be stopped by friendly drivers wanting to know if we needed a ride. We refused, we like to walk, it was hard to get enough exercise with a floorspace of around 3 sqm, but they were baffled.

Air-conditioning is something I craved now though; climate control. Temperature was a constant consideration, changing with the direction of the boat, the physical exertion of simply walking down a road or the upwellings of a blue hole. Temperature dictated more of how I lived through each day than it ever had before I became a sailor.

It was only twenty metres along the road and I saw the sign. A north-facing 'Bear Right' sign on a pole larger than it needed. That was it, the description online for how to find the cave. Immediately across the road the path should begin, and it did.

The path was barely noticeable in the dense undergrowth and reaching branches. Within a few minutes, we'd taken to wielding dead branches to stop us from walking straight into vast spiders' webs where the only visible part was the huge, black and yellow spider sat waiting patiently in the centre.

Large, eight-legged marvels they might've been, but I didn't want one in the face and I wilfully broke their webs, strung across the path at intervals. Don't look at me like that, we've all watched David Attenborough: these beasts can weave the most complex web in ten minutes flat, it was hardly an inconvenience.

"This is more like it" I said to Alex, "we should've known the last one was too good to be true." After all, so far the only way we'd found actual caves, was by following the path less travelled. Frost was clearly a caver.

True to form, the path diverges in two and we swatted whining mosquitoes from our faces and surveyed our options. We took a winding uphill route, ridden with thin tree stumps and biting things but the path petered out; another Bahamian road to nowhere.

The second was low and even at my stature I had to walk heavily hunched down to avoid the overhanging trees and bushes. The spiders had woven thicker, tighter webs along here and I wondered if I would've walked this path years ago, with stripy arachnids, with a propensity for jumping, hanging from broken webs. Possibly not. Probably not.

A sharp turn to the left and I spied the top of a ladder, hidden in a swarm of mosquitoes. We'd liberally applied repellent beforehand but it was mostly irrelevant, these creatures drank DEET for breakfast and it was only through speed and good hand-eye coordination that we got down the ladder and into the darkness below without more than one bite each.

No slow entry to this cave, light merely trickled from the hole we'd come down.

"You brought the torches," said Alex, "right?"

I turned on my torch and walked along the tunnel, the smell of guano filling my nostrils and the squeak of bats emanating from the ceiling. I flicked my torch up and there is one, two, three, more and more, hooked onto the rock by tiny feet and squirming, elbows wriggling.

They were leaf-nosed bats, tiny and loud and here in their multitudes. The deeper I went the more there were, swooping around me, small wings shifting air just centimetres from my ears.

There were no mosquitoes there, presumably any stray ones instantly became a welcome snack and instead the bats are left alone with a population of ginger cockroaches, antenna waving curiously in the otherwise emptiness of their surroundings.

The tunnel divided and its floor was a maze of holes, some natural while some looked man-made – leftover diggings from the era of guano harvest. I turned off my torch and stopped for a moment, trapped in absolute darkness. The bats chittered and flitted above me, around me and they passed so close I felt I could grab one.

With my torch back on, I'd lost the distant twitching light of Alex and continued along the tunnel with him somewhere up ahead. The screech of the bats became louder and further up above me just a couple of metres away was a churning huddle of hundreds.

A mass of vibrating, shivering bodies writhed above and bats flew in and out, the huddle reorganising itself every second. It was truly stunning. Bats on the outside stretched wings and extended their comparatively huge ears. The torch light didn't seem to bother them so much as any movement I made.

As I walked on, I started sinking into dense earth and turned the torch to my feet. The ground was thick with bat faeces, as thick and bouncy as freshly laid compost and I sprang up and down a few times, the chattering a roar around me. I wondered if the cuts on my flip-flopped feet would be an entry way for disease… you can't get rabies from bat guano. Right?

The cacophony unnerved me and I propelled myself forward across the blanket of guano and deeper still along the tunnel. The bats died down and the ceiling was bare with only the odd creature squirming from its foothold.

"Alex!" I called. I heard a faint response.

The tunnel was narrow before it opened up into a huge cavern with multiple routes off. The piece of filthy string that had been tied to the ladder and lead into the cave when we arrived, had long since given up and collapsed into a hole.

Light crept in somewhere ahead and I could see the outline of Alex as he made his way towards it. Shafts of sunshine cut through the blackness and as I reached the open cavern, a forgotten cathedral of rock.

I could see perfectly vertical tree roots coming down from the rock ceiling and grappling firmly into the cave floor. Twisted and strong, these pillar-like roots gave the impression of holding up the ceiling and they'd plaited themselves neatly together. The roots splay out when they hit the ground and clawed at whatever earth and rock they found, cementing themselves to the cave and running feelers out for water.

I was staring at the crack in the cave where rocky crevices were slung below the flood of sunlight when an owl, pale and silent, swooped through the cave and out, startled by our presence. I opened my mouth to say something and another lifted from its unseen perch and followed its mate. Neither beat a single wing, rather glided as an artist on a flying trapeze.

The cave meandered along under the dry and barren land above and forked often. Tiny cairns sat at the entrances to various tunnel mouths, leading explorers into the unknown depths of the labyrinth. The cairns were too numerous and too indiscriminate to trust and besides, who trusted a partially collapsed pile of stones when navigating a cave system sans map?

Instead I turned around after each new fork to pick out marks and features, to remind myself of how to get back. At the bit that looks like an ear, turn left. When the rusty lines spread over the cave ceiling like blood running down, turn right.

Each new turning and I ran all the previous ones back through my mind like a navigator's version of the supermarket game; 'I went to the supermarket and I bought…'

When I eventually made it back out, through the immense piles of guano, it was like I've emerged from the underworld. The Bahamas were littered with cave systems and each is like another world, cooler, darker and full of troglodyte creatures that have no place in the intensely bright world above.

In Rock Sound, a bay in Eleuthera's south, there is a flooded vertical cave half a kilometre inland that is said to be haunted. Strange things appear and disappear in its huge, circular mouth and while it looks tempting to swim in in the heat of the day, there is undoubtedly something eerie about it. Somewhere within its depths though is the answer; a cave system that connects the vertical blue hole to the ocean underground, feeding it confused fish and turtles and sucking out rubbish and other detritus thrown in.

With so many islands, we found ourselves sailing almost continually back and forth between them, looking for quiet anchorages or food shops or anything to entrance and interest us. The charts were littered with intriguing creeks and bays and handfuls of aeroplane wrecks, the numerous tiny airstrips always on the edge of the water and easily missed in strong winds.

The shallow waters meant that I often saw things lost on the sea floor without having known they were there. As we sailed from Great Guana Cay in the Exumas across its shallow 3 metre sound to Staniel Cay, I spotted something decidedly odd. The boat was gliding along in light downwind airs and the bank was so protected there was barely a ripple. The large dark patch ahead was probably just a coral head, and I turned the wheel ever so slightly so we would pass right by it.

When I looked over the side at this dark shape contrasted against the bright turquoise, it didn't look like coral. It was oblong. Alex was below making tea and for a moment we carried on sailing as I pondered.

"Alex?" I called. He stuck his face around the companionway in response. "I think we just sailed past a car," I said.

"Out here?"

"Well… I don't know," I said, at a loss. We were miles from land, how could a car be out here?

"Let's turn around and have a look," said Alex. I turned the wheel and we set the sails to the new direction, picking up speed as we close-reached back to the very obvious black patch.

So clear was the water that I could confidently steer the yacht within inches of the object and know for certain that I wouldn't touch it. We both peered over the side as we slid past and I had been right, we were looking at a pickup truck sat quietly on the sandy floor.

Providing a long sought after anchoring point for coral and seaweed, the truck looked like it had a happy community of fish and had turned itself into a thriving artificial reef. The Exuma bank is so barren that I was often disappointed by its lack of interesting sea life but it wasn't that there wasn't any, it was just that they all hugged the reefs, the only place where food could be found.

The truck, the aeroplanes and the underwater sculptures that abounded in the Bahamas weren't irresponsible pollution by humans, although undoubtably some had been originally. Instead they had been claimed by the sea and turned into something useful, something that gave a perfect habitat for life.

Once more I was reminded of the dystopian worlds of J.G. Ballard's novels. The withering, rotting buildings reclaimed by the jungle or the sea or the desert, depending on which of his books you read. There are already ghost towns on this earth, their inhabitants having been evacuated or fleeing some disaster or, more simply, leaving after the gold rush, the oil rush, the fuel rush. They squat alone, slowly being consumed by the natural world and assimilated back in as novel habitats for nesting creatures.

The further north we sailed through the Bahamas, the more built-up the islands became. Huge motorboats pumped out music, filled with cheering tourists that would speed past us, causing huge surges of wash that would knock the light winds from our sails.

I had little desire to visit the Bimini Islands where Hemingway had spent much of his time. Less than fifty miles from the Florida coast, I had been told that they were merely an extension of a Florida beach, filled with bars.

I had been tempted by the Abacos though, seaward of the Biminis and right on the edge of the Atlantic Ocean. Marsh Harbour had been touted as the best place to go for provisioning and, while it did have large supermarkets, it wasn't a good place to anchor and we were swiftly driven out to the surrounding cays for shelter. The nearest and safest was Man-O-War Cay.

Like a tropical version of Sark, there was a slight feudal atmosphere about Man-O-War Cay. The houses were the best kept I'd seen in the Bahamas and the gardens were thriving with colourful bushes and fruit trees.

The few roads were dusty and lined with hedges, something I hadn't seen at all in the rest of the islands. With neat signs painted in pastels and even picket fences, it didn't take long for me to feel distinctly odd.

With no cars on the little island, the few residents that were travelling around passed me on golf carts and didn't meet my eye. Again, strange considering the majority of Bahamians were so cheerful they'd practically run you down just to say 'hi' and smile. Also, everybody who passed me and turned into their huge houses, was white.

The cay was beautiful in an entirely different way to the other Bahamian islands farther south. While the outer islands were rugged with flat scrubland and wild, white beaches; Man-o-War Cay was groomed, preened, planted and organised. If the outer islands were parkland, Man-o-War was the palace gardens.

As I wandered around I started wondering if it was some kind of enclave for the richest white Americans, after all, every house had a little hand-painted sign at the gate with the family's name and a bell with which to announce yourself. Everybody drove around on golf carts. It was so unlike any of the Caribbean or Bahamas I had previously been to that it was almost like a part of Universal Studios. It just didn't feel real.

But the cay wasn't a piece of paradise exclusively for rich Americans, it was more an example of the intriguing history of this enormous and scattered archipelago and how there is really no such thing as a typical Bahamian island.

Man-o-War Cay is, in fact, a historic Loyalist community and most of the residents are related to the original settlers who fled America at the tail end of the civil war. You could be forgiven for thinking you've travelled back in time as you walk around the staid island.

Settled in the late 1790s, the Cay received a shipwrecked boy, Benjamin Albury, whose legacy can now be seen everywhere on the island. There remain many Alburys on the island and the graveyard is almost exclusively filled with members of this island family name.

Boatbuilders by trade, the Albury boats gained a great deal of local fame and the shipbuilding work sustained the island community for decades. With the settlers originating from New England, the island is said to closely resemble a New England seaside village – I wouldn't know because I've never been to New England but I can imagine it's true.

Staunchly proud of their history and familial loyalties to this slice of Bahamian paradise, there is still, nonetheless, a bizarre feel to the island. Its bizarreness is highlighted in its historic and continued racial segregation.

The late Michael Craton, who specialised in Bahamian and Caribbean history, studied the archipelagic community and wrote:

Today, except for a handful of government officials the entire population of the original settlement remains 'Conchy Joe' white, the majority are blood relations and more than one quarter rejoice in the single surname Pinder. Similar configurations, (albeit with a higher 'sprinkling' of blacks) are also found on the offshore cays in the Abacos including Guana Cay, Elbow Cay, Man o' War Cay and the mainland settlement of Cherokee. While the obvious and explicit forms of racism may have subsided in these communities, their values and preference for living apart from others encourages social distancing and latent forms of racism.

Bay Sreet, Black Power and the Conchy Jones,
Michael Craton, 1998

Nearby Spanish Wells, for instance, soon became an all-white island shortly after settlement to the extent that black people weren't allowed to stay overnight on the island. Michael Craton and fellow author Gail Saunders write in their book *Islanders in the Stream: A History of the Bahamian People*:

This precedent has allowed the modern inhabitants of Spanish Wells to justify their tradition of racial segregation by perpetuating the myth that it originated from an abhorrence of the slavery system which equated race with class, conveniently ignoring the fact that at least some early white inhabitants of St George's Cay were slaveholders who kept their slave bondsmen on the nearby mainland.

Regardless of the historic choices for racial segregation or not, the exclusive atmosphere of the Cay got to me. Not only did it highlight my sheer ignorance of Bahamian history and culture but it also made me feel as though I was walking through the past, and not in a good way.

The Albury surname proliferates in a way I had never encountered in a community before and, after reading up on the island's history, and that of the nearby Loyalist Islands, genuine dedication to genealogy also proliferates – after all, the Loyalist islanders needed to know just how closely related they were to each other before they could marry within their community.

So it was walking around the alcohol-free and historic boat building island of Man-o-War that I really discovered the complexity of Bahamian culture and just how little I knew about the island nation that I was living in.

Over three months we'd worked our way north from Great Inagua and

Mayaguana, the two most southerly islands, all the way up to Marsh Harbour in Abaco, the northern-most. Hurricane battered and utterly flat, the Bahamian islands were easy sailing by my standards.

Even with the fickle, clocking winds, the Bahamas felt like a safe place to sail. Almost always sheltered from the true Atlantic, there was always an island within a day sail and always a safe anchorage within a 24-hour sail, usually much less. But I was finding myself increasingly restless with island after island of flat scrubland.

Walking on Elizabeth Island in the Exumas, I came across one of the reasons for my lassitude. A bird, singing in the low bushes overlooking the cliffs. It was a songbird, chortling away before pausing, listening for a reply and then continuing with its song. It caught my attention because I couldn't remember the last time I'd heard a bird singing. Real birdsong, not just the call of a hungry seabird.

I stopped and looked at the bird and then I realised something, where were all the animals?

I hadn't seen a land mammal since Providencia, I realised. Aside from dogs on yachts, I hadn't seen any sign of pets in the Bahamas whatsoever and certainly nothing wild. The Bahamas do have resident communities of endemic iguanas but they can only be found in very specific places and seemed to be one of the largest non-human creatures in the country at all.

I didn't know what I needed to see, but something, some life. Instead, the barren islands yielded little birdlife and not a single mammal I could find. The Bahamas technically does have animals but they keep themselves hidden and are nothing like the eruption of life I saw in Panama. The absence of mammals made sense, the land was arid and the islands very small, it would be difficult for mammals to excel surely. But it made an impact on me, I realised how much I needed to just hear other animals, hear the calls of birds, the rustling of mammals and sight of a cat curled up on a wall.

Having grown up in the New Forest in England, large mammals were as integrated into my childhood as the forest itself. They were always there. Roaming free across the national park, horses, ponies, cattle and donkeys had ownership of the roads of my childhood, not the motorists. Deer in their multitudes would stop munching and stare at me on walks mere miles from my house before bounding off.

With the seafront less than a mile from my father's house, as an irate teenager I would take sulky walks to the clifftops and pause in the dark, hearing the thumps of rabbits as they alerted each other to my presence and leapt for the safety of their burrows, tails flashing in the dark.

Above, there were endless buzzards circling, and below, hedgehogs would squeak and rustle in the garden. Frogs proliferated in the pond and crows would bounce around the lawn, infuriating my step-mother's cat lying in the sunshine.

Animals and birds were such a deeply ingrained part of my life in the UK without me having much to do with them at all. They were there and I loved them for it.

As Alex and I were walking back to our dinghy, lugging heavy bags of freshly cleaned laundry, I noticed that there was a lizard sat on his shoulder. I stopped him and pulled him to the side of the road, laughing at the tiny hitchhiker who eyed me curiously.

'You've made a friend,' I said, reaching up and scooping the lizard up. The little creature climbed nonchalantly onto my hand and cocked its head, showing no fear or wish to flee. We stared at him, appreciating this rare connection to an animal, so starved of it were we.

I crooked my finger and the lizard rearranged himself so he remained upright, his miniature hands spread out across my skin. I wanted to keep him forever, name him and talk to him, look after him and let him live on my boat as if it were his. But he didn't need looking after, he was a lizard already in his ideal environment. It was my selfish need for animal company that he would be serving.

With great reluctance, I found a large leafy tree and pressed my hand against it. The lizard didn't budge. I gave him a nudge with another finger but he climbed onto that one instead and looked at me. I looked imploringly at Alex.

"Come on, we still need to buy vegetables," he said, "and I'm getting hot." I all but picked the lizard up and placed him on a big flat leaf where he contentedly sat.

"Bye," I said to him and walked away, determined not to look back.

With flat land and many islands, the Bahamas had the best 3G signal of any Caribbean or Atlantic island I had visited. Most inhabited islands had BaTelCo mobile towers and with the Bahamian SIM card that I improbably bought in the far outpost of Mayaguana, I had constant and fast access to the internet.

But it had been two years since I last had an on-demand internet connection on a daily basis. I had grown very used to spending just fifteen minutes here and there on poor connections replying to emails or checking my bank balance. In the few places I found internet good enough to use, I spent it solely working or gathering research for my freelancing copywriting work.

With the abundance of 3G connection in the Bahamas, I was drawn back into the orgy of information that is the internet and with it I felt the world around me blur and fade out. So instantly absorbing and so utterly full of seemingly fascinating things, news stories, gossip, potential opportunities, guidance, funny pictures, networks of people and everything else... I could quickly glance at my phone and not look up for another 30 minutes, wondering if I had even breathed in that time.

People of my generation were eased into the internet at exactly the same time we began being eased into the adult world. We never learned to live without it in adulthood or even our teenage years and it grew insidiously until we were flies trapped in its incomprehensibly large and tangled web.

It wasn't until I really got back onto the internet that I realised the all-encompassing nature of its distraction or its incessant whispering in your ear. As soon as I was back looking at all the social media sites, even the news, the idea that I was not doing enough, not achieving enough, not making the most of my life, reared its head again.

Straight away I was bombarded with travel blogs that were raking in the money, why didn't I have a blog? Why did I shut down my blog two months into the voyage when surely that was when I should've been focusing on it the most? Why wasn't I already successful in life (whatever that means)? Why didn't I have a huge following? Why wasn't I uploading pictures of my lunch every day?

I could see all those people running huge blogs, writing books, creating courses, setting up global meetings and generally being wonder-people. What was I doing with my Instagrammable lifestyle and Tweetable experiences? I was lazily making pancakes for breakfast, snorkelling around the boat and spending an inordinate amount of time reading books and looking at charts. Most of the time, I forgot the internet even existed, it just didn't have much of a bearing on my day-to-day life because it simply wasn't there.

But once I was in the Bahamas I suddenly realised that I wasn't doing enough, I wasn't working enough, pitching enough, building my career enough, replying to my actual editors often enough and generally not doing as much as other 27 years olds. I didn't really know what they were doing either but with '30 Under 30' lists I could see what my age group were capable of. And all I'd done was sail around an ocean.

I went from basking in the sailing life to worrying endlessly about if I had just wasted the last two years exploring when I could've built a travel blog of 100k subscribers. What could I quantify in my achievements? In a world where everything must be quantified and validated by the masses, most people just looked at me a little stumped when I said I wasn't sailing around the world, I was just… sailing.

I felt like I was missing something, especially because I was in the Bahamas and surely everybody loves the Bahamas? A word is synonymous with 'luxury, beach paradise', I'd never imagined I would one day wind up on these islands. They seemed like a place honeymooning celebrities would go to and so surely they must be marvellous.

I was charmed by the Bahamas, by the expanse of islands, the truly clear water and the unadulterated friendliness of most of the islanders. But I suddenly missed the sprawling jungle of Panama, the volcanoes and hills of the West Indies and the constant chattering of the birds and animals. The Bahamas felt, in a way, barren.

With American foods clogging up the supermarkets, Georgetown in Exuma had the distinct feeling of an extension of Florida. Hundreds upon hundreds of American yachts, catamarans and motorboats dropped their anchors in Elizabeth Harbour at the beginning of the winter season and didn't move again until spring. It was suffocating.

We sailed in and out of Georgetown after weeks to other parts of the Bahamas, always returning for the unrivalled shelter and free water supplies put on by the main supermarket for sailors. When we arrived at night, sailing through the tricky, reefy entrance by wind alone, the lights of the anchorage never failed to shock me. After two years, never had I seen so many boats in one place, their anchor lights at the top of their masts in the American way, in no way showing the exact location of the boat but instead providing a new milky way of lights.

The cruiser society that swarms into Georgetown every year for 6 months does huge amounts for the local economy. In fact, cruisers can add an extra thousand or more to the small population of the Exumas. Georgetown is well set up to cope with them as well and it is, in general, a symbiotic community.

But it was so… American. Each morning came the radio net, a VHF radio conference call of sorts that is so at odds with how European sailors use their VHF radios that I found it utterly bemusing. American sailors have a tendency to use VHF as if it were a mobile phone, with invitations for lunch, chats about last night and discussions on the basket weaving lesson about to take place on the beach. European sailors use the VHF for emergencies, yacht-to-container ship communications and when entering marinas. And not even for most of that.

I'd had my first taste of VHF radio nets in Grenada, where another semi-permanent American cruising community resided. The nets have an agenda, or sections that remain the same every day. Typically beginning with urgent items and weather reports, the nets then go into new arrivals, departures, community events, buying and selling (or swapping, for the purposes of customs listening in).

Conducted with amazing zeal and almost always at 8am on the dot, the radio nets have certain voices that you get to know. A fairly matriarchal basis, the nets are filled with what my Canadian friend terms a 'Barb', the loud, boisterous women who collect people around them like a mother hen, are never afraid to put anyone in their place and selflessly give help and advice to any who require it. And who are almost always called 'Barb' in fictional depictions.

With Ladies Bible Study, basket weaving, volleyball, talks, conch horn making classes and myriad other events, the Elizabeth Island side of Georgetown resembled the Floridian retirement village of my imagination. With outboards big enough to power a dinghy twice the size, every day cruising couples would power the mile across from Elizabeth Island's anchorages, favoured for their shelter from prevailing winds, and tie up to the dinghy dock in Georgetown's harbour. From there they'd fan out, visiting the two supermarkets, the post office and filling up the open air bars with their laptops and tablets, arranging t-shirt designing competitions and regattas with dog parades and coconut throwing events.

Few of these cruisers, having motored south from the USA, ever travelled further than the Exumas but they had undoubtedly found their niche. Nowhere in the Caribbean was as easy to live on a boat with the possible exception of Grenada and Martinique, but Martinique's Frenchness and EU status turned off the Americans.

European sailors weren't very prolific in the Bahamas, most probably because, having almost exclusively sailed west across the mid-Atlantic, they were too busy exploring the West Indies. In the year or two most cruisers take to complete their Atlantic circuit, the Bahamas, (with its hurricane history), just doesn't fit into the timetable. It's also too far north to be a good place to set off on the return Atlantic crossing, most sailors preferring Antigua or Saint Martin.

So it was understandable that Americans and Canadians had the monopoly on the Bahamas. The chain requires no overnight passages for those who didn't want them. After all, the Bahamian islands of Bimini are just 40 miles from Florida and you can island hop by day from there south through the chain. Sailing simply becomes a lot harder south of the Bahamas, out of protection of the islands and into the ocean. Few American sailors I met in the Bahamas had even been as far south as the Bahamian outer islands. Georgetown and its neighbour Long Island, were as far as the Americans went south and Saint Martin was often as far as the Europeans went north.

The only exception were the sailors heading for the Virgin Islands, an expensive place to sail with buoy charges and few anchoring spots but a territory half owned by the USA, allowing Americans the ease of working. The Virgins were also a hub of charter companies, another reason the average cruiser may want to avoid them.

The Bahamas has hundreds of uninhabited cays and islets and yet few of the inhabited islands have any real semblance of provisioning. In Mayaguana we stepped into a crumbling shop, the door opened to us by the owner, only to find the shelves completely empty with a single tin of American hotdogs on the dusty wood. The owner left briefly, presumably to give us time to pick and choose what we wanted to buy and Alex and I stood staring at each other in total confusion.

"What does he think we're going to buy?" I whispered.

"Stand next to that shelf, I want to take a photo," said Alex.

Sailors become preternaturally obsessed with sourcing food. It doesn't take much time at all for sailing to utterly break down even the choosiest of eaters and much time is spent finding out where to restock. I had no idea before we left Europe just how hard it would be to find food and it was a constant source of distraction but also amusement.

The West Indies were rich in fruit and tropical vegetables as well as rice and eggs. The French islands were havens of outstanding food, often flown in from mainland Europe on the regular Paris flights but the Bahamas, for all its luxurious marketing, was the hardest place to find food. Growing almost nothing in-country, almost everything is imported from the USA with huge prices attached.

The Bahamas was the only place I have ever seen an onion priced separately, slightly moulding, at $1.71. Fresh fruit and vegetables were immensely expensive as was tinned food. Meats and tins were from

America, packed full of salt, sugar and long lists of ingredients that simply shouldn't ever reach the human digestive system.

Unable to spearfish due to laws and the ciguatera poisoning that affects north Caribbean reef fish, our quality of nutrition was waning frustratingly. I was worrying about how we were going to adequately provision in a country with such limited quality and expensive food.

Provisioning for a projected 3-week-long journey would mean stocking up with enough food for 2 months as a minimum. With excellent weather, we could reach the Azores in around 20 days but with storms, calms or breakages that could turn into 8 weeks or longer with no great difficulty. The North Atlantic is a very different place from the mid-Atlantic's balmy trade winds.

Restocking in the Canaries had been one huge day of Supermarket Sweep. With cheap tins and jars of every vegetable under the sun and vast ranges of rices, pastas, grains and legumes, the packing away of our mountain of food had filled me with excitement of all the future meals I'd enjoy across the rolling ocean.

But in the Bahamas, the tins were at least twice the price and contained less nutritional value. We sailed north 200 miles to Marsh Harbour after we heard the provisioning was excellent but found just bigger supermarkets similarly filled with American food.

We flirted heavily with the idea of sailing back down to Saint Martin and watched the forecast for days, but it soon became apparent that we were just too late in the season, the trade winds were bending northwards meaning Saint Martin would be directly into the wind.

As the voyage back across the Atlantic loomed in my mind and in my immediate future, I grew more and more restless. It was the start of the return journey, it was real and I felt as though I had reached the tipping point; the summit of the rollercoaster. From now on all I could think of was Europe.

Chapter 13

Riding The Gulf Stream Home

One does not discover new lands without consenting to lose sight of the shore for a very long time.

Andre Gide

We'd been at sea for ten days when it occurred to me that I'd changed quite a lot. I was helming the boat with the engine on, under full sail while trying to drink a cup of coffee and keep an eye on the huge squall immediately abeam. I was also totally naked. Even at this latitude the spitting rain was chilled and when the boat needs you, the boat needs you, no time for clothing.

The concept of helming naked after two hours of sleep overnight, in the rain somewhere around 800 miles away from land would've horrified me, if it had been suggested before this trip. Not the nakedness itself, per se. More like the sheer discomfort of the situation. I don't like being uncomfortable with such a vehemence that I've avoided plenty of probably enjoyable things in life purely so I could remain warm.

So what then was I doing out here, in the deeply ruffled Atlantic Ocean? What exactly was I doing on what would turn out to be a 27-day ocean crossing during which not only would I not sleep for more than 2 or 3 hours at a time, but in which I would also be permanently too hot, too cold and increasingly underweight? If I truly hated discomfort, then why was I living, long term, aboard a boat with a floor space of around 3 sqm?

Within just three days of leaving the Bahamas, I had spotted lightning on the horizon. There are lots of frightening things at sea when you're an offshore sailor (or even coastal sailing) and while hitting a submerged container was probably close to the top, it was really lightning that truly frightened me.

While the number of containers lost from ships per year is difficult to pin down, it seems that at least hundreds per year fall into the sea during bad weather as a result of poor stowage and that number could be far higher. Considering that some containers are capable of floating for months on end, often just below the surface and certainly invisible at night, there was a constant niggle in the back of my mind. Especially as there was a much larger amount of commercial traffic in the North Atlantic than the mid-Atlantic.

But while floating containers worried me, it was lightning that really concerned me. Because when there's lightning it's right there, in your face, threatening you.

There is no real consensus about what happens to yachts that are struck by lightning. Plenty are, but the results seem utterly dependent on where the lightning struck the yacht, what type of yacht it was and the general temperament of the lightning itself. Sometimes the damage was dead electrical items, sometimes small fires, sometimes holes punched in the hull and sometimes nothing at all. But lightning burning through the hull below the waterline would sink a boat in a flash, quite literally, and, although we were only a few hundred miles offshore, I didn't fancy floating around in our liferaft. And for that matter, would the liferaft even open? Many didn't.

These worries were mine alone, Alex chose to worry about things as they happen rather than soak himself in the endless and destructive anxiety of 'what if?' But, as I sat below deck in my heavy weather clothing, the sail-less boat rolling sickeningly from side to side in a strong squall, and closed my eyes against the blinding lightning, I discovered something. It wasn't that bad.

Due to the relentless squalls, the pleasant 12 knot wind had become alternately 28 knots gusts or 3 knot calms. We'd opted to take the sails down entirely with the exception of a small scrap of genoa and simply wait out the thunderstorms. Although the sea had been incredibly flat before, the vicious squalls were kicking up an equally vicious sea and, without the pressure of the mainsail up, our full-keeled boat was practically rolling the gunwales under.

I was on watch while Alex lay wedged in his bunk and normally this scenario, i.e. complicated and stressful night watch, would have troubled me no end. Yes, of course I was wishing it was over as I tried to support myself in the violent motion, but really, it wasn't that bad.

We didn't get struck by lightning and I didn't even exert too much energy in cursing the weather because it was finally beginning to sink in that it wasn't really the weather that was the problem. It was my reaction to it.

So I was standing naked at the helm in the morning light and it was only the very beginning of my watch. Fickle, squally winds were particularly tricky because you have to constantly adjust the boat to deal with them. Stable winds of any velocity are far easier because you can set the correct sail plan to cope and monitor the situation from there. Even when the winds get very strong you can just simply take down the sails, stick some warps out the back and relax. But fickle winds were a constant battle.

At least, that's how I had always viewed them. In fact, that's how I had always viewed most uncomfortable situations: as a battle. But why were some people so readily able to deal with challenging situations, if not with actual relish, then certainly some level of keenness? And why did I struggle and hate it so much?

Sailing across the Atlantic is better for the soul than a meditative retreat because, at some level, it is a meditative retreat. With added squalls. I spent most of the crossing considering my personality; mainly its bad points. I traced irritations, dislikes and discomforts back to their cause and, while you'd think this would be a painful process, it was actually incredibly liberating.

That's how I worked out one thing, possibly the most crucial part of enjoying sailing. When it's raining in England and I'm without a coat or umbrella or a place to shelter, I know I'm truly done for. I no longer hurry, I don't run or stand beneath a leaky tree. I slow down and I marvel at the rain. I relax, relinquish and allow myself to become absolutely and utterly soaked, right down to my underwear, to my skin, to my bones.

It seems like a silly thing to do when I dislike being cold and wet. But at some point in my history I must've worked out that the rain doesn't respond to dislike and there's nothing worse than being partially wet. Nothing worse than that pervading dampness when your jeans have gotten wet and the water seeps through to your thighs as you sit down. But in the same way, there are few things more pleasurable than being absolutely and utterly soaking wet and fully clothed.

The key to my acceptance of being the type of English woman perennially ill-prepared for the downpours my country is famous for is just that, acceptance. Stop resisting the difficult things and they suddenly stop being so difficult.

To this end, I wasn't tense and irritated standing at the helm. I was relaxed and curious about the situation and not only a little amused at how I would look to the average landlubber. I wasn't dancing in the rain, but I was enjoying the feel of sub-tropical freshwater on my naked skin as I tried to drink freshly made stovetop espresso from the old Wedgewood mug that came with the boat.

"Tropical storm Bonnie heading NE to South Carolina. Expect…" The SSB radio made a sequence of white noises and from then on it was just, "squalls… strong… north of… tschhhhhh…"

This wasn't the first time we'd heard about Bonnie. Or, *Bonnie*, as we were increasingly coming to know her as, with an exasperated exhalation. We'd first picked up a weather report about her progress as a tropical wave travelling westwards from the Cape Verdes and then again as a depression near the West Indies but all had gone quiet on the Bonnie front for almost a week. I'd thought her gone for good after exhausting herself on the hot beaches of the Caribbean. But no.

We hadn't picked up any weather reports for the first three quarters of our passage westwards across the Atlantic, having only SSB receiving available to us. The eastward passage started with strong radio forecasts on clear nights as we were considerably closer to Boston and Florida, the nearest transmitting forecast stations.

But it's not really down to distance so much as atmospheric conditions. I didn't know the sun affected radio signals. I was still learning every day.

SSB radio signals work best when there is little atmospheric disturbance to scatter the signal. Without disturbance, they can practically travel around the world. Clear nights saw the forecasts coming through as though the host was sat in the next room (had we had a 'next room' anyway). But cloudy or squally nights scatter the signals and all we got was fuzziness. However, the further east we travelled, the earlier the sun rose and, within two weeks, the forecasts were almost impossible to pick up.

The scraps of forecast we'd got, combined with the odd yacht close by who we could hear on the radio talking to the forecaster in Florida, were all we had for the majority of the journey. Occasionally we'd pick up a pressure chart that was just about readable and watch as Bonnie disappeared and reappeared along the US's Eastern seaboard.

Alex was in charge of attempting most of the forecasts as I'd lie in my bunk, pillow jammed over my head to stop the aggressive white noise and chatter of the SSB. Days went past and Bonnie again reared her head, being visited by US Airforce Hurricane Hunters to establish her status.

With no consistent forecasts, Bonnie weighed heavily on my mind as the pressure charts we could receive suggested she had plans to follow us across the Atlantic. Further north a yacht was already facing gale-force winds and huge short swell due to another low pressure careering across the north Atlantic.

Repeatedly it looked like Bonnie would be upon us within days and she doggedly stuck to our tail. Each time I awoke the first thing I'd ask was about the weather, was she here yet, could she be seen approaching on the western horizon?

It wasn't Bonnie in the end that got us, although by that point I almost wanted to meet her face to face. I still couldn't believe that a tropical wave, a weather scenario I hadn't even heard of before, could be causing so much concern three weeks later. As we neared the Azores I knew we couldn't stay at such a southern latitude forever, it was time to head north.

With lows leaving the US eastern seaboard every few days, I'd come to terms with the high probability that we'd be caught by something. As Alex always received the forecasts while I was sleeping and then turned off the ailing laptop (I had spilt a glass of red wine over it in the Bahamas) to preserve power, so I rarely got to see the actual charts.

I trusted him to give me accurate rundowns of the weather forecasts though, as long as I picked the right moment. Prone to exaggerating when tired or in a bad mood, it wasn't uncommon for me to receive a 'there are three lows, all of which will probably turn into tropical storms, merge and head right for us,' at which I'd purse my lips and leave him to sleep, knowing that when he woke up rested the forecast would've miraculously turned to, 'a couple of disintegrating lows, maybe maximum winds of 15 knots or so.'

So when he told me that two lows were in fact peeling off the US mainland and heading directly for where we'd be soon and that one at least would be a gale and 'Bonnie will probably come up behind it and squash it against the high, causing the low to stall over the top of us,' I didn't think much of it.

When Alex woke up three hours later I broached the subject again, knowing that his forecast would've moderated as he slept and we'd jaunt off up to Flores in a nice force 4. Except his forecast hadn't changed, it was just now delivered with a rueful smile as opposed to a clipped dismissal.

Within three hours it was gusting 30 knots.

While I was slightly outraged that his boy-cries-wolf habit had tricked me into thinking nothing serious lurked on the horizon, his justification for not telling me about it sooner (he'd known I didn't believe him before) was that I'd only worry about the imminent prospect of getting caught up in a gale. In his opinion, which I shared, there would've been no point in us heading south as we couldn't have sailed fast enough to avoid the strong winds and would just be going further out of our way.

We always knew this and, while we'd altered course to avoid the lows in the previous weeks, we were now too close to the path of the centre for it to be worth it. In fact, it was due to our slow speeds that we hadn't worried about our lack of forecasts on the Canaries to Caribbean crossing. After all, in the trade winds the winds will either be light, middling or strong, you just had to deal with whatever came up.

The pressure had been dropping but then it plummeted. While we had been sailing along in 1014 millibars, the barometer was now down below 1000 and falling.

Sailing in 35 knots was a lot more pleasant than thinking about sailing in a 'gale' and the relative ease of doing 4 knots without having any sails up was surprisingly restful. After all, you don't have to worry about reefing if there aren't any sails to reef.

The sea state changed quickly, the profound blue changing to a dull grey with spume flying off the waves. As the seas built, a slight cross swell formed, bringing three metre waves sloshing over the deck from the aft quarter. Sloshing perhaps isn't the right word. More like slamming.

The warps that we were now towing out the back were slowing us down so that we wouldn't zoom off down the faces of the waves and instead the stern merely slumped off the back of them. Down below from my bunk it felt like we were practically gliding along in near flat water. I kept thinking the wind had simply gone away.

After a non-eventful watch where I spent most of my time wedged on the top step of the companionway, I woke Alex up and handed over. It was around 9am and I was more than looking forward to my three hours of cosiness, even if sleeping would be difficult in the daylight.

As I climbed into the nest I had created within my lee-clothed bed, we heard a clank against the mast. It wasn't loud enough to be shocking or even really marked enough to pay much attention to in that second but when it happened again and again a few seconds later, the strangeness of the noise registered.

Alex stuck his head out the companionway hatch and I buried my head under my pillow away from the light, please don't be anything, please don't be anything.

"Ah" said Alex, before going on deck. He came back a few minutes later and started making a cup of tea.

"Well?" I managed from my bed of duck down.

"The spinnaker snap-shackle chafed through its loop and has wrapped itself around the forestay and the mast," he lit the stove and looked at me as though this was a minor inconvenience.

"That means we can't put any sails out. At all!" I said, horrified. He nodded.

"Yes," he said thoughtfully, "it is a problem."

His casualness was infuriating me as I left my warm nest and went out to look for myself, hoping there was an easily solvable solution and he was just keeping it from me. But no, the spinnaker halyard had indeed rapped itself around the top of the almost entirely furled forestay and then the top of the mast including a few loops around the stays for good measure. The heavy snap-shackle on the end was, in some balletic display of liberation, waving around and intermittently banging into the mast creating new tangles with itself.

"What are we going to do?" I asked him.

"Well I'll have a go at trying to flick it free," he said. I thought, well that's not going to work.

He spent at least half an hour on deck with the bottom end of the halyard, trying to jerk the tangled end free but it was well and truly overjoyed with its new-found freedom and was too busy embarking on the Atlantic's greatest example of a cat's cradle to take any notice.

I lay in bed creating doomsday scenarios where we'd be drifting for days, waiting for the sea to calm sufficiently so that one of us could go up the mast and retrieve it, by which time we'd be far south of the Azores and would have to beat up into the wind for more days.

By the time Alex came back below, having failed in his attempt but in no way disheartened, I was convinced that it was an impossible mission and the following lows would ensure the sea was never flat enough to ascend the mast. We didn't carry enough fuel to motor the remaining 140 nautical miles to Horta and Flores, just 30 nautical miles away, was soon to be directly upwind as we drifted along in the waves beneath it.

The wind did in fact begin to drop, but that only made us roll more as the large swell remained. Although we could have easily raised the mainsail to 3rd, or even 2nd reef, we were worried that the spinnaker halyard would foul the main halyard, preventing us from lowering the sail again should the wind increase. The only thing worse than not being able to hoist the sails was to have the sails up but not be able to lower them again.

I smothered a pillow over my head and tossed and turned, desperate for sleep but knowing that the motion and the frustration would keep me miles from it.

"We might be able to hoist the gaff to the top of the mast," mused Alex out loud.

"No," I said. "We can't have the gaff waving around on a rope, it'll kill us!" He lapsed into silence again.

Around an hour later, Alex asserted that he had a plan and that it would work. Although it involved the gaff, complete with its savage hook, sloshing around the top of the mast, I didn't have the energy to dispute the likelihood of it working and instead got on my wet weather gear and hunkered down in the cockpit to do as I was told.

First we tied the main halyard around the boom to support it and removed the topping lift to use for the gaff as it had a better angle, being craned slightly off the top of the mast. We then tied the topping lift to the top of the gaff and another rope to the bottom of the gaff and the other end of the topping lift, in order to create a pulley system. In squally drizzle and three metre waves, I cannot describe how spurious this all looked.

Alex sent me up on deck to the mast so I could slacken off the spinnaker halyard slowly as he used the gaff to pull it down; in theory. I huddled at the mast, one hand hanging onto a free cleat and one on the end of the halyard. The violent motion of the boat was far more pronounced on deck, even though the mast was just three metres further forward from the cockpit and less than a metre higher.

I thought about my suggestion of me trying to go up the mast and saw immediatley how impossible it would be. Holding on at deck level was difficult and I would've been afraid had I not been clipped on. Holding on at spreader level or masthead level? Completely ridiculous.

Controlling the direction of the gaff hook was not only difficult because of the simple rope pulley system, but the rolling of the boat sent it swinging to and fro continuously. Alex repeatedly managed to hook it over a section of the tangled spinnaker halyard but the hook would immediately swing free.

Then I watched in amazement as the hook held and Alex tugged down, slipping the tangled end free of at least several of its complex wraps. He called to me and I eased off the halyard slightly, the halyard dragging out its tangles. The hook swung free but now we knew, now I knew, it was possible.

I was jubilant twenty minutes later when we'd freed and pulled through the spinnaker halyard. I just couldn't believe that such an outlandish idea had worked in these conditions. A giant rusting hook on a pulley system while the boat was rolling around all over the place? Not for the first time I was amazed at what the skipper was capable of.

By evening the seas had lessened to the point where it was possible to close reach up to Flores. The idea that we might make landfall by first light was barely comprehensible after the lengths I'd gone to to convince myself that we'd be stranded for days. As I sat out in the cockpit in the distinctly cool night air, I watched the loom of Flores' southern lighthouse sign out its unique code and felt the anticipation rise within me.

I fell asleep gratefully at midnight after what felt like days of sleepless off-watches. And I did manage to sleep, the deep and complete sleep that only comes from relief.

I woke up at 4:15am and jumped out of bed. How had I slept for four hours? I was expecting to be woken up at 2am for my next watch as we'd arranged the night watches so that Alex got four hours of sleep followed by just a two hour watch to enable him to rest enough.

I stuck my head into the cockpit to find Alex nodding his head distractedly to whatever was playing through his headphones and looking perfectly at home in his bright yellow Guy Cotton jacket. Because we'd been lackadaisical about changing time zones as well as not being 100% sure what time zone the Azores were in anyway, the sun had already risen and the ocean was bathed in the coral glow of post-dawn.

"Good morning sleepyhead!" he said, pulling his headphones down around his neck.

"You didn't wake me up!" I croak, extremely glad of this fact.

"You looked like you could use the sleep," he replied, "and I'm not tired. I had a cup of coffee"

Alex only drinks decaffeinated coffee as a general rule, so when he has a caffeinated espresso he's not unlike someone in the middling stages of a speed binge.

"Look," he said, "Flores!"

I looked around the cloudy sprayhood and, sure enough, Flores was there like a shock of green and grey. An impossibly huge body of land after 27 days at sea. We were only 7 miles off, a distance that, in the low-lying Bahamas would render land invisible but here so grand were the verdant cliffs that it looked considerably closer.

Waterfalls poured from the heights, straight into the ocean and patchwork fields blanketed the hills in the landscape version of a sign saying 'Europe'. A cloud sat exclusively on the very top of the island, a damp hat promising endless supplies of fresh mountain water awaiting us.

The idea of freshwater as a rarity had become firmly embedded in my mind over the last two years and even more so during my time in the Bahamas where it never seems to rain at all.

For a month we'd been using freshwater as frugally as physically possible as we lacked any method of making it at sea but really we'd been doing it much longer than that. Flores, in contrast, promised an orgy of freshwater and even from sea I could see that the island was rich in greenery that only comes from the oft-rained upon.

I heard the familiar whoosh of a dolphin exhaling nearby and a small but merry band had raced to join us as we closed in on the island.

I struggled into numerous layers of clothing and took the helm in the brightening morning as Alex went below to make coffee and porridge.

Looking at the island brought more emotions than I had expected because I still imagined the Azores to look foreign. In reality they were sub-tropical Portuguese islands but in my heart they were home, because they were green and forested and farmland and damp and European. My veins sung with the call of familiarity after 18 months in the bitter heat of the Caribbean and the barren lands of the Bahamas.

Flores Marina was small and tight, but as I handed a spring line to another British sailor who'd put aside his cup of tea to help us, I could've kissed the pontoon. I jumped off the boat and secured the bow, holding onto *Berwick Maid*'s pulpit from an angle only possible in a marina berth, and clutching it, gripping it to let her know she'd down well, she'd got us back to our continent.

I looked around to find the marina full of European flags, boats from Germany, the Netherlands, France and Norway all flapped gently in the wind. Each yacht showed signs of offshore sailing, of serious effort and sleepless nights. And that was the thing about the Azores I would come to realise. While the liveaboards of the Bahamas were day sailors and motor sailors, the sailors of the Azores all had to cross at least 900 miles of open ocean, North Atlantic Ocean, just to get here. Most had come further. As your eyes met across the pontoons, you'd disregard the wind-burnt skin, the tangled hair and the lines of exhaustion etched underneath the lashes, you'd know exactly how each other felt.

As the most remote island of the Azores, Flores is not only two thousand miles from North America and a thousand from mainland Europe, it's also 130 miles from the next Azorean island to the west. It's often the first stop for trans-Atlantic sailors who sail boats less than 40 feet as they can fit into the tiny marina and the majority of yachts resting in the berths when we arrived flew yellow quarantine flags; a symbol that not only had they most probably come from the Americas (otherwise they'd have checked into a previous Azorean island) but also that most had arrived within the last day.

As it turned out, the marina manager had been storm-bound in Horta, Faial, for the last week and the maritime police had taken it as an excuse to not bother checking anybody in during his absence. He arrived the same day as we had, having been trapped in the gale that we'd been swamped by and, within fifteen minutes of our arrival, the maritime police turned up en masse, or at least as en masse as the police workforce could be on such a small island.

Very polite and self-conscious of his English, the policeman who sat in our cockpit filling out paperwork merely looked at our passports and registration documents and had checked us into the country within five minutes. None of the eye rolling or sighing or reasonless waiting that we'd been met with so frequently in the Caribbean islands.

"Welcome to Flores," he said with a bashful smile as he climbed off the boat.

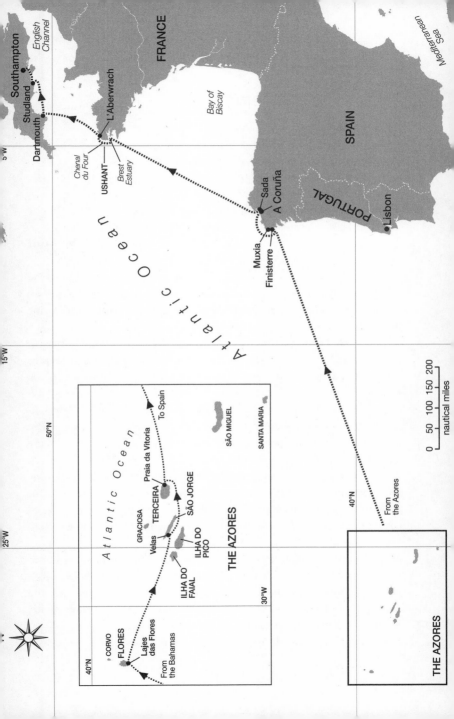

Chapter 14

The Outpost Island

Thousands of tired, nerve-shaken, over-civilised people are beginning to find out
going to the mountains is going home; that wilderness is a necessity.

John Muir

The Azores are remote by anyone's standards. Around 900 miles from the nearest land, they are the ambitious tips of volcanoes drawing everything towards them.

Sat firmly in the path of North Atlantic storms, the sudden heights of the islands rising straight out of the sea from 4000 metre depths creates the near ever-present clouds that continually mist the rolling hills.

So verdant are the nine islands that they are almost entirely self-sufficient food-wise. Extensively farming everything from cows, sheep and bees to bananas, potatoes and even grape vines. Sao Miguel, the largest island, even has a tea plantation.

Fishing was, and is, a huge part of the Azorean culture and economy and more and more the underwater life is becoming the reason for tourism income. This is probably one of the few places where, when you sign up for a whale watching tour, you really are guaranteed to see some whales.

Drenched from a furious rain that trampled over the boat without much warning, the sky cleared all at once as I helmed in fickle winds from Sao Jorge to Terceira. Just there, slightly off the path of the morning sun, I saw a pod of whales idling towards me like small aquatic steam trains, puffing vast clouds of spray into the air.

The islands create huge upwellings of nutrients in an otherwise profoundly large ocean. It seemed as though all species of fish and marine mammals collected there, each species eating the one below it like a game of trophic dominoes.

A perfect snack-stop for every marine creature imaginable, the Azores lie on the migration paths of everyone; tuna, whales, sharks, dolphins, turtles, jellyfish and long-distance sailors. The late spring is a non-stop party as the fish spawn, the water warms and the fishermen take out their tiny day boats and simply pluck tuna out one at a time.

The tuna turn up in their millions each spring for the bait fish that swirl and swarm just beneath the surface and the marinas are more for small fishing boats than trans-ocean yachts.

Much of the fishing is just solo fisherman, bringing back enough to make a little money at the fish market on the quay, enough for dinner. Flores, the most remote of the Azores, is visited by a supply ship once a fortnight and even less if one of the many yearly storms is dragging its heels.

The Floreans simply have their own allotments, neatly laid out behind their small stone houses. With island cheese, meat and vegetables, they want for nothing if the ship is delayed.

This isn't to say that the Azores are some kind of rural backwater. Far from it. The sense of community is evident in every town and village and seldom does a weekend go past in the summer without some form of street party or festival.

I hadn't left the boat all day one Tuesday in Terceira and after dinner Alex suggested we go for an amble. The town of Praia da Vitoria is small and a perfect example of the atmosphere in Portuguese towns where nothing is open before 10am but long evenings are filled with promenade strollers and children eating ice cream.

While beers are €1, it's espresso cups that litter the tables of street cafes and as we walked into the single street of the old town we were considering an after-dinner coffee.

Expecting a fairly empty square, I instead quickly realised that the amount of people milling around was out of proportion for the hour of 9pm. And they were all casually holding little white bowls as they chatted.

The entire street had been turned into a community soup kitchen, where €5 would get you a bowl and you could walk around the many tables, hosted by local communities of old ladies and sample their soups. It was, literally, a soup festival. On a Tuesday night.

Rather like the kinds of jumble sales that haunt school halls at the weekend, each table had a line of ladies sat proudly behind. Some knitting, some drinking and some unveiling dinner plates with squares of orange cake for 40 cents apiece. The lady at the head of the table would wield her ladle at interested parties and spoon soup into outstretched bowls.

'We shouldn't bother with dinner anymore,' I said to Alex, 'we should just trawl the street for pop-up food festivals.'

The week before we'd gone for a leg-stretch in the streets of Velas, a smaller town than Praia, on the neighbouring island of Sao Jorge. We didn't find soup on that amble but we did come across a street where the town's entire population were gathered to eat fresh sardines and drink red wine. In the street. For free.

Disgusted at the lack of exercise I had been doing in the last few months of being at sea and moored in colder water, I decided to start running in Terceira. The marina was tucked deep inside the long, protected bay behind a breakwater and the town had a promenade that ran for two miles from the marina almost all the way down to the commercial port to the south.

Up in the 6:30am fog that often enveloped the town and lent it a damp Dickensian atmosphere, I ran along in the manner of someone who's forgotten that the last time they ran was for a train four years previously. Otherwise known as the stop-start-oh-god-what-am-I-doing manner.

On the third such attempt of the week, the fog was so dense that I was only twenty metres away when a huge stage loomed out of the opacity. Considering it was directly opposite the marina and we hadn't seen it the night before, it must've sprung up overnight.

By mid-afternoon, the stage had an array of huge speakers and a couple of Super Bock bars were hovering on trailers. Another unspoken festival was in the making.

It turned out to be a rock festival, sponsored by Super Bock, the main lager brand of Portugal, and none other than Amigos Açores, the Azorean motorbike club. With an incredible array of Harley Davidsons and classic choppers parked along the promenade opposite the stage, the first evening was dominated by sound loud enough for a stadium and an audience of around a hundred people, a quarter of which were children under ten.

But this wasn't a surprise. Ever since arriving in the Spanish rias over two years previously, I'd quickly come to realise that crowd expectation was unrelated to the size of the stage and the impressive effort put into the lighting displays.

We'd once watched a rock festival in a tiny Spanish town where long-haired rockers belted out their music to five elderly couples, an attentive line of small, cross-legged children and the odd passing jogger. No one seemed perturbed.

So there is nothing remotely sleepy about the Azores. After all, it's an island chain where communities regularly put terse bulls on 100 metre long ropes and let them run into large crowds.

I'd been excited about seeing the famous tourada à corda (literally bull on rope) because, unlike Portuguese bullfighting, which ends in injury and often the later death of the bull, the animal isn't harmed at all. In fact, the bull on the rope is the Portuguese equivalent of setting off a firework in a small room.

While tourada à corda events often take place in the streets, the first one I watched was on the commercial quayside in Velas, Sao Jorge.

A large portion of the dock had been completely hemmed in on three sides by shipping containers with Maersk and Hapag-Lloyd sprawled across the sides. The fourth side was the quay edge leading to chilly water with the odd Portuguese Man-of-War jellyfish sunning itself on the surface.

Four bulls were already huffing in their boxes within the space as perhaps two hundred people clambered up rusting metal and sat on stacked containers, legs swinging over the edge. As many times as I've driven past the huge container farms of Southampton dockyard wanting to get a closer look, not once did I ever think I'd be casually sat on top of one eating an ice cream.

Milling around the central space was around twenty local men complete with jeans, t-shirts and potbellies. A few more spritely 20-something guys were kicking a football around as a long rope was laid out from the bull box across the concrete.

The Pastores, four men in billowy white shirts and black hats picked up a section of rope and a firework was set off to display, as I would come to learn, that there was a bull on the loose.

The door to the box was lifted by a man standing on top and a bull cantered out, looking around to get its bearings. Already many of the people had positioned themselves on the quay edge, ready to jump into the water at a moment's notice but one clearly had his eye on starting the action.

With a pale rag, he sprang in front of the sceptical bull and in a series of sudden, jerky movements, had its full attention. As he danced and jogged around it, it too began to move, running at anyone in its eye-line with a half-hearted spurt of movement.

This wasn't so bad, I thought. It was sort of silly, a safe-ish dance where anyone could jump around and still flee the bull quickly. But it didn't take long for the confusing and erratic movements of the amped up men to irritate it into charging.

The Pastores whipped and twitched the rope to further anger the animal and it pawed the ground as a man squatted low on the ground and waved at it. Bulls do paw the ground. Head low, nose skimming the concrete, the bull lined the man up as it looked out from under its horns.

It charged within seconds at incredible speed and the man took off, looking for an escape. He ran around the bull in a large enough circle for it to no longer see him as a threat and it jogged to a halt, whipping its head around to assess the other people nearby.

A young guy in jeans and a grey t-shirt unravelled a sheaf of carpet and approached the bull. It eyed him, huffing and pushing the rope out of its way. He started running in a tight circle around it, challenging a creature with a larger turning circle and he was close enough to draw the cheers of the audience. Having looped the following animal, he slowed his pace but the bull wasn't giving up. It shot into a burst of energy and he skidded to the ground as he tried to double back behind it.

Horns to the ground, it scooped him up and threw him backwards over its head as though he weighed nothing at all. He landed hard on the concrete but was up in seconds, sprinting off for a gap between the containers, red oozing from a gash on his elbow. The crowd cheered more but the Pastores had done nothing to prevent his injuries and, in fact, couldn't have anyway given the sheer length of the rope and the position of the bull. The rope, I eventually gathered, wasn't for crowd safety, but to enable them to irritate the bull more easily and to aid its eventual reigning in.

After fifteen minutes of this daring game, the bull was reigned in by the men on top of the box pulling in sections at a time, ever-shortening the rope until the bull was half-pulled, half-walked into its box. The firework shot up again and the crowd went to refill their beers.

The second bull was bigger, and the third bigger still, and both seemingly more irate each time. Many men went swallow diving, fully clothed into the water to escape the encouraged charge of the bull, who managed to halt centimetres before going into the water itself. On several occasions it was the bulls horns that threw them in.

While there were moments of panic, for the most part it was all good-humoured. With even slightly injured people brushing themselves off with a smile of pride. The point was to touch the bull on the forehead, right between the horns, and flee without getting hurt.

One of the containers at ground level was open at one end and had a resident population of five beer drinking locals who stuck their heads out and banged on the metal to bring the bull their way before they'd hide inside.

Using large sheets of cardboard they'd found in the container, they flapped them at the bull and shrieked with delight as the bull charged towards them, halting in confusion as they disappeared before its eyes. It took multiple jeers for it to finally learn where they had gone.

Board-shorted and baseball-capped, a man in his mid-twenties danced around the entrance to the container, waving his arms and throwing packing materials in the direction of the bull. It sniffed and pawed the ground with its monstrous hooves. As it charged, the man darted inside the container, his companions' heads all disappearing with him. But while the bull slowed its pace, it didn't stop.

It sniffed the door and then, almost jauntily, trotted inside the container. I clamped my hand over my mouth in horror as bangs and shouts erupted from the huge metal box. The Pastores barely even lifted the slack off the ground. The crowd was half cheering, half waiting. But all I could think was, there is no way past the bull for those men.

With a couple of half-hearted tugs of the rope and a bystander banging the neighbouring container, the bull emerged into the sunlight and jogged out into the space. The men appeared once more at the container's doorway, cheering, filled with adrenaline from their narrow escape. The bull turned and ran at them again and they screamed and ran back inside the container as the bull once more went straight in behind them.

I could not believe what I was seeing, were they insane? If the bull managed to reach them at the end of the 40ft container there would be no stopping it. The banging from inside the container was hideous, like the caged T-Rex in the opening of *Jurassic Park: The Lost World*.

The bull emerged again and charged directly for a man waving at in on the quayside. Surprised by its swift response, he tripped over a huge ship's cleat behind him and jumped into the water.

The fourth and last bull was enormous. A shuddering mass of muscle, horns, hooves and irritation at the heat, the crowd and rope around its neck. It charged at a group the moment it was out of its box, forcing some into the water and some to climb lightning fast up the side of a container, hands hanging down to pull them up. The danger of it was absurd, but it seemed as though the narrower your escape, the more glory you felt.

Each container lining the makeshift arena had a gap between it and the next just wide enough for a human. Little groups huddled in each gap, four or five at most, and would lurch out into the space to distract the bull and make it charge at them, before they ran yelling with excitement back into the gap. But these weren't at all like the bouncy young man at the beginning, who was tossed violently into the air and escaped with a graze and a grin. These were 50, 60-year-old men with shirts tucked into their belted jeans and white hair.

Playing with bulls was most definitely not just a game for the trained and the fit. In fact, no one except the Pastores were there in any formal capacity. The men waving at the bull and opening umbrellas in its face were just locals from the town.

The gap between two of the containers was uneven and here one container had been placed at an angle to extend the arena. This meant that as people ran in, they couldn't keep going to the other side, the gap had a finite capacity.

But people were milling about everywhere, confident of their ability to find an opening somewhere in a hurry or the sea if they could reach it. A group of men spread out from the gap and waved erratically at the huge bull. Some shouting, some waving towels.

The bull looked at them and then looked back to a few guys jeering in the opposite direction. Even boys as young as 14 were crouched on the quayside, ready to jump into the water if the bull came their way. The bull looked back and forth, deciding where the greatest danger lay and the Pastores flicked and slapped the rope against it, riling it into making a decision.

It turned on its heels and threw itself into motion towards the men from the uneven gap and they yelled and ran back to the space between the containers. It was part of it, the chase, the momentary adrenaline rush, the possibility of the bull catching up. But it was the risk that was enjoyable, they didn't expect to be hit.

The gap filled up in a microsecond, perhaps there was an extra person or two who had used it instead of the next one. Who knows. But as the last two men tried desperately to push their way in, the bull caught up to them and slammed into them with extreme force.

It lifted them both up and threw them like rag dolls over its head. Two grown men, one in his thirties, the other pushing 60. They bounced across the bull's back but it was cornered by their bodies, the strange, almost right-angled positioning of the containers and the rope that was catching around its rear ankles.

The younger of the two was dragged into the gap by clawing hands but the bull shunted its horn along the ground as the older man was getting to his feet. It threw its entire, monumental weight into his back, slamming him face first into the side of the shipping container, one of its blunted horns directly on his spine. It bucked its head, lifting him off the ground and I looked away, shoving my head over Alex's shoulder and jamming my lips together.

Whatever I thought I could watch, I just couldn't. I couldn't turn around. I looked at the crowd on the ramp below me and wondered what they thought was happening. The bull was well out of their line of sight, all they would be able to hear was the shouting.

"It's okay, the bull's run off," said Alex. I looked back, reeling from shock. I had never, ever felt like that before. I'd seen plenty of stupid stunts on TV or online, I'd grown up in the era of Jackass, but I'd never seen anything that horrendous in person. So close.

The man was around 30 metres away, lying unmoving on the concrete. His arms and legs were all in line, his head to one side, as though he'd just lain down for a quick nap. But he was utterly still.

The bull had cantered off to the centre of the concrete and, without anyone waving at it or jeering, it seemed quite sedate. It simply stood, wondering what the ceasefire was all about.

The man lay on the ground in full view for several seconds before it was clear that the bull was not going to return, despite its presence nearby. Then a rush of people from the gaps between the containers came and crowded around.

Still the Pastores did not pull the rope in.

An ambulance had been parked behind the container nearest the injured man for the duration but, because the arena was secured to prevent the bull escaping, a sort of huge telehandler had to be driven in to lift the massive container off the ground and move it to enable the paramedics to reach the casualty with a spinal board.

I kept looking from the huddle to the bull and back. The bull was calm and gazing over the sea to the cliffs, no longer interested in the people around it so long as they weren't interested in it.

The paramedics lifted the man onto the spinal board and carried him back to the ambulance without him showing any signs of consciousness that I could see.

The telehandler replaced the container... and the game continued.

A month later we were in the marina in Terceira, at the tail end of a huge festival week, and watching another bull barrelling towards daring men. This time the bull had the full length of Praia Grande to run down, the main beach in Praia da Vitoria town and some sort of obstacle course had been set up.

I hoisted Alex up the mast on an ancient wooden seat with a bag of binoculars and beer and made my way to the end of the pontoon. It was low springs and, although there was a three metre channel cut around the end of the pontoon, Praia Grande beach began just ten or so metres away.

A Portuguese family had set up a picnic table and chairs right on the end next to their small motor boat, and were busy unpacking Eski boxes and shouting to each other to pass the snacks.

There were hundreds of people lining the promenade that ran high up along the back of the beach and at least a further hundred on the beach itself, playing in the tiny surf or just standing around and chatting.

Instead of the open space in Velas, here there were huge tractor tyres partially buried in the sand, providing shelter for the runners. An exaggeratedly large see-saw also stood firmly in the sand and a swing with a seat strung around six feet high sat in the centre.

A commercial green bin had been almost entirely buried in the sand with just its lift-top lid visible and a pole, not unlike a giant swing ball set, was set in the beach to run up, grab and swing around out of the bull's way.

Unlike the bare concrete of the quayside in Velas, this was more than a decades old tradition of running in front of a bull. This was a game.

The first bull sprung out from its crate and cantered along the beach, immediately spotting the mass of people to the right and jogging towards them. The first bull is always the smallest, but adult bulls are between 500 and 1000 kg, so even the small ones are powerful.

The four men on the rope ran after the bull across the sand as the bull swerved down to the sea and careered into the surf, sending swimmers and cocky teenagers scattering for cover.

The day before I'd seen vacada on another beach, young bulls who weren't on a rope but hemmed in by high breakwaters. Hot from their crates, they'd each plunged straight into the sea and swum a good distance before a jet-ski herded them back each time. For animals with such huge bodies and relatively skinny legs, they could swim a lot faster than the average person.

The bull was pulled back onto the sand and stood briefly, dripping from its refreshing swim, before sauntering off down towards the other end of the beach. Even for the brief moments it passed behind the motorboat moored in front of me, I could always tell where it was and which way it was going due to the immense scattering of people in certain directions.

While the bull had been testing the waves, some sort of crack team of bull players had taken up positions on the outsized playground. Dressed in fluorescent yellow t-shirts and blue shorts, they were on the see-saw, the swing, hanging around the swing ball pole and others holding swathes of fabric.

It didn't take long for the bull to charge at one of these curious people and the most shocking thing when a bull picks a target is the sheer acceleration there are capable of. They just keep speeding up and can reach 35 mph. In short, the idea of out-running a bull in a straight line is preposterous.

As the bull charged at the man on the down-end of the see-saw, he pushed off at the last second sending his partner flying down to the ground. The bull barely paused and set off to the newly downed man. He pushed straight back off the ground and the bull reared its head with frustration and continued running down the beach. The crowd cheered.

As seemed to be the case in all bull-running events, there were four bulls in total in ascending order of size. Kept in crates only barely big enough for each, the larger bulls were angrier and far faster to lunge than the smaller ones, either because they'd been kept enclosed and hot for longer or they simply knew the score.

Naturally though, bulls are social animals. While they use their size and violence to establish hierarchy in the herd at first, after their position is known by other bulls and cows, they're much more sedate and happy. It's wildly theorised that it's their isolation and breeding that makes them prone, even guaranteed, to attack.

As the third bull ran into the crowd in the water and sought the refreshing coolness of the sea, the swarm of people around him splashed and yelled. Someone threw a beach ball that bounced off his hind quarters and he jerked his head in confusion.

Solid and huge, the four men on the rope could do no more than jerk his head as they tried to encourage him from the shallows. But he just stood there, calmer, surveying the mad crowd.

I felt sad then, sadder then I had in Velas. In Velas there were perhaps twenty people taking it in turns to shout and jump out in front of the bulls and it seemed more like a harmless sport. Harmless for the bull at any rate. But here it was different.

With a hundred people on the sand where the bull could run, more in the water and yet more on the sidelines, each bull was constantly confused and overwhelmed by the sound and distractions from all sides. To see a bull enjoy wallowing in the sea before being driven back onto the sand was to catch a brief glimpse of solace from an animal so separated from us.

Was this really any better than children digging into ants' nests? Pulling wings off a fly? Kicking a dog?

Bulls aren't stupid. In fact, cows are regarded to be quite intelligent animals and I knew that. I had worked on a tiny dairy farm one summer in the US. I'd seen how the fifteen cows came in for milking every day in the same order because they knew how to and at what time.

I saw how they hid their newly born calves under hedgerows while they went to be milked, to keep them safe and I saw the thinking going on in those same calves' eyes when I fed them from a bottle after stealing them from those hedgerows.

Was it really okay that a tradition of tourada à corda justified the continuation of it? Just because the bulls weren't injured, and in fact did the injuring, didn't mean they didn't suffer.

My previous amazement at the event waned until I couldn't watch anymore. As the bull rampaged along the beach towards a jeering man, I turned and walked back along to the boat. I could hear an ice cream van jingle along the promenade.

I was waking up in states of despondency by July, my insides fluttering erratically. I found myself thinking of returning to the UK and would gasp for air, pushing myself back into a corner inside my head. When I went back it would be over. I would go back to a world that hadn't changed and so it would be like I hadn't changed. For all my delirious Bahamian dreamings of well-stocked supermarkets, the idea of walking into a Tesco store made me itch with fear. How could I just go back?

I hadn't seen my family for two and a half years but it didn't feel like that. It felt as though I'd seen them last week. It felt as though I was living in a different world, a whole separate bubble that existed through the wardrobe. I didn't think about the time that had elapsed for them, the tectonic shifts that had occurred in their lives, the differences that there would be when we reunited. I felt like time hadn't passed at home, that it had only passed for me.

"You're worrying again," said Alex.

"No I'm not," I replied, "why do you think I'm worrying?"

"Because you were tossing and turning in your sleep last night. It's like sleeping next to a steam train," he said. My heart sank. I wondered just how much I was destroying myself by endless worrying. And worrying about what? Did I have such a hard life? I could wake up whenever I pleased, wonder around new and interesting places and open up the rum dead on five. I cringed at how easy each day was, in theory.

But the worries gnawed at me day in, day out. Had I changed, really? Was I now any different from the girl three years before who twisted her hands in a doctor's office, being told that her anxiety would ruin the best years of her life if she didn't get a handle on it?

I thought I was keeping it under control, but it was clear some days that I was just keeping it in. I felt like I was deep in a tangle of wool, fighting to get out, knowing it was real but each struggle would tangle me tighter. I could see it was a simple extrication process, I just needed a pair of scissors to snip snip snip on through and then I'd be free. I'd be able to think with decisive clarity. But I didn't have a pair of scissors.

Chapter 15

A Circle Has No End

Coming back to where you started is not the same as never leaving.
Terry Pratchett

It's always the same, arriving home from travelling or living abroad. There's an immediate sense that the second you left, your life and the lives of everyone you left behind, split.

It sounds utterly arrogant and self-righteous and those who are naïve enough to say it out loud would remain the victim of many a smirk and eye roll. But it doesn't negate the fact that this sense of split is there. The Before and the After.

It sounds like it should be life-changing and end in one burning multitudes of incense sticks and spurning the fast and relentless merry-go-round that is our modern world. But in reality, it lasts, in all its force, for about a week.

After a week you've been exposed to so much finely-honed advertising that you've already started filling up your imaginary house with items from the John Lewis department store and have embroiled yourself in a complex and instantly gratifying relationship with Amazon.

After a week the errands are subsiding and you've caught up with the most important and closely related people and you can scarcely believe that just eight days ago you were somewhere else. Someone else.

You're wearing your clothes from before the adventure, having discovered holes in the ones you brought home and months of foreign dust embedded into fabrics. You wash your hair frequently and use deodorant, because your skin never smelt outside, out there but here in modern Britain it inexplicably does.

You've almost completed your transformation from butterfly to caterpillar. You're beginning to forget the last two years in unfamiliar shores, working on island time, swimming with sea turtles. You're getting irritated with erratic drivers and the queue in the supermarket.

But the transformation never completes. The last piece never clicks in. You can never go back. You don't start burning incense (after all, it is only a more pleasant smelling version of passive smoking) but you remain one degree away from who you were before you left. It may take a forest to make a book but that book contains so much.

And there, in that one degree of change, is the constantly burning flame of, 'let's do it again'.

It's easy to see why offshore sailors gravitate to offshore sailors. In the same way that many people in strenuous professions gravitate to those doing the same thing. You strive to be understood. To see the knowing in someone else's eyes. Someone who will say, 'yes, I've been there, I know'. Someone who will nod and say, 'it's true, container ships are always on a collision course at midnight'.

I find myself at Southampton Boat Show the day after landing in England. It's busy, the preview day. Thousands of people milling around in their Musto jackets and their Dubarry sailing wellies as though expecting an impromptu storm and no room left in the gastro tents.

I'm there to meet a magazine editor primarily but after our meeting I'm lost in the sea of Breton tops and Crew Clothing polo shirts. I'm lost on pontoons of brand new yachts with no locker space or grab rails.

I find myself on a Nordhaven because Alex wants to show me the insides of the motor boats we saw everywhere in the Bahamas.

"So do you sail at all?" asks the owner on the bridge. And it is a bridge. With more screens and buttons than your average airliner.

"Well, we've just finished sailing for two years around the Atlantic in our Nicholson 32," says Alex.

The owner almost falls off his chair.

"Good god! I thought you were yuppies!"

We take shelter on a Dutch tall ship named *Artemis* which, thankfully, has a fully stocked bar. It looks conspicuous and proud amongst the impossibly shiny SunSeekers and is at least five times the size of the largest.

I am, admittedly, not in the uniform of the tribe. I'm wearing black skinny jeans, a checked shirt and a fur-lined hooded gilet. I do, if anything, look like a country bumpkin. Or a wannabe country bumpkin at any rate. I certainly don't look like someone who has just spent the last 2 plus years living on a ten metre boat in tropical climes. I don't look like someone who's done 3 hours on, 3 hours off, across the Atlantic in gales.

As I wander around the vast show, I wonder who else dressed innocuously is also recovering from a long sea voyage. I'm dressed in the comforting fabrics of high street shops because, well, I've been wearing ragged sailing clothes for the past two years. I'm hardly going to dress as a sailor if I'm not literally sailing. Just like I wouldn't wear a wetsuit if I wasn't literally about to go into the sea.

I was on a beach in the Bahamas, painting anti-rust paint onto some parts, when an English couple came along. I'd seen them dinghy over to the island from their yacht and we got chatting the usual sailor talk: where have you come from, where are you going.

The woman, in her thirties, asked me, "where did you sail out from?" It seemed like a strangely worded question, after all, she knew I sailed from England.

"Portsmouth Harbour," I said, figuring it for the most specific starting point I could really muster short of, 'the pontoon'. By her slightly confused expression, I knew I'd said something wrong but she was polite enough to smile and nod a beat too late.

"She meant what yacht club do you belong to," said Alex after the couple had left.

"Huh? Why didn't she ask that then?" I said. This wasn't the first time I'd been bamboozled by yachting lingo, I just didn't have the background these lifelong sailors did. I didn't know what you should say to illustrate your status in the sailing world.

"That's just what's said, so you might sail out of Royal Corinthian or Hamble River Sailing Club," he said.

"But what would be the point of me being in a yacht club halfway around the world? I sailed across the ocean, isn't that good enough?" I demanded. The couple hadn't done that, they'd bought their boat in Florida. "Even if I had been part of a yacht club I'm hardly going to continue paying club fees if I'm abroad... sailing."

Alex laughed and told me it was all posturing that kept the sailing circles happy. Where do you sail out of? Pfft, being part of a yacht club hardly makes you a sailor.

But the Southampton Boat Show seemed to be full of people who knew. They knew how to speak, what to say, what the lingo was, how to describe a yacht. They were the sailors, I had just sailed. After three years, I still didn't know the right things to say because I hadn't been around the racers, the lifelong regatta sailors that spoke in such tongues. I felt like a fraud more than ever.

Sitting on *Artemis*, hiding from the modernity outside, a man leaned into me and Alex.

"Have you been in *Yachting Monthly*?" he asked me. If I was ever going to get recognised anywhere for my writing then it would be the Southampton Boat Show, probably the event with the highest concentration of *Yachting Monthly* readers in the world and my appearances in other magazines were certainly rare enough to never be recognised from them.

"Er, yes," I said, "I write for them!"

David and his wife were keen sailors but, at the same time, fairly new to it. They had a coastal cruiser and often took her out in the Solent but preferred tying up to buoys and rarely, if ever, anchored. They asked me how we found anchoring all over the Caribbean. A couple, in their fifties, asked me how to anchor.

I would like to say I nodded thoughtfully before dispensing my hard-earned advice, experience gathered over several years of anchoring in many different conditions. In reality, I panicked slightly at the thought of implying that I knew anything about sailing and immediately deferred to Alex, who did dispense thoughtful and hard-earned advice which they gratefully listened to.

And it made me wonder: did I not belong in the sailing world because I kept pushing it away? I was the one who refused to admit that I was a sailor, no one else. Plenty of highly experienced sailors were my age or younger, some by ten years or more. Was it really my attitude that was stopping me, yet again, from doing something?

But the more I thought about it, the more I couldn't work it out. If I dropped my attitude and joined in with the sailor chat then perhaps I could belong there. Perhaps I could talk about weather and the cut of a jib and the lines of a boat. But that still wouldn't be me, that would be me talking in someone else's language. Besides, in all honesty, I found it mostly boring to talk about a lot of sailing, boat construction and the finer points of sail trimming. I sailed to explore, to connect with the wind and the waves and to smile at dolphins when they dropped by for a chat. Did that make me a real sailor? Or did that just make me a traveller whose method of motion was the wind?

The next week I was sat at my laptop, reading travel blogs and trying to work out just where I was going with my writing. I wasn't a blogger, I had deliberately chosen not to blog in any real sense, wanting instead to focus on travel writing. But the lines were blurring so heavily that I wonder if I wasn't tuned in enough to what modern travellers really wanted to read.

"Do you want to go for a walk?" asked Alex, appearing in the room.

"Yes, sure," I said. We were staying on the edge of the New Forest for two months before heading to Austria, refusing to pay rent in the UK when we could pay in somewhere with a better view and an unlimited selection of cheese and bratwurst. I'd never been to Austria or even any of its border neighbours and, without the boat, we needed somewhere to live.

"You'll need your walking boots," he said, "and we're driving." He paused, a shadow of a smirk on his lips, "and we have to leave in the next 15 minutes." I eyed him closely, he was clearly up to something.

We could walk to the forest from the house in less than two minutes and Alex hated driving. He's also excellent at keeping schtum though and I knew better than to press him for details lest I become embroiled in imaginative yet possibly believable lies until we reached our destination.

It was my birthday in a few days but I couldn't fathom where he was taking me until we got onto the Salisbury road out of Southampton. The thing with having grown up in a particular area that's 70% countryside is that it becomes quite easy to narrow down your destination.

Before we even got to Salisbury I suspected that he was taking me skydiving. After all, there's almost nothing else to do on Salisbury Plain except pretty river walks, Stonehenge and possibly a military museum. Not that I'm pooh-poohing Stonehenge but, having lived an hour away from it for two thirds of my life, does take the novelty out of it somewhat.

I didn't query Alex because I was quietly terrified and there's was always the possibility that he was taking me to fly a nice friendly bird of prey or something similar. Skydiving was something I had always wanted to do. After all, how could you not want to fall through the air from a great height? I loved heights, I loved the freedom I felt when standing on a sheer drop but I was starting to realise, in the car possibly on my way to a skydiving centre, that I had always wanted to skydive in the abstract.

It's easy to want to do something when there's very little danger of actually doing it. I thought back to Peru the year before. We'd taken a short flight there from Panama, leaving the boat in a marina during hurricane season and spending a couple of weeks exploring the Peruvian historical centres of Arequipa and Cusco. One morning, walking along Cusco's Incan street, Alex spotted a sign for bungee jumping and less than three hours later we were jumping from a cage 150 m off ground, 3000 m above sea level.

Bungee jumping had also always been one of those things that I always thought I'd give a go. It wasn't particularly dangerous and substantially cheaper than skydiving. But standing on the brink looking over the valley and the sheer amount of air beneath me was frightening in a way that I had never experienced before. I couldn't believe how afraid I was.

"Are you ready?" asked the guy at the top, shoving a video camera in my face, filming a film that I would certainly not be paying for.

"No," I said, honestly. I wasn't ready, I didn't want to jump. Every fibre in my body was telling me not to jump. In fact, I wasn't even sure how I could physically do it, physically override my survival instincts. This wasn't doing something that my sense perceived could go wrong, this was something that, evolutionarily, would absolutely kill me.

He laughed, "that's not what I want to hear!" I wasn't ready but then again, I never would be. I couldn't go down again, I had far too much pride for that. So I stood with my toes just on the edge of the cage, put my hands around my chest straps and leaned forward.

The next split second was a rushing inhalation and my lungs strained to do their job. Utter weightlessness and a pure euphoria so exquisite that I couldn't even comprehend it. I was falling, plummeting, I would've laughed if I'd had the sense.

The bounce was violent but not as violent as I had imagined. It was followed by another momentary fall and another bounce. And then I started laughing. I was lowered down slowly, enough for all the blood to rush to my head but the exhilaration… it was astounding.

My immediate thoughts were, 'why doesn't everybody do this?' I found out later that night.

I was wrenched from sleep with such agony I screamed out. Alex immediately grabbed me and told me it was okay, it was only a nightmare.

"No, no, I'm awake, it's my knee," I gasped. The pain was equally exquisite as the jump. I couldn't move my right knee for fear of feeling the agony again. Eventually I managed to put it in a position in which I could sleep without moving it at all until morning.

I can only imagine that the jump had pulled something in my knee which had then swollen during the night, causing screaming agony when I moved in my sleep. The pain became muted the next day but my knee hurt walking Peru's endless winding hilly streets for the rest of the trip and weeks afterwards.

It was the fear of the bungee jump that had cemented itself in my mind, although I can still conjure the blissful sense of falling at will, so heavily stamped in my memory is the unique feeling. But it was that I was so surprised at the fear that struck me in the car past Salisbury.

Suddenly I didn't want to skydive. I needed more time to think about it, to mull it over, to worry, to plan, to prepare. In an hour or two I could be jumping out of a plane, how was that even possible, was this really happening? Had Alex really organised a skydive? How had he kept that a secret? When had he been planning it since? Maybe it'd be called off, maybe squalls would turn up, I thought looking into the cloudless blue sky.

The game was up when Alex realised he needed me to navigate to the out-of-the-way centre. He told me that Google Maps was open on his phone in the glove box, and that I needed to tell him which lane to take. I looked at the phone.

GoSkydive was the name where Google's handy blue line ended. I was going skydiving. Imminently.

"Oh my god, I knew it!" I said with far more enthusiasm than I felt. Or half of me felt. I did want to go skydiving, but I wanted to be able to worry about it for at least a week in advance. "I'm going skydiving," I said, "are you going skydiving too? Right?" Alex laughed and nodded.

"How long have you been planning this?" I asked, amazed at his secrecy.

"I just called them up this morning, they had a cancellation and said that if we could be there by noon we were in," he said. Serendipitous beyond measure considering the centre turned out to have a huge waiting list of previously cancelled to-be-rearranged jumps backed up from cloudy summer days.

For the next ten minutes I was consumed with what some generously call butterflies and others called outright anxiety. I still couldn't tell if I wanted to do it. My mind raced through every possibility that it might just not work out, that we wouldn't be able to jump. But I did want to jump. There was something inside that was telling me I didn't, a tension within that made me want to pull the brakes.

"And how did you feel when you woke up this morning and knew you were going to skydive today?" asked the instructor leading our induction. We were in a room with 9 other people, most of whom were set to jump as well and just two there for their friends' moral support. She looked at me.

"I actually woke up like normal, because I didn't know we were coming here until half an hour ago," I said.

"Ha, me neither!" said a girl, leaning forward from just along the bench and looking at me. It was none other than Dodie Clark, a ukulele-playing truth-telling YouTuber whom I secretly adored and was there representing Coke TV. She was only 21, another example of the success that I didn't even know existed at that age.

The jump would be from 15,000 ft, the highest jump offered by the centre. We would be taken up by a light aircraft, already strapped in to our tandem instructor and then… you know, jump out and fall to earth. It was a Friday in late September and the centre was trying to fit in as many jumps as possible. After all, the later it got in the year the harder the weather was to predict.

We got dressed up in our jumpsuits, practised our landings while suspended from the ceiling and then went out to the picnic tables to wait our turn to be called. Cloud was forming and lowering gradually as the afternoon wore on and Alex had asked around, discovering that they don't jump when the cloud base is below 5000 ft. This is because that's the latest they should technically open their chutes but in cloud, they wouldn't be able to check they were clear of others to open.

I became antsy, I was here now, I'd done my induction, I was wearing the gear, if I couldn't jump today all this pent-up anxiety was for nothing. I needed to jump, I wanted to jump. I went alternately between excitement and fear, back and forth.

Finally, our names were called and we went into the pen area with similarly nervous jumpers. As the instructors came over from their previous jump, the two of us were taken aside by our induction instructor.

"I'm afraid you guys are going to have to be on the jump after this," she said. "One of your instructors is quite new and he says he doesn't feel comfortable jumping in these cloud conditions this late in the day." So our jump was delayed again.

The cloud base was lowering all the time and now sat around 5000 ft – anymore and we wouldn't be jumping at all. The current jump was the last 'tourist jump' of the day and we would be going up in the plane with the instructing students who were all trying to gain their 800 jumps before they could be instructors. As the plane took off, we gathered with them and the atmosphere changed entirely.

There was no nervousness anymore, the students had done this hundreds of times already, sometimes multiple times a day if they could fit it in. There was banter and laughter, equipment checks and a general air of total relaxation. If these guys did it every day, why on earth should I be nervous?

I met my instructor, a Dutch skydiver who had literally tens of thousands of jumps under his belt. He had already done around ten that day but was still amped up and excited, determined to ensure I would have the best possible experience. As I climbed into the plane and got strapped to his chest, the students poured in around us, lining up on the military like benches that would enable us all to fall out in order. I didn't feel anxious anymore, just awed.

The plane climbed to 10,000 ft where the students began to drop out, rolling forward as though there was nothing unusual at all about falling from such a height. They didn't hesitate. Four got together at the brink and held hands, ready to jump in synchronisation. Another didn't jump far enough and his backpack clipped the step on the outside of the plane, eliciting a roar of laughter from the more experienced jumpers.

"Ready, yes?" shouted my instructor. I made the Okay sign and we shuffled inelegantly to the edge of the plane. There was no time to tense up, we were out and falling in moments.

It only took a few seconds for me to overcome my shock and then it was clear, I was falling to the earth at around 120 mph and I could see nothing below me but white, fluffy clouds. I had to drag air into my lungs, probably not because it was any harder to breathe up there, but because I had to consciously remind my body that it could operate as usual.

Free fall from 15000 ft until parachute deployment is around 60 seconds, which gave me an abundance of time to process what was happening. There is simply no other way to experience falling. Bungee jumping happens too fast to think but skydiving allows you shock, exhilaration and finally appreciation of the feeling. I stretched out my arms and felt the air resistance, almost like a pillow I could rest my body on. Like when in water, your muscles are supported, but this was air, just air and yet I could just relax.

With only cloud below and blue sky above, it was next to impossible to gauge the speed of our descent and so I existed in a strange sensation of suspension, technically hurtling to Earth but oddly incapable of comprehending it. Eventually the cloud did get closer and then the mind bending began again because it looked as though I was going to smash into a solid substance, so opaque was the cloud.

I knew rationally that we'd simply fall through it, but it looked so solid. As the cloud approached at startling velocity, I felt myself taking a deep breath as I braced for an impact that logically wouldn't come. Suddenly we were plunged into the grey haze of the deep cloud and then yanked upwards (or rather, it felt like it was upwards) as my instructor pulled the parachute.

As we descended upright through the cloud base, the whole of Salisbury Plain opened up to me and we began our five-minute weaving drift to the ground. He pointed out the Solent to me and I could see the power station next to my house, then Stonehenge and Old Sarum Castle. Most of all, I could see the area as a whole, the endless patchwork of fields and cows, the individual villages dotted along narrow, winding roads and the River Avon, its shimmering network of marshes and oxbows and curves in all of its dawdling glory.

I took over the reigns, pulling my right arm down to bank right and left to weave left. The control was immense, so much more than I had ever realised. Previously confused at how skydivers could ever land in a specific place, with the chute controls in my hands, I felt the power of the air in the canopy and for those few minutes, finally understood how birds could glide through the air without a single beat.

Just like with bungee jumping, once I began to laugh, I couldn't stop. It seemed impossible to see why humans weren't spending their whole lives jumping out of planes when it felt like this! When it was this easy! No wonder those students were as relaxed as could be as they rolled, jumped and laughed their way out of the plane, they were about to get a euphoric hit so good it'd make you swear off stimulants for life. The simple act of a body flying through the air, touching clouds and riding physics was as pure a sense of freedom as you could get. Just as I used the wind and the ocean to travel across huge distances, these skydivers used the air to fly above the earth with the ease and control of a bird.

There is something about using the natural world in this way that brings out vivid life in people. Harnessing the power of the wind, the sun, and the waves brings us closer to who we really are, who we've evolved to be, than anything before.

It's surely why people become so-called adrenaline junkies, why the most exhilarated you can get is always directly to do with the natural world. We get so lost in the world we've created, in the digital abyss of the internet and in the enclosed spaces of our homes, offices and cars, that we often forget that to feel something so powerful as unbridled exhilaration and euphoria isn't a weird and rare thing, it's just what happens when we absolutely give ourselves up to nature, and embrace it.

In the weeks after I arrived back in England, I thought a lot about what it would've meant if I had never gone. If I had told the truth to Alex over two years ago, 'I don't think I can do this, I don't know if I want to do this, why don't we just…stay?' If I had let my fear of the unknown, my insecurities about what I was capable of stop me from embarking on the greatest adventure of my life so far, then nothing would have changed. I would have confirmed my own fears in an instant; if I hadn't have gone, I wouldn't have succeeded, I would've failed off the bat.

It is so easy to not do something. I've spent so much time not doing the things that came across my path and idolising those who took a chance, who took a risk and did take the opportunity. I thought it was because they were capable and I was not. I thought it was just who we were in the same way that I am blonde and others are brunette. Some. Things. Just. Are.

But most are not. The American comedy writer and actress Mindy Kaling released her second autobiography while I was sailing. It was called *Why Not Me?* And that's what she said to herself when she looked at the typical white, thin, all-American women in the industry she wanted to be in. I'm not clamouring to have my own American comedy show but the logic is the same. Why not me?

Why did I spend so long coming up with reasons that I couldn't do something? And why was that the first thing I would always think of? I'd even invent reasons I couldn't do something (sometimes I still do) just because I didn't want to try and fail.

I didn't want to sail only to discover I wasn't a sailor. I thought that sailors had some big sign above their heads and in their hearts that said SAILOR. Except that no one is a sailor before they sail. To some it's a burning love, and to some it's an enjoyable hobby, but they were all born not sailors.

When I returned to England, it was as though the whole world had opened up. Suddenly, things I 'couldn't' do, were there, ready and waiting. It no longer seemed to matter very much that I might fail at something, at least I could try the something in the first place. I couldn't speak German, but I could learn. I might pronounce some words wrong and get a laugh, but the world wouldn't end. I no longer had to have any guarantees.

After all, I no longer had a leg to stand on. Every single time I'd said I couldn't do something, it had turned out that I could. And did. Because why couldn't I? Why not me?

Chapter 16

The Final Stretch

The real voyage of discovery consists not in seeking new landscapes, but in having new eyes.

Marcel Proust

In September 2016 we had left *Berwick Maid* on the Azores island of Terceira to fend for herself until the following spring. The North Atlantic had shown no intention of delivering us a good forecast to sail to England and we had seen the astronomical prices of south coast marinas. We decided to pay the tiny amount of money it would cost to leave her on hardstanding in this mid-ocean chain and return to the UK.

Those months flew. After two days exploring the streets of Lisbon we touched down in Terceira's tiny airport and took a taxi in the rain the two miles to the boatyard. I stared out the car window like a child looking at a new landscape, aching for a glimpse of our yacht.

Over the past winter I had watched the Atlantic weather charts closely, monitoring the winds that would affect her, the rain that would wash her decks and the storms she would have to weather. So, when she finally came into view, propped up just as we had left her, I felt great relief and an even greater sense that I was home again.

As I ran my hands along her hull and climbed up the ladder to the cockpit, it felt as though I had never been away. Here she was waiting for us to return. Alex worked tirelessly sanding the hull and re-antifouling as I sat in the saloon copywriting for distant companies.

We knew that we would have to sell her soon. We would be finishing the voyage in just a few months and there was no way we could afford to keep her in England. We neither wanted the thought of her sitting in a boatyard for the few weekends we could spare her nor the vast expense of doing so.

It was unreal to me no matter how much we discussed it. Completely unreal that one day she would not be ours. That we wouldn't walk her decks or sleep in the cocoon of her forepeak. But there was a lot of ocean between us and that. For now.

We put her back in the water and the feeling of home was even more immense. To feel her suspended in the marina again, to feel her tilt slightly as we stepped off, to feel her relax – no longer affected by the gravitas of dry land. It was like all three of us were home.

We left the Azores on the 4th June 2017, a year after we had arrived from the Bahamas. It was a stunning day with light winds but an incoming depression that we intended to use. Pilot whales dipped off in the distance and we set the cruising chute and were pulled along under its vivid colours.

I felt an ounce of nerves. I didn't like leaving land behind and whenever we set off I always waited impatiently for it to fall off the horizon before I could truly relax. But the day was beautiful and easy and it was everything that sailing should be.

We were sailing for Spain, an easier goal given the tempestuous nature of this part of the ocean. Heading for England looked unpleasantly like we'd be caught up in a storm and, while I hadn't initially been keen to cross Biscay proper again, heading for Spain would be the safest option. And we were right.

The first five days were good with dolphins streaming alongside and blue skies. But the storm we had seen hints of caught up with us eventually and plummeted us into fierce winds. Still days from the shipping channels of Spain, we took down the sails and languished on the southern edge of what we would later discover was one of the worst storms for years.

With 60 knot winds further north plus 15 metre waves, the storm sent the OSTAR sailing fleet running for safety while one yacht was rescued by the *Queen Mary* cruise ship. We knew it was big but had no idea how big.

Blissfully unaware of the havoc caused just a few hundred miles further north, we hoisted the sails after the storm had gone and continued under cruising chute for several days. The weather was fickle but on the eighth day we were flying along, hand steering the chute down big ocean waves and surfing at 8 knots.

"I think we might be going too fast," I called to Alex. He came up into the cockpit just as a gust sent us roaring forward.

"Yeah," he said, looking at the speed, "too fast for the chute anyway."

The wind strengthened rapidly and by the time I was sat with my legs wrapped around the mast to release the chute it was already far stronger. We wrestled it down and set the main and genoa with heavy reefs in.

The wind and waves calmed into the night before strengthening again at dawn with lines of squall clouds trooping along up ahead. We were coming up to the Finisterre shipping lanes and, while we had aimed to head north-east to A Coruña, it was very obvious that we wouldn't make it.

It was as though the waves came out of nowhere, so huge had they become in such a short amount of time. Just as we began a lengthy crossing a four vast and busy shipping lanes, our AIS died.

The waves were obscuring our view of oncoming ships and, travelling at 20-25 knots, these behemoths were not something you could even take your eyes off for a second. We hove-to at the edge of the first lane as a phenomenally huge car transporter chugged past us, its huge vertical sides towering over us.

I began to feel truly scared. Not just nervous, not just anxious, but extremely frightened. We were now in the high wind area of Spain's west coast where winds funnel around the north-west corner and ploughs south, kicking up huge, rough seas. We could no longer aim north-east to the corner and we couldn't even aim due east, the waves were too severe. With each slam I though the side of the boat had caved in. Never had we experienced such violent seas and such humongous short chop. With the added unreliability of the AIS, we not only had to get through the waves at horrendously slow speeds but we also had to be critically aware of the speed and location of every single ship bearing down on us.

We couldn't turn back because who knew when the winds would calm? These weren't the product of a storm, they could last for days or longer. We simply had to cross the lanes and get to the safety of a bay.

We steered more and more downwind, constantly battling the need to progress with the avoidance of simply sailing south which would mean staying in the shipping lanes for longer. Alex helmed for hours straight, using every ounce of his strength to keep the boat going in the right direction. With every huge wave thumping into us, the bow would career off, leaving him to struggle to regain control. I was constantly at the AIS and looking around for ships. It took us hours to cross the south-bound lanes before having an iota of rest in the few miles that separated them from the north-bound lanes.

I prayed for safety. I had never been so afraid for our lives. So rough were the seas that books had long ejected themselves from our usually secure shelves and were littering the saloon floor. There was seawater in the saloon and everything was covered in salt. It didn't matter. Nothing mattered except getting across these shipping lanes.

"Kit!" yelled Alex. I leapt up into the companionway and wedged myself there between the handles.

"What's wrong?" I asked, terrified of what he might say.

"Dolphins!" he said with a laugh as another monstrous wave tipped our little boat over so that water rushed along the gunwales and covered the coachroof. And sure enough, there they were. A pod of dolphins leaping out of the waves and zooming along beside us like guides in this frenzied sea. It's as though they can sense when they're needed.

It took twelve long hours to get through the shipping lanes, Alex battling with the helm the entire time. In the lee of the mainland, we could finally turn downwind and roll our way in flatter water to Finisterre lighthouse. As we turned the corner north into the flat water of the bay, we had stepped into a different world. The wind was almost gone, unable to make it over the land and we glided silently along in the moonlight.

As we anchored under Punta de Sardiñeiro we were both grateful to have reached land. More than land. Mainland.

It was several weeks before the northerlies subsided and light westerlies cloaked the coastline in a thick fog. We took the opportunity to motor north, taking the silent coastline bay by bay until we reached A Coruña. The Spanish coastline is infamous for this all-or-nothing weather. With fierce northerlies or foggy westerlies, it hardly seems there's anything in between.

Once we reached A Coruña there was a certain level of completeness. We had been here exactly three years before, green and salty, fresh from Biscay and my first night sail. And now we were back, same boat, same people. But different.

We meandered the easy streets of this glass city, where the sun reflects from every building. We ambled and ate tapas and watched the fires burn along the beaches during Noite de San Xoán, the Night of St John. We spent hours upon hours walking the city and weeks went by. That's the thing about A Coruña, it's just the easiest place to be.

All this time, Biscay was very much being itself. Rough and changeable with northerly winds always set dead against us. It took us a long time to leave Spain and two attempts. The first attempt I bailed. No. I couldn't do it in that, it would have meant beating to windward for several days. So we deferred for a week to a nearby bay until the wind abated and finally provided us with a good forecast.

And it was good. It was Biscay at her finest with good winds and little swell. We reached Brittany and anchored for the night in the entrance to Brest before catching the flood tide up through the Chenal du Four and past the lighthouses that have graced many a painting.

Arriving in L'Aberwach that evening was blissful. We spent a night at anchor before heading into the marina the next day. The tiny town above had croissants and a tiny, cheese-filled supermarket. The marina showers were delightful and I was thrilled to be in France after many years.

We stayed for just a couple of days before it was time. It was time to cross the English Channel and return to our home country. I was both excited and terrified. How could this truly be happening? We only left yesterday and now it's... over?

We sailed out of L'Aberwach and began a slow and light-winded journey. It was comical really, how short it was. Just two days. And that was because there was little wind and we kept deviating our course further and further east. Three years before the Channel crossing had been the most frightening thing I could've imagined. The Channel had seemed vast and uncrossable in such a little boat.

Now I was afraid, but not of the water. I was afraid of what was the other side of it.

Fog descended upon us in the night. The kind of fog that makes you feel as though you're the only thing in the whole world. As magical as that feeling can be, it meant a sleepless night for both of us as we navigated around ships by ear and stood back to back watching the dark greyness for container ships. Our AIS worked only intermittently having never recovered after the storm off Spain. We glimpsed fishing boats in the gloom and breathed sighs of relief as huge ships ghosted astern, no one using fog horns.

When dawn finally broke and the fog turned patchy, there she was. England. She was so beautiful. So green with mist hanging on her cliff tops. Sea birds were everywhere; following fishing boats, bobbing on the water or circling above us.

Even though we had been in England only months before, it was so different to sail back. Before we had been visitors. Now we were coming home and we were bringing *Berwick Maid* home.

We sailed into Dartmouth, where we knew we'd have shelter from every wind and besides, it's Dartmouth. There is no more English place for a sailor to visit than Dartmouth with its incredible array of boats of every description from the oldest to the youngest.

There's nothing like sailing past the Naval College high up on the hill and imagining my dad there when he was only 20. Nothing like seeing the cadets patrol the river and speed after their camouflaged peers.

There's nothing like picking up a buoy and turning off the engine and sitting down in the summer sun and knowing. Knowing that you've just completed the most extraordinary journey of your life.

Sources

Chapter 1: I Bought A Boat
Introductory quote: Cheryl Strayed, *Tiny Beautiful Things: Advice on Love and Life from Dear Sugar*

Chapter 2: Spanish Horizons
Introductory quote: Alan Watts

Chapter 3: A Secret Island
Introductory quote: Pico Iyer, *Why We Travel*
Extract: T. D. A. Cockerell, *Flora Of Porto Santo*, Torreya Journal, 1922

Chapter 4: A Familiar Ocean
Introductory quote: Arthur C. Clarke

Chapter 5: Full Sea
Introductory quote: Robin Lee Graham

Chapter 6: Racing Grenada
Introductory quote: John A. Shedd, a collection of sayings *Salt in my Attic*

Chapter 7: Tropical France
Introductory quote: Lawrence Durrell, *Bitter Lemons of Cyprus*

Chapter 8: Caribbean Crossing
Introductory quote: Neil Gaiman, *The Graveyard Book*

Chapter 9: Sloth Hunting
Introductory quote: Gregory Maguire, *Wicked*

Chapter 10: Beating Through Rainbows To Paradise
Introductory quote: Tennnessee Williams, *Camino Real*

Chapter 11: The Sky, The Sea And The Wind
Introductory quote: John Ruskin

Chapter 12: Northern Bahamas
Introductory quote: Malala Yousafzai
Extract 1: Michael Craton, *Bay Street, Black Power and the Conchy Joes: Race and Class in the Colony and Commonwealth of the Bahamas, 1850-2000* in Howard Johnson and Karl Watson (eds.) *The White Minority in the Caribbean*, 1998
Extract 2: Michael Craton and Gail Saunders, *Islanders in the Stream: A History of the Bahamian People*, 1999

Chapter 13: Riding The Gulf Stream Home
Introductory quote: Andre Gide, *Les faux-monnayeurs* [The Counterfeiters]

Chapter 14: A Circle Has No End
Introductory quote: John Muir, *Our National Parks*

Chapter 15: The Final Stretch
Introductory quote: Terry Pratchett, *A Hat Full of Sky*

Glossary Of Nautical Terms

Abeam	At right angles to the boat.
Aft	Near the stern of a boat.
AIS	Automatic Identification System: an automatic tracking system used by ships to identify and locate each other using electronic data exchange.
Anchor	Device to moor a boat in open water on the end of a line.
Anchorage	Location where boats anchor.
Aries	Self-steering system used on *Berwick Maid*.
Autopilot	Self-steering system.
Baggywrinkle	Soft covering for rigging to reduce sail chafe.
Bare poles	Boat at sea with no sails up, just the spars.
Beam	Mid part of the boat or maximum width of the hull.
Beam reach	Sailing with the wind directly abeam.
Bear away	Steering away from the wind.
Beneteau	A French boat builder.
Berth	Place where a boat is parked in a marina.
Bilge	Bottom of the inside of a boat.
Bimini	Open-front canvas top for the cockpit of a boat.
Boom	Spar attached to the mast and the foot of the mainsail.
Bow	The front of a boat.
Bowsprit	Spar projecting forward on the bow
Bows-to	Mooring with the bows pointing to the shore.
Broad reach	Sailing with the wind further astern than the beam.
Bunk	Bed onboard a boat.
Buoy	Floating mark.
Butterfly hatches	Rectangular hatch, both sides open upward.

Capsize   Boat on its side with the mast in the water.

Chandlery   Nautical store stocking items for boats.

Chart   Nautical map.

Chart table   Table in boat for looking at charts.

Clew   Lower, aft corner of a sail.

Close-hauled   Sailing close to the wind (beating).

Coachroof   Raised part of the cabin roof.

Cockpit   Well near the stern from which a boat is steered and the crew sit.

Combing   Vertical surface on a boat designed to deflect or prevent entry of water.

Companionway   Entry from the cockpit to the cabin.

Deck   Upper surface of the hull.

Ebb tide   Outgoing flow of the tide.

Echo sounder   Device to measure the depth below a boat.

Fender   Air or foam-filled bumper to keep boats from banging against things.

Foredeck   The deck in front of the mast.

Foremast   Front mast.

Forepeak   Cabin in front of the mast.

Furl   To roll up a sail.

Gaff   Spar which holds the upper part of a gaff sail.

Gaff-rigged   Boat rigged with a traditional four-sided mainsail.

Galley   Kitchen on a boat.

Genoa   Large headsail that overlaps the mainsail.

Grab bag   Bag containing essential items when abandoning ship.

Grab rail   Low rails which provide a hand-hold on a boat.

Guard wire   Wire around the deck to stop people falling off.

Gunwale   Upper edge of a boat's side.

Hatch boards   Boards to close the opening of the hatch into the cockpit.

Headsails   Sails set forward of the main mast.

Hove-to   When a boat is stationary at sea, head to wind with the jib backed.

Hull   Main body of the boat.

Jib   Small headsail.

Kedge anchor   Light, temporary anchor.

Keel   Structure under the hull which prevents sideways drift and counterweight to the boat's heeling.

Keel-stepped mast Mast which rests on the keel.

Knot   Unit of speed: one nautical mile per hour.

Lee-cloth   Piece of fabric that acts like a safety net to keep a sailor in their bunk.

Leeward   Side away from the wind.

Liferaft   Inflatable raft used when abandoning ship.

Lockers   Cupboards onboard a boat.

Main mast   Larger mast.

Mainsail   Principal sail set on the mainmast.

Marina   Place for parking boats on jetties and pontoons.

Nautical mile   Unit of distance used at sea: 1.15 statute miles.

Pay off   Let out.

Port   Left hand side of a boat.

Pontoon   Floating structure that serves as a dock.

Preventer   Line to stop the boom crossing the boat unexpectedly.

Pulpit   Tubular structure at the front of a boat.

Pushpit   Tubular structure at the back of a boat.

Rail   Raised piece of wood on the deck of a boat.

Reaching   Sailing with the wind coming from the side of the boat.

Reef   Reducing the area of sail which is hoisted.

RIB   Rigid inflatable boat, with a rigid bottom and inflatable sides.

Rigging   Wires that hold the mast up.

Rowlocks   Brace in which an oar is held when rowing.

Rudder   Foil at the back of a boat, used for steering.

Rudder stock   Structure which holds the rudder.

Sea breeze   Onshore wind which is generated when the

	land heats up.
Schooner	Boat with fore and aft sails on two or more masts.
Shackle	Metal link with a pin to connect two things.
Sheet	Rope used to trim a sail.
Shroud	Wire which supports the mast.
Side deck	The deck around the side of the boat.
Squall	Sudden, short-lived increase in wind.
Starboard	Right hand side of a boat.
Stay	Wire which supports the mast.
Stern	Aft extremity of a boat.
Switch panel	Panel to which electric wires are led.
Tack	Steer a boat through the eye of the wind.
Tidal range	Difference in the height of the tide between low and high tide.
Tide	Six-hourly rise and fall of water caused by the gravitational pull of the moon.
Toe rail	Raised piece of wood on the deck of a boat.
Topmast	Top part of the mast on a gaff-rigged boat.
Topping lift	Rope/wire which holds the end of the boom up.
Trade winds	Wind blowing steadily towards the equator from the north-east in the northern hemisphere or the south-east in the southern hemisphere.
Transom	Surface that forms the stern of a boat.
Trimming	Adjusting the sails.
Veer	Clockwise shift of the wind.
Warp	Rope used to moor a boat.
Watch	Period of time when a person or group are responsible for a boat.
Winch	Cylindrical mechanical device to tension sheets and halyards.
Wind force	Wind strength as measured by the Beaufort Scale.
Wind vane	Part of an autopilot device which keeps the boat in a constant direction relevant to the wind.
Windshift	Change in the wind's direction.
Windward	Side towards the wind.